Time Out

SHORTLIST

Buenos Aires

WHAT'S NEW | WHAT'S ON | WHAT'S BEST

www.timeout.com/buenosaires

Time Out

Buenos Aires

Contents

Buenos Aires by Area

Essentials

Published by Time Out Guides Ltd
Universal House
251 Tottenham Court Road
London W1T 7AB
Tel: + 44 (0)20 7813 3000
Fax: + 44 (0)20 7813 6001
Email: guides@timeout.com
www.timeout.com

Managing Director Peter Fiennes
Editorial Director Ruth Jarvis
Business Manager Dan Allen
Editorial Manager Holly Pick
Assistant Management Accountant Ija Krasnikova

Time Out Guides is a wholly owned subsidiary of Time Out Group Ltd.

© Time Out Group Ltd
Chairman Tony Elliott
Chief Executive Officer David King
Group General Manager/Director Nichola Coulthard
Time Out Communications Ltd MD David Pepper
Time Out International Ltd MD Cathy Runciman
Time Out Magazine Ltd Publisher/Managing Director Mark Elliott
Production Director Mark Lamond
Group IT Director Simon Chappell
Marketing & Circulation Director Catherine Demajo

Time Out and the Time Out logo are trademarks of Time Out Group Ltd.

This edition first published in Great Britain in 2009 by Ebury Publishing
A Random House Group Company
Company information can be found on www.randomhouse.co.uk
Random House UK Limited Reg. No. 954009
10 9 8 7 6 5 4 3 2 1

Distributed in the US by Publishers Group West
Distributed in Canada by Publishers Group Canada

For further distribution details, see www.timeout.com

ISBN: 978–1–84670–159–7

A CIP catalogue record for this book is available from the British Library.

Printed and bound in Germany by Appl.

The Random House Group Limited supports The Forest Stewardship Council (FSC), the leading international forest certification organisation. All our titles that are printed on Greenpeace approved FSC certified paper carry the FSC logo. Our paper procurement policy can be found on www.rbooks.co.uk/environment.

Time Out carbon-offsets all its flights with Trees for Cities (www.treesforcities.org).

Buenos Aires Shortlist

The **Time Out Buenos Aires Shortlist** is one of a new series of annual and biannual guides that draws on Time Out's background as a magazine publisher to keep you current with everything that's going on in town. As well as Buenos Aires's key sights and the best of its eating, drinking and leisure options, it picks out the most exciting venues to have opened recently and gives a full calendar of annual events from January to December. It also includes features on the important news, trends and openings, all compiled by locally based editors and writers. Whether you're visiting for the first time in your life or the first time this year, you'll find the *Time Out Buenos Aires Shortlist* contains all you need to know, in a portable and easy-to-use format.

The guide divides central Buenos into six areas, each containing listings for Sights & museums, Eating & drinking, Shopping, Nightlife and Arts & leisure, and maps pinpointing their locations. At the front of the book are chapters rounding up these scenes city-wide, and giving a shortlist of our overall picks. We also include itineraries for days out, plus essentials such as transport information and hotels.

Our listings give phone numbers as dialled within Buenos Aires. From abroad, use your country's exit code followed by 54 (the country code for Argentina), 11 and the number given.

We have noted price categories by using one to four peso signs ($-$$$$), representing budget, moderate, expensive and luxury. Major credit cards are accepted unless otherwise stated. We also indicate when a venue is NEW.

All our listings are double-checked, but places do sometimes close or change their hours or prices, so it's a good idea to call a venue before visiting. While every effort has been made to ensure accuracy, the publishers cannot accept responsibility for any errors that this guide may contain.

Venues are marked on the maps using symbols numbered according to their order within the chapter and colour-coded as follows:

❶ Sights & museums
❶ Eating & drinking
❶ Shopping
❶ Nightlife
❶ Arts & leisure

Map key

Major sight or landmark	
Railway station	
Subte (metro) station	●Perú
Park	
Hospital	✚
Area	**RETIRO**
Avenue	
River	
Church	✚
Airport	✈
Highway	
Pedestrian road	

Time Out Buenos Aires Shortlist

EDITORIAL
Editor Jeremy Helligar
Managing Editor Mark Rebindaine
Copy Editors Katie Buckland, Matt Chesterton, Patrick Welch
Editorial Assistant Amanda Guerrero
Proofreader Emma Clifton

DESIGN
BA Art Director Gonzalo Gil
BA Designer Javier Beresiarte
Ad Make-Up Sofia Irtube

Art Director Scott Moore
Art Editor Pinelope Kourmouzoglou
Senior Designer Henry Elphick
Graphic Designers Kei Ishimaru, Nicola Wilson
Advertising Designer Jodi Sher
Picture Editor Jael Marschner
Deputy Picture Editor Lynn Chambers
Picture Researcher Gemma Walters
Picture Desk Assistant Marzena Zoladz
Picture Librarian Christina Theisen

ADVERTISING
Commercial Director Mark Phillips
International Advertising Manager Kasimir Berger
International Sales Executive Charlie Sokol
Commercial Director BA Andres Castro
Advertising Sales Mau Banach, Sara Blaylock, Juan Faieraizen, Maria Dolores Martínez

MARKETING
Marketing Manager Yvonne Poon
Sales & Marketing Director, North America & Latin America Lisa Levinson
Senior Publishing Brand Manager Luthfa Begum
Marketing Designers Anthony Huggins

PRODUCTION
Production Manager Brendan McKeown
Production Controller Damian Bennett
Production Coordinator Kelly Fenlon

CONTRIBUTORS
This guide was researched and written by Katie Buckland, Matt Chesterton, Elizabeth Gleeson, Amanda Guerrero, Cate Kelly, Dave Lowe, Maraya Loza-Koxahn, Layne Mosler, Sophie Parker, Sanra Ritten, Scott Young and the writers of *Time Out Buenos Aires*.

PHOTOGRAPHY
Principal photography Emily Anne Epstein, Marc Van der Aa.

Additional photography by Matt Chesterton, Gonzalo Gil, Elizabeth Gleeson, Jeremy Helligar, Stéphan San Quice, Mark Rebindaine and Ricardo Watson.

Cover photograph: Painted houses, La Boca, Buenos Aires, Argentina.
Credit: © Chris Coe/Axiom.

MAPS
Nexo Servicios Gráficos.

About Time Out

Founded in 1968, Time Out has expanded from humble London beginnings into the leading resource for those wanting to know what's happening in the world's greatest cities. As well as our influential what's-on weeklies in London, New York and Chicago, we publish more than a dozen other listings magazines in cities as varied as Beijing and Mumbai. The magazines established Time Out's trademark style: sharp writing, informed reviewing and bang up-to-date inside knowledge of every scene.

Time Out made the natural leap into travel guides in the 1980s with the City Guide series, which now extends to over 50 destinations around the world. Written and researched by expert local writers and generously illustrated with original photography, the full-size guides cover a larger area than our Shortlist guides and include many more venue reviews, along with additional background features and a full set of maps.

Throughout this rapid growth, the company has remained proudly independent, still owned by Tony Elliott four decades after he started Time Out London as a single fold-out sheet of A5 paper. This independence extends to the editorial content of all our publications, this Shortlist included. No establishment has been featured because it has advertised, and no payment has influenced any of our reviews. And, for our critics, there's definitely no such thing as a free lunch: all restaurants and bars are visited and reviewed anonymously, and Time Out always picks up the bill.
For more about the company, see www.timeout.com.

Don't Miss

Basílica Nuestra Señora del Pilar p11

Sights & Museums

When it comes to world-famous, must-see attractions, Buenos Aires may be no match for such metropolises as New York, Paris or Rome, but the city's cultural and visual treats are considerable. In addition to the museums, architecture and parks, in a town this buzzing, some of the best sightseeing can be done by grabbing a sidewalk seat in a vintage cafe and watching the (really rather beautiful) world go by. For though it's still something of a bargain destination for travellers from Europe and North America, it is easy to forget that for the first half of the 20th century, this was one of the world's wealthiest cities.

These days, BA's grandeur, though somewhat faded (literally and figuratively), continues to impress. Exhibit A: the exciting new art gallery Colección de Arte Amalia Lacroze de Fortabat (p147), in Puerto Madero. It showcases edgy, contemporary Argentinian art in a futuristic space. The gallery's permanent collection features pieces by Chagall, Dali, Turner, Rodin, Brueghel, and a portrait of the gallery's patron by none other than Andy Warhol.

More museums

Artists from both Argentina and abroad are represented in Museo Nacional de Bellas Artes (MBNA, p84) in Recoleta. Its collections include the most important

Argentinian 19th- to 20th-century artists as well as masters such as El Greco, Rubens, Rembrandt and Goya. Argentina's past is the main attraction of Museo Histórico Nacional del Cabildo y de la Revolución (p51) on Plaza de Mayo – a proud square that was founded in 1580, at the same time as the city. In it stands the Cabildo, BA's old town hall, and its bell tower like a hologram from a frontier-era town. The Cabildo's museum collection is particularly good on the English invasion of 1806.

Nearby, in the Microcentro, BA's commercial centre, you'll find the Museo Histórico y Numismático del Banco de la Nación Argentina (p61), a museum dedicated to the financial history of the nation. One barrio over, in Monserrat, one of the oldest parts of the city, the

Museo Etnográfico (p72) delineates Argentina's indigenous tribes region by region.

Right next door to Montserrat, San Telmo feels even more antiquated, with its centuries-old mansions, street lanterns and cobblestone roads. The barrio also contains several important museums. The Museo Histórico Nacional (p51), with its Tuscan-looking façade, houses a collection that provides insight into what colonial-era Buenos Aires must have been like. After that, clothes horses will want to gallop to the Museo del Traje (p74), a fashion atelier-museum hybrid. El Zanjón de Granados (p74) is also worth a visit; it was a derelict 18th-century mansion that is now part archaeological museum, part event space.

MALBA p102

Of BA's proper museums, Malba: Colección Constantini (p102) is perhaps the most fêted. The works of Frida Kahlo and Diego Rivera, among many others, adorn the walls of the contemporary art museum. Apparently, the building was too small to accommodate Constantini's entire collection, and an entire new 'wing' is under construction underground. Finally, it's impossible to overestimate the importance of Evita Perón in Argentinian culture – the life and times of the former First Lady are explained at the Museo Evita (p102).

Beautiful BA buildings

The posh, tree-lined barrio of Recoleta contains some of BA's most opulent residences and avenues. Compared to the ostentation of its surroundings, the sombre simplicity of the Basilica Nuestra Señora del Pilar (Junín 1904, 4803 6793), an early colonial church (1732), and its crypt, is all the more sobering. Adjacent to Recoleta, Retiro is noteworthy for Plaza San Martín and the impressive buildings that surround it, including Palacio Paz (Avenida Santa Fe 750), the largest private residence in BA. Galerías Pacífico (p63), a grand shopping mall located on the pedestrian calle Florida, is perhaps of more interest to shopaholics, but it's as noteworthy for its spectacularly baroque design as the retail outlets inside. A short distance past the heart of the Microcentro, on Plaza de Mayo, is the Catedral Metropolitana (p51), which has undergone numerous renovations since its construction in 1791 but retains its splendid, neo-classical grandeur. On the large public square, surrounded by all this historic architecture, you can watch the changing of the guard outside the presidential mansion, which,

SHORTLIST

Best new gallery
- Colección de Arte Amalia Lacroze Fortabat (p147)

Grand reopening
- Fundación Proa (p82)

Gorgeous graveyard
- Cementerio de la Recoleta (p84)

Most electic architecture
- Palacio Barolo (p51)

Best international collections
- MALBA: Colección Constantini (p102)
- Museo Nacional de Bellas Artes (p84)

Best specialist museums
- Museo de Armas de la Nación (p65)
- Museo Nacional Ferroviario (p65)
- Museo del Traje (p74)

Great gardens
- Jardín Botánico Carlos Thays (p100)
- Jardín Japonés (p101)
- Jardín Zoológico (p101)

Iconic Buenos Aires
- Caminito (p81)
- El Obelisco (p54)

History lessons
- Casa de la Cultura (p51)
- Catedral Metropolitana (p51)
- Manzana de las Luces (p72)
- Museo Histórico Nacional (p51)
- Museo Histórico Nacional del Cabildo (p51)
- Museo Mitre (p61)

Religious experiences
- Catedral Metropolitana (p51)
- Tierra Santa (p152)

Touching tributes
- Museo Evita (p102)

owing to its colour, is known as the Casa Rosada (Balcarce 50).

Along Avenida de Mayo, the wide, tree-lined boulevard that extends from the Plaza, you will find such architectural wonders as Palacio Barolo (p51) and the quaint, 150-year-old Café Tortoni (p51). The buildings right next door in the barrios of Congreso and Tribunales are just as impressive. Here, the Palacio del Congreso (p55), with its dome-and-columns design, is both reminiscent of and inspired by the US Capitol building in Washington DC. Those with less political and secular leanings will appreciate the religious wonders of Monserrat. Like almost all BA buildings of its type, the Iglesia de San Ignacio, on the corner of Alsina Adolfo y Bolívar, has undergone various alterations over the years; but in this case, the early 18th-century character has been largely preserved. Attached to it is the equally archaic Manzana de las Luces (p72), or block of enlightenment; ironically, it is famous partly for its mysterious underground passages, the original purposes of which are still unknown. Just behind both is the Farmacia de la Estrella (Defensa 201), a pharmacy that has been open since 1834, with a carefully preserved interior and frescoed ceiling.

Open-air attractions

Perhaps the best-known of BA's sights is the Cementerio de la Recoleta (p84), the resting place of Eva Perón. The cemetery is laid out like a well-planned, miniature metropolis and makes for a great afternoon's stroll. Not quite as iconic but nonetheless a quintessential BA point of interest is Avenida 9 de Julio. This is said to be the widest avenue in the world, and it certainly feels like it. Looming over it is the giant,

needle-shaped monument known as El Obelisco (p54), which was once as controversial in BA as the Eiffel Tower was in Paris.

South of here is La Boca – literally named 'the mouth' for its position along the Riachuelo River. The barrio is perhaps best known as the home of BA's legendary football team, Boca Juniors, and the Bombonera stadium, though it has several other worthwhile attractions. These include the Fundación Proa (p82), a large contemporary-art space a short walk from Caminito (p81), one of BA's most tourist-heavy streets.

Palermo, by far the city's largest neighbourhood, is less about sightseeing and more about sampling its myriad cafés, bars and restaurants, but there are also plenty of cultural diversions as well. Outdoors types will appreciate the Parque Tres de Febrero (p88), one of Palermo's loveliest parks; the Jardín Zoológico (p101), the city zoo; the Jardín Botánico Carlos Thays (p100), a botanical garden; and the Jardín Japonés (p101), which is one of the largest Japanese gardens outside of Japan.

Touring tips

It's a good idea to call before visiting museums and galleries, as opening hours can sometimes change without notice. For a guided approach to BA's sights, Tangol (4312 7276, www.tangol.com), Eternautas (5031 9916, www.eter nautas.com), Opción Sur (4777 9029, www.opcionsur.com.ar), and Bike Tours (4311 5199, www.biketours.com.ar) all offer various tours of the city's major landmarks. Artists' Atelier Tour (mobile 15 4049 6107,www.art tour.com.ar) introduces visitors to Palermo-area artists in their working environments.

Standard p112

Eating & Drinking

In recent years, several ingredients – an influx of foreigners, a heightened health consciousness and perhaps boredom – have merged to broaden Buenos Aires's palate and drastically alter the restaurant scene. Since the majority of Argentinians can trace their roots to Spain, Italy or the Middle East, these cultures have long been on the capital's culinary radar. Now *porteños*, or BA locals, are expanding their menus to include Indian, Mexican, French, Southeast Asian and other South American cuisines. The biggest boom has been the proliferation of Japanese and Peruvian eateries. In the case of some, including Osaka (Soler 5608, 4775 6964), one of the city's most popular restaurants, the two have united in one kitchen, spawning a unique flavour. Meanwhile, TÔ (Costa Rica 6000, 4772 4578), will open in April 2009, bringing the Kaiten-zushi, or conveyor belt sushi, to BA.

Inspiration in the kitchen isn't just coming from overseas. One recent trend is the development of Argentinian cuisine beyond the *parrilla,* or grill. Internationally famed chef Francis Mallmann of Patagonia Sur (p82), as well as dozens of others, are producing a new brand of Argentinian haute cuisine. Restó (p55), Manero (p153) and Freud & Fahler (p107) all offer menus that are not quite French, not quite Italian, but rather *porteño* with a twist.

Northern Argentinian restaurants, such as Cumaná (p86), tend to be more casual and

traditional, with menus offering *empanadas* (Argentinian pasties), *locro* (pork and bean stew) and *humita* (grated, cooked sweetcorn). Patagonian restaurants, like Divina Patagonia (p107), are fancier, with the iconic Patagonian lamb being a menu centrepiece. And others, like El Baqueano (p75), focus on introducing indigenous Argentinian meats, such as *yacaré*, an alligator from the north; *jabalí*, a wild boar; and *ñandú*, an Argentinian ostrich.

One of the newest trends in BA restaurant culture is downsizing, creating more intimate dining experiences in which the chefs have more control over the menu. Super chef Germán Martitegui recently opened a small Palermo restaurant, Tegui (p115), which seats considerably fewer people than his grander properties, Olsen (p111) and Casa Cruz (p105). This desire for intimacy also helps explain the *puerta cerrada* (closed door) phenomena, where chefs and owners open their homes to serve a small number of guests.

Naturalist vegetarian restaurants are also sprouting like wheatgrass in Buenos Aires. Pura Vida (p61) in Microcentro and Recoleta, Bio (p103) in Palermo, and VerdeLlama (p142) and Kensho (p141) in Chacarita are just a few.

The barrio scene

BA's various neighbourhoods offer a mixed bag of culinary options. The majority of the noteworthy, fine-dining establishments are clustered in Palermo. Puerto Madero restaurants are famed for their posh atmosphere, but the food is hit or miss. Recoleta, home to Argentina's old money, is also home to some of the city's most exclusive (and expensive) restaurants. San Telmo's food haunts tend to be more on the

SHORTLIST

Best New
- 70 Living (p75)
- El Baqueano (p75)
- Fervor (p86)
- Tegui (p115)
- Vintage Bar (p77)

Best bargains
- Las Cabras (p104)
- Chan Chan (p55)
- Manolo (p76)
- Plaza Asturias (p54)
- Sarkis (p141)
- Status (p56)

Best beef
- Cabaña de las Lilas (p148)
- La Cabrera (p104)
- Don Julio (p107)
- El Trapiche (p115)

For popping the question
- El Bistro (p148)
- La Bourgogne (p85)
- Cluny (p105)
- Manero (p153)
- Nectarine (p86)
- La Vinería de Gualterio Bolívar (p77)

Most locals
- Aramburu (p75)
- Cantina Pierino (p133)
- Don Chicho (p153)

For wine connoisseurs
- La Cava Jufré (p141)
- Gran Bar Danzón (p86)
- Limbo (p107)
- Mira Vida Soho Wine Bar (p111)

Best pizzerias
- Banchero (p55)
- Filo (p66)
- Los Inmortales (p55)
- Piola Pizzerie Italiene (p91)

Beautiful-people watching
- Le Bar (p61)
- Bar Uriarte (p103)
- Olsen (p111)

tô

traditional side, and restaurants in other less touristy neighbourhoods continue to draw increased traffic, including Pura Tierra (p154) in Belgrano, Pan y Arte (Boedo 878, 4957 6702) in Boedo, and Thymus (p141) in Villa Crespo.

The endless and ever-growing number of restaurants in BA can make choosing where to dine a daunting task. A good place to start is with the source of Argentina's national gastronomical pride: grass-fed, free-range beef. Parrillas, restaurants serving *asado*, or barbecued meat, offer the quintessential Argentinian dining experience. There are greasy spoons; unpretentious neighbourhood family joints, like El Obrero (p82); and more upscale affairs, such as La Cabrera (p104) and La Brigada (p75). And there are even *tenedor libre*, or all-you-can-eat parrillas, like Siga La Vaca (www.sigalavaca.com), which has locations throughout the city.

As many are dutiful descendants of Italians, Argentinians carry on two of the most important Italian culinary traditions: pizza and ice-cream. Avenida Corrientes in the Microcentro is home to the historic pizzerias, Los Inmortales (p55) and Banchero (p55), where you can try authentic Argentinian classics *fugazetta* (cheese and onion pizza) and *faina*, a chickpea-flour bread. For more elaborate gourmet pizza options, Filo (p66) is a top destination. There are probably just as many ice-cream parlours as pizzerias. The most well-known chains, Volta, Freddo and Persico, stay open into the wee hours and offer delivery service well past midnight. True to BA's Parisian aspirations, café culture is just as important as restaurant culture, and it's epitomised by Café Tortoni (p51) and Las Violetas (p142).

Drink up!

A visit to Argentina wouldn't be complete without a few bottles of sultry malbec or a crisp torrontés. Luckily, you don't have to go all the way to wine country to sip on an excellent glass of wine. Many

Filo p66

restaurants have sommeliers to create elaborate wine lists covering every grape variety and region in the country. You don't even have to go all the way to Mendoza to experience wine tastings: Alvear Palace Hotel (p171) and 0800 Vino (Anchorena 695, 0800 122 8466, 15 5771 0259 mobile) are just two of the places where you can indulge and learn at the same time.

As for the harder stuff, the Argentinian classic, Fernet and Coke, can be found in most bars. To experience BA mixology at its best, head to Green Bamboo (p107), 878 (p107) and Milion (p86), source of the most killer mojito in town. Pisco and cachaça spirits, also very popular, are shaken and stirred into delicious concoctions at the Standard (p112) and Le Bar (p61).

Tips for dining out

Charging a *cubierto* (cover) remains a common practice in BA. Usually just a few pesos, it's an additional fee per person for bread and use of the plates and silverware that's included in the final bill. Don't confuse it with the tip: the standard gratuity is ten percent of the total bill. Many places only accept cash, so check with the restaurant first if you are planning to use a credit card. Water is always served bottled, with or without gas, and don't even think about lighting up: it was banned in restaurants and bars in 2006, though some have designated smoking areas.

Breakfast consists mostly of sweets, pastries and coffee. Lunch is generally served from noon to 3pm, and it's not uncommon for restaurants to close afterwards for a siesta. Many cafes serve *meriendas* (an afternoon snack similar to breakfast), between the hours of 3pm and 8pm, when most restaurants re-open. Argentinians don't go to dinner until much later: the peak hour is from 10pm to 11pm, and at the weekend it's not uncommon to see packed restaurants past midnight. It's advisable to make reservations in advance; aside from a few top restaurants, you can usually get a reservation the same day.

Sarkis p141

ROSSI & CARUSO
ARGENTINA

SINCE 1868

Posadas 1387 T. (5411) 4811-1538/4811-5357. Recoleta
Av. Santa Fe 1377 T. (5411) 4814-4774 • Galerías Pacífico. 1ºpiso T. (5411) 5555-5308
Huesca, España. Calle Mayor Nº23 Jaca T. (0034) 974 363003
Mail: info@rossicaruso.com | Web: www.rossicaruso.com

La Dolfina p95

WHAT'S BEST
Shopping

Lured by a period of prosperity, a flood of foreign visitors and the spending power of the country's affluent upper class, high-end designer brands began returning to Argentina in recent years. Exclusive labels like Armani and Ermenegildo Zegna opened multiple stores in BA's well-to-do neighbourhoods; local polo-inspired label La Dolfina (p95) has been branching out into new geographical areas, and Carolina Herrera is due to open a store in the elite Patio Bullrich mall (p97).

Soaring inflation and the current international economic climate may mean that more *porteños* are leaving their credit cards at home, but BA's retail sector continues to prosper as the rich keep spending.

And the moneyed crowd continues to do it on Recoleta's exclusive Avenida Alvear, where palatial properties house international couture names and swanky jewellers sit alongside leather goods outfitters and upmarket art galleries. Follow the fashion trail along the surrounding streets toward Patio Bullrich and pick up outstanding garments and accessories from celebrated Argentinian designers like Jessica Trosman and classy menswear label Etiqueta Negra.

More for less

If top-drawer threads and big-ticket bags are not your thing, check out the chain stores and cheap shoe shops along Avenida Santa Fe.

Work your way up this busy thoroughfare from Avenida 9 de Julio to the stretch around the Alto Palermo shopping mall (p115). With a mix of decent local brands like Desiderata (p95) and independents specialising in throwaway rather than timeless items, this is perfect hunting ground for disposable fashion and wardrobe top-ups.

For bargains with more emphasis on the classic, hit the outlets on Avenida Córdoba for past-season and end-of-line stock. In the ten or so blocks on either side of Avenida Scalabrini Ortiz, the mostly mainstream names include Levi's and Argentinian heavyweights Kosiuko (p121) and Chocolate (p92).

If up-to-the-second trendy is more your style, head to Palermo Viejo. From avant-garde Argentinian womenswear designers such as Cora Groppo

(p118) and modish menswear from the likes of Bolivia (p116) to urban casual wear from Diesel and Adidas, the area is also a hub for the up-and-coming, and destination stores like Creative Circus (p118) round up the funkiest finery from an assortment of promising labels.

For the love of leather

High-quality, affordable leather goods have long topped tourist shopping lists here, and the city has plenty of purveyors of premium products. The traditional Casa Lopez (p67) specialises in sheepskin, suede and leather from indigenous animals including the carpincho (a large rodent found in the north of the country) and the yacaré (a South American caiman). Footwear is also abundant, with top-class tango shoes from Comme Il Faut (p92) and cool, throwback leather trainers from 28 Sport

Galerías Pacífico p63

(p115). The budget-conscious should head to the *calle* Murillo in the Villa Crespo neighbourhood, where numerous outlets offer leather jackets, accessories, luggage and even sofas at discounted or wholesale prices. Don't forget to pay attention to quality while the staff sweet-talk you.

Malls and markets

Feeling overwhelmed by the city's shopping options? A comfortable compromise is one of BA's many malls, with their familiar format of fashion, food court and family entertainment. From the elegant Galerías Pacífico (p63) and Patio Bullrich (p97) to the popular Abasto (p133) – which has everything from mid-range clothing stores to electronic dealers and music and bookshop chains Musimundo and Yenny – the majority of the 'shoppings', as they're known, provide a good introduction to Argentinian brands, interspersed with international names, and usually feature multi-screen cinemas.

If you find the 'shoppings' a little soulless or are dying for some fresh air, try the city's weekend craft markets. Recoleta's extensive Feria de Artesanías stretches along the green spaces by this neighbourhood's famous cemetery, providing a pleasant browsing environment for tourists seeking *mate* gourds, ceramics, knitted textiles, leather accessories and jewellery. Feria de Mataderos (p156) and Feria San Pedro Telmo (p77) in Plaza Dorrego are also worthwhile options.

Fashion backward

When it comes to vintage garb, BA may not have the stats to match other international cities, but tucked away in San Telmo are a couple of treasure troves well worth

S H O R T L I S T

Best leather
- Casa Lopez (p67)
- Murillo 666 (p142)

Best antiques and vintage
- El Buen Orden (p77)
- Feria San Pedro Telmo (p77)
- Gil Antigüedades (p78)
- Mercado de las Pulgas (p154)

New import
- Penguin (p123)

Best wine
- La Botica del Vino (p63)
- Lo de Joaquín Alberdi (p121)

Best traditional craft items
- Feria de Mataderos (p156)
- Feria Plaza Francia (p95)
- Kelly's (p63)

Best books and music
- El Ateneo (p92)
- Boutique del Libro (p118)
- Miles Discos (p121)
- Walrus Books (p79)
- Zivals (p56)

Best original gifts and home accessories
- L'Ago (p78)
- Papelera Palermo (p123)
- Sabater Hermanos (p124)

Best menswear
- Balthazar (p116)
- Bensimon (p116)
- Bolivia (p116)
- Félix (p119)

For shoe lovers
- 28 Sport (p115)
- Comme Il Faut (p92)
- Mishka (p121)
- Ricky Sarkany (p156)

Best multi-brand design stores
- Autoría BsAs (p62)
- Puro Diseño (p124)

Best books and music
- Fedro San Telmo (p77)

investigating: El Buen Orden (p77) and Gil Antigüedades (p78). If you like your vintage shopping experience scenic and unsanitised, take a trip to the Mercado de las Pulgas (p154), an alternative to well-trodden San Telmo. Whether it's antiques or atmosphere you're after, this flea market – located beyond Palermo in the Colegiales neighbourhood – provides both.

Buying tips

BA may be a bargain when it comes to beer and beef, but shopping can be harder on your bank account. Visitors benefit from the Global Refund system where, in participating stores, foreign shoppers are entitled to a subsequent reimbursement of taxes paid on purchases over AR$70. Along with your receipt you'll be given a refund cheque to fill in.

Before passing through airport security on your way out of the country, present these for stamping at the counter indicated. Have your purchased goods accessible as you will be required to present them. After your forms are stamped, you will be directed to a refund desk.

The city suffers from a chronic shortage of coinage, and producing a large note for something that costs a couple of pesos may provoke a less-than-cheerful reaction. Some smaller establishments don't accept credit cards or may take only one brand. It's also worth noting that discounts are sometimes available when paying in *efectivo*, or cash, rather than with plastic. These offers may mean that refunds are not given: ask about returns policies as these vary from business to business.

Bolivia p116

Crobar p127

Nightlife

It might not have the clubbing
kudos of London or Berlin – note
the disco balls, the omnipresent
generic electronica and cheesy
1980s pop, and the fact that every
advertising agent with a laptop
calls himself a DJ. Despite all of
the above, though, Buenos Aires
remains a party hub, the best in
South America.

There are still aftershocks
from the Cromagnon disaster of
December 2004, when more than
4,000 clubgoers got trapped inside
the burning nightclub, resulting in
the deaths of 194 people and the
subsequent impeachment of then-
mayor Aníbal Ibarra. Tighter rules
regarding building capacity and
codes have changed BA club
culture in the years since, but
legalities aside, this remains a
nocturnal town, and if you want to
play with the *porteños*, you have to
stay up with them. Clubs don't get
rolling until well past midnight,
peaking after 3am. The brat pack
arrives between 4am and 5am, and
things don't wrap up until close to
breakfast time, when the action
moves to an after-hours venue and
later, sometime post-noon, to the
after after.

Everybody dance now

Like the haircuts inside them,
boliches (as Argentinians call
nightclubs) go in and out of
fashion, but Buenos Aires' biggest
megaclubs have been pumping
out house and electro for ten-plus
years now and most of them are
still going strong – and loud.
Crobar (p127) packs strobe-

addicted twentysomethings into its massive, maze-like domain on Friday nights; Pacha (p152), an international DJ mecca and the King Kong of the Costanera club strip, takes champagne-driven Saturday nights as seriously as *porteñas* take body hair removal. Pacha's chichi, now-defunct neighbour Mint has reinvented itself as Rouge (p152); Caix (p152) still rules after-hours and beyond, when sleepless party rats scurry to the dancefloor for the Sunday afternoon DJ set; while across town, Amerika (p142) remains king of the straight-friendly cheesefests (Gay Maps, www.gaymaps.org, available in shops, bars and hotels, offers good gay listings).

There's more to BA night music than the thump thump thump of techno. In-house beat makers Villa Diamante and G-Love of Zizek (see Niceto, p127) keep party animals on their feet with a mix of hip hop, cumbia and reggaeton. Resident DJ Bad Boy Orange spins drum 'n' bass at Tuesday night's +160 fiesta at Bahrein (p63). Pack -'em-in Cocoliche (p63) and the clandestine hipster fest War Club (www.warclubmember.blogspot.com, address available upon request) cater to alternative night-owl culture. Decade-old Club 69 at Niceto Club (p127) carries on, though it's now more tourist attraction than fringe orgy/spectacle.

Live music is well represented too. As the city continues to draw an increasing number of A-list superstars – recent arrivals have included Madonna, Kylie Minogue, Elton John, Cyndi Lauper and Alanis Morrissette – more pop and rock 'n' roll fans are joining the party in top downtown concert venues like Luna Park (p63) and Teatro Gran Rex (p64).

Watering holes

From the chichi to the downright grungy, BA has an impressive volume and variety of drinking dens, with new spots popping up every week (at the expense of others, like San Telmo's La Farmacia, shutting down). Froufrou cocktails are best enjoyed in equally fabulous surroundings: Milion (p89), with its famous frozen mojito, is a must for its old-mansion setting, while the what-if-Shanghai-gave-birth-to-Buenos Aires'-baby vibe at 647 Club (p74), recently singled out by the *New York Times*, is the ultimate aphrodisiac.

A less glitzy vibe can be found on the rooftop terrace at Carnal (p126), at moody La Cigale (p63), or at Palermo's Mundo Bizarro (p127), where a stockpile of slick indie-artsy regulars choose from 50-odd house cocktails. Dutch import Van Koning (p131) is a veritable beer palace, an anomaly in this oenophile's paradise. Several clubs and bars around town, such as Museum (p80), host a Wednesday night 'After Office' that's a great excuse to party in the middle of the week.

Opening and closing times as well as holidays are all extremely unpredictable, regardless of posted hours, so it's best to call first or come up with a plan B before dropping by and finding out that the owner of your destination venue took off to Brazil on holiday, the bartenders are on strike, or government officials have suddenly, mysteriously, decided that the place needs a break.

Club style

Ditch the hiking boots before hitting the scene: BA's good-looking club crowd is serious about looking effortlessly cool – even if the guys must spend hours getting their seemingly gravity-defying hairstyles just right. Those neon shades and that Kraftwerk tee that you thought would never again see the light of day – or night – will come in handy here.

Despite the emphasis on appearance, there's no official dress code. That said, guys should keep in mind that some of the eagle-eyed super-club doormen might scoff at anything scruffier or more revealing than long trousers and shirts with sleeves. Girls typically enjoy waived or reduced cover charges early in the night. Otherwise, admission prices can be upwards of AR$30 (just under $US10) and are often *con consumición*, entitling you to a drink with your ticket stub.

Mind your manners

Night-owl *porteños* are an outgoing and varied lot (expect to encounter guys and girls, both gay and straight, and plenty in-between, at the increasingly mixed venues), and foreigners can expect to be treated with friendly curiosity from chatty, amicable locals. But when in BA, do as *porteños* do, and imbibe in moderation. Locals aren't likely to guzzle cocktail after cocktail in wild inebriate-me-now fashion.

If you're intent on living it up anyway and would prefer to do so free from disapproving *porteño* stares, tourists and expatriates congregate in popular foreign-run establishments like Sugar (p128) and the Shamrock (p88), where the drink-'till-you-drop party ethic lives on. Meanwhile, Casa Bar (p88) has a daily happy hour, and Gibraltar (p79) dishes up downright tasty pub grub to accompany your pint, granted you can find a mug- or elbow-free surface on which to rest any of it.

DON'T MISS

S H O R T L I S T

Best new
- Belushi Martini Bar (p126)

Best makeover
- Rouge (p152)

Best gay and lesbian
- Ambar la Fox (see El Teatro p156)
- Amerika (p142)
- Glam (p99)
- La Preciosa (p80)
- Sitges (p80)

New York style
- Asia de Cuba (p149)
- Crobar (p127)

Best cocktails
- 878 (p142)
- Mundo Bizarro (p127)

Best pub style
- Gibraltar (p79)
- The Kilkenny (p67)

Excellent tunes
- Bahrein (p63)
- Rumi (p127)

Best happy hour
- Casa Bar (p88)
- Museum (p80)

Super clubs
- Caix (p152)
- Pacha (p152)

For expats
- The Basement Club (p99)
- Shamrock (p88)
- Sugar (p128)

Best underground
- Cocoliche (p63)

Something for everyone
- Niceto Club (p127)

Hip-hop nights
- Club Aráoz (p127)
- Fugees 99 (p99)

Best late-night bar
- Único Barra (p128)

Rojo Tango p150

WHAT'S BEST
Arts & Leisure

Mention the words culture and Buenos Aires to anyone, and tango is no doubt the first thing that comes to mind. Yes, tango is king in BA, but when it comes to the arts, it's hardly the only spectator sport in town. This is a city full of creative people, drawn to the arts, in some cases, by personal impulses, and in others, out of necessity, as Argentina is sorely lacking when it comes to industry. As the quantity and quality of film and art schools and programmes in the capital continue to grow, so does the number of artists and performers.

The result: a city brimming with more art than ever before. The strains of various music forms fill concert halls and dives; movie houses are plentiful; and the stage tradition is booming, with local theatres recently or currently launching productions of such Broadway fare as *Chicago, Sweet Charity, Hairspray* and *Closer*. Whatever you're dying to see or hear – performance-related, of course – you can probably find it somewhere in BA.

Dance

No visit to BA would be complete without a little heel-clicking tango, and the offerings run the gamut from dinner shows staged in restaurants all over town to the naughty cabaret-style Rojo Tango (p150) spectacle at the Faena Hotel + Universe (p179) to amateur couples putting on impromptu shows on the sidewalks of San Telmo and La Boca. For a straightforward, tango-through-the-ages introduction, reserve a table for the nightly show at Café Tortoni (p51), or check out Señor Tango (Vieytes 1652, 4303 0231) in the southern barrio of Barracas for a sexy spectacle that's pure showbiz. Drawing crowds in BA and the rest of the world, the Tangokinesis (www.tango kinesis.com) troupe puts on a show of tango-infused modern dance. They're set to tour Europe in the summer of 2009 but will return to local stages shortly after.

If you'd rather do more than watch, BA's tango classes continue to multiply. The best are held in faded-glory cafés, dilapidated social clubs and old-fashioned community-centre basements. Many of them take place just before the evening's *milonga* (a tango dance party) gets underway and are open to beginners as well as more advanced *milongueros*. Try La Catedral (p144) for electronic tango, La Viruta (p130) for human diversity, Confitería Ideal (p65) for a touch of elegance and Centro Región la Leonesa (p72) for increased *porteño* sightings.

For ballet lovers, Julio Bocca directs the traditional Ballet Argentino company (www.julio bocca.com), which performs in theatres around town. Aerial dance, which combines contemporary dance and acrobatics for a dazzling circus-like spectacle, is also represented in BA: the Brenda Angiel Aerial Dance Company (www.aerialdance.com) has long ruled the local fusion scene and has spent the past few years touring around the world, and Circo del Aire (Peru 856, 4582 5309, www.circodelaire.blogspot.com) offers alternative weekend performances. Consult the websites

DON'T MISS

SHORTLIST

Best new milonga night
- Mondays at La Catedral (p144)

Best tango
- Confitería Ideal (p65)
- La Marshall (p65)
- Sabor a Tango (p139)
- Salón Canning (p129)
- La Viruta (p130)

Best multiplexes
- Cinemark (p150)
- Village Recoleta (p100)

Best mainstream revues
- Teatro Astral (p59)

For classical music
- Casa de la Cultura (p51)
- Catedral de San Isidro (p157)

Multi-purpose venues
- Centro Cultural Borges (p64)
- Centro Cultural Recoleta (see Museo Participativo de Ciencias, p100)

Most awaited reopening
- Teatro Colón (p59)

Oldest theatre
- Teatro Liceo (p59)

Best experimental
- Belisario Club de Cultura (p58)
- Espacio Callejón (p137)

For arthouse lovers
- Lorca (p58)
- Sala Leopoldo Lugones (p59)
- Centro Cultural Ricardo Rojas (p137)

Most eclectic programmes
- Teatro San Martín (p59)

Best gym
- Megatlón (p100)

Best spectator sports
- Campo Argentino de Polo de Palermo (p128)
- Estadio Alberto J Armando (p82)

www.danzabuenosaires.com.ar and www.danzaerea.com.ar for information on other BA-based dance troupes.

Theatre

BA's theatre tradition covers a lot of ground. According to a November 2008 article in Argentina's *La Nación* newspaper, there are 187 registered theatres in BA – more than in New York, London and Paris. The offerings here range from Broadway-style cheesefest spectacles launched in the bright-lights venues concentrated mainly on Avenida Corrientes, to quirky experimental works staged on a mostly donation basis in dive bars around the Abasto barrio. You can catch open-air theatre during the summer months at the Centro Cultural Recoleta (see Museo Participativo de Ciencias p137), and for a more left-of-centre off-Broadway-style experience, there's the Abasto playhouse El Camarín de las Musas (p136). Check the English-language *Buenos Aires Herald* or on www.wipe.com.ar for live-theatre schedules.

The government-sponsored theatre circuit is the Complejo Teatral de Buenos Aires, with five venues scattered around the city centre. Teatro San Martín (p59) is the flagship, and tickets for all can be picked up at the box office or website, www.teatrosan martin.com.ar.

Film

There's no shortage of cinema options in BA. Choose from modern multiplex theatres

Estadio Monumental p156

specialising in mainstream Hollywood fare (ticket fees are reduced from Monday to Thursday; see www.pantalla.info for listings) or avant-garde art-house nickelodeons for the best in independent releases. Cosmos (p137) and Centro Cultural Ricardo Rojas (p137) both offer diverse flicks. During the warmer-weather months, Ciudad Cultural Konex (p137) and Centro Cultural Recoleta (see Museo Participativo de Ciencias, p137) have outdoor summertime series, screening, respectively, classic films and contemporary movies, and indies.

Music

We're still drumming our fingers, waiting for the light at the end of the renovation tunnel at Teatro Colón (p59), the continent's grandest opera house; it shut its doors for a makeover in 2006 and has yet to reopen them. Luckily, there are other options for those with highbrow music taste as classical and opera flourish elsewhere in BA. The Casa de la Cultura (p51) holds chamber music concerts every Friday, while San Telmo's gorgeous Spanish-style Teatro Margarita Xirgú (p81) and La Manufactura Papelera (p81) also feature classical music. Just north of town, the Catedral de San Isidro (p157) puts together free afternoon chamber performances. For a symphony of strings, track down the long-running ensemble Mozarteum Argentino (www.mozarteumargentino.org) from April through October at the Teatro Coliseo (Marcelo T de Alvear 1125, 4816 5943).

Sports

Right up there with tango among essential Argentinian pastimes is football. The two major national teams are River Plate and Boca Juniors, whose home is Estadio Alberto J Armando (p82), affectionately known as 'La Bombonera' (the chocolate box), in the La Boca barrio. River Plate's in-town games play out in Estadio Monumental (p156) in Nuñez. For Boca or River Plate matches, you can get tickets through Ticketek (52377200, www.ticketek.com.ar). For any other team, tickets can be bought at the relevant ground (cash only). The better a team is doing, the higher the ticket price. Standard prices range from AR$24-$60, rising to AR$100.

Coming in a not-so-close second among sports fanatics is rugby. The season lasts from March to November, and many of the games play out in the San Isidro Club (p157). Polo, an up-and-coming favorite among *porteños* and visitors, is spawning not only numerous disciples to the game but nearly as many fashion victims (see box p155). Matches are concentrated mainly in the northern, upscale barrios, but you can catch games centrally in Campo Argentino de Polo de Palermo (p128).

Further information

To find theatre, music and film schedules, log on to www.whats upbuenosaires (in English) and www.vuenosairez.com (in Spanish). Daily newspapers *La Nación*, *Clarín* and the English-language *Buenos Aires Herald* have the most up-to-date cultural calendars, and www.bue.gov.ar has a seasonal city guide listing tons of free events. Tickets for stage productions, including concerts, are sold at www.ticketek.com.ar, www.online seats.com/buenos-aires and through Ticketmaster (4321 9700). Try the discount ticket counters first: www.123info.com.ar and www.unica-cartelera.com.ar are quick references.

Calendar

Chinese New Year

The following is our selection of annual events. Always confirm dates before making travel plans.

January

Late Jan-early Feb **Chinese New Year**
On Arribeños 2000-2200, Belgrano
Chinese Embassy 4541 5085

February

Ongoing **Chinese New Year**
(see Jan)

Mid Feb **ATP Buenos Aires, Copa Telmex**
Buenos Aires Lawn Tennis Club, Palermo
www.copatelmex.com
For one week in Feb, male tennis players compete on clay courts for a cup victory.

End Feb **BA Fashion Week**
La Rural, Palermo
www.bafweek.com

Feb-June **Torneo Clausura**
Various venues
www.torneo.cablevision.com.ar
The football tournament that closes the regular Division One season.

March

Ongoing **Torneo Clausura**
(see Feb)

Mid Mar **Código País Festival de Música y Diseño**
Tribuna Plaza, Palermo
www.codigopais.com
Five days of the latest in local productions, from music and design to technology, gastronomy and children's products.

End Mar **Nuestros Caballos Exposición Internacional Equina y de Industria Hípica**
La Rural, Palermo
www.nuestroscaballos.com.ar
A week-long international equine and horseriding exhibition.

End Mar-early Apr **Buenos Aires Festival Internacional de Cine Independiente (BAFICI)**
Abasto shopping centre and other venues
www.bafici.gov.ar
Two-week independent film festival.

End Mar-early Apr **Copa República Argentina**
Hipódromo de Palermo
www.aapolo.com
Over two weeks, teams compete in the final round of this national polo cup.

End Mar-early Apr **Quilmes Rock**
Club Ciudad de Buenos Aires, Nuñez; Estadio Monumental, Belgrano
www.quilmes.com.ar
Big-name rock festival, with four dates over the course of two weeks.

April

Ongoing **Torneo Clausura** (see Feb); **BAFICI** (see Mar); **Copa República Argentina** (see Mar); **Quilmes Rock** (see Mar)

Mid Apr-mid May **La Gran Via de Mayo**
Avenida de Mayo
www.bue.gov.ar
On weekends, Avenida de Mayo is a month-long backdrop for dance, theatre and musical performances.

Late Apr-early May **Feria Internacional del Libro de Buenos Aires**
La Rural, Palermo
www.el-libro.org.ar
Three-week-long international book fair.

Apr-Nov **Gallery Nights**
Various venues
www.artealdia.com
Participating galleries open to the public for free visits at 7pm on the last Fri of each month.

May

Ongoing **Torneo Clausura** (see Feb); **La Gran Via de Mayo** (see Apr);

Feria Internacional del Libro (see Apr); **Gallery Nights** (see Apr)

Late May **La Feria de los Chicos**
Centro de Exposiciones, Palermo
www.revistaplanetario.com.ar
Products, activities, plays, music and puppet shows for kids, over three days.

Late May **arteBA**
La Rural, Palermo
www.arteba.com
Five-day contemporary art fair.

June

Ongoing **Torneo Clausura** (see Feb); **Gallery Nights** (see Apr)

Mid June **Ciudad Emergente**
Centro Cultural Recoleta
www.ciudademergente.gov.ar
A five-day rock and pop music festival with an indie vibe, featuring local and foreign talent.

July

Ongoing **Gallery Nights** (see Apr)

Mid July **Arteclásica Feria de Arte Moderno y Contemporáneo**
Centro Costa Salguero, Costanera Norte
www.arteclasica.com.ar
Five-day classic and contemporary art fair with conferences, chats and round-table discussions.

20 **Día del Amigo (Friend's Day)**

August

Ongoing **Gallery Nights** (see Apr);

Late Aug **Festival de Tango**
Various venues
www.festivaldetango.gob.ar
Ten-day tango festival leading up to the world championship.

End Aug-early Sept **Buenos Aires Percussion**
Various venues
www.buenosaires.gov.ar

Fight Club

Whether you're looking to release a little mid-vacation steam or just indulge in some harmless fun, grab a pillow and prepare to rumble at BA's spring Lucha de Almohadas (pillow fight). Any pillow will do, but one filled with feathers is best, according to Marina Ponzi, 25, of Buenos Aires, who launched the event in 2006. Inspired by a YouTube video of a similar *lucha* in San Francisco, Ponzi, who works as an event organiser, decided Buenos Aires needed to host one too. 'It seemed to me an original, creative and different idea,' she says.

Every kind of pillow – some fluffy and full of goose feathers, others stuffed with foam, some square, some rounded and some rectangular – was used to slug it out for more than two hours in Palermo in front of the BA planetarium in November of 2008. Small bands developed, and they bombarded unsuspecting victims with gaggles of pillows before moving on to someone else. Besieged participants escaped

to the sidelines of the fray where they rehydrated and inspected the damage to their own pillows. The contents of many erupted onto the lawn, giving the grass a snow-like coating on the hot spring day.

The first pillow fight in 2006 attracted more than 3,000 pillow-wielding combatants. After a year-long hiatus in Spain, Ponzi returned, and so did the pillow fight. The second Lucha de Almohadas attracted a smaller, but no less energetic crowd of 1,500 *porteños* and travellers. Ponzi says she hasn't committed to a specific date for future pillow fights, but she likes them because they're fun and free. Once plans are finally underway, you can follow the progress on her blog, at www.luchadealmohadas.blogspot. com. With more than 7,500 members in her Facebook pillow-fight group, she is sure to find plenty of interest when the next battle breaks out. That leaves plenty of time to buy an extra pillow and maybe loosen the stitches along the edge.

Two-week long percussion festival, featuring clinics and workshops as well as performances.

End Aug **Mundial de Tango**
Various venues
www.mundialdetango.gob.ar
Tango world championship, over ten days.

Aug-Dec **Torneo Apertura**
Various venues
www.torneo.cablevision.com.ar
The football tournament that opens the regular Division One season.

September

Ongoing **Gallery Nights** (see Apr);
Buenos Aires Percussion (see Aug);
Torneo Apertura (see Aug)

Early Sept **Buenos Aires Feria Internacional de la Música (BAFIM)**
Centro de Exposiciones, Palermo Chico
www.bafim.buenosaires.gov.ar
Four-day international music festival.

Early Sept **South American Music Conference**
Centro Costa Salguero, Costanera Norte
www.samc.net
A one-day celebration of electronic music, art and dance culture.

Early Sept **Vinos y Bodegas**
La Rural, Palermo
www.expovinosybodegas.com.ar
Four days of all things wine-related.

21 Día de la Primavera (First Day of Spring)

Late Sept **La Semana del Arte**
Various venues
www.lasemanadelarte.com.ar
Galleries, museums and cultural centres participate in a week-long art celebration.

Late Sept-early Oct **Brandon Fest**
Various venues
www.brandongayday.com.ar/brandonfest

Feria Internacional del Libro p34

Selected films are shown at this week-long international LGBT film festival.

Late Sept-early Oct **Pepsi Music Festival**
Estadio Obras Sanitarias, Nuñez
www.estadioobras.com
Seven days of national and international rock music.

October

Ongoing **Gallery Nights** (see Apr);
Torneo Apertura (see Aug); **Brandon Fest** (see Sept*)*; **Festival Guitarras del Mundo** (see Sept)

Early Oct **Festival Internacional de Teatro de Buenos Aires**
Various venues
www.festivaldeteatroba.gov.ar
Two-week international theatre festival.

Mid Oct **Expo Trastiendas**
Centro de Exposiciones, Palermo
www.expotrastiendas.com.ar
Galleries and private collectors gather to showcase works by more than 500 national and international artists, over one week.

Mid Oct **Festival de Cine & Latinamericano de Buenos Aires**
ATLAS Recoleta
www.festlatinoba.com.ar

A week-long series of conferences, chats and workshops leading up to the gay pride parade on the first Saturday of November.

November

Ongoing **Gallery Nights** (see Apr); **Torneo Apertura** (see Aug); **Buenos Aires Photo** (see Oct); **Ciclo de Música Contemporánea** (see Oct); **Buenos Aires Rojo Sangre** (see Oct); **Personal Fest** (see Oct); **Semana del Orgullo** (see Oct)

Early Nov **Creamfields**
Autódromo de Buenos Aires, Villa Lugano
www.creamfieldsba.com
One-day electronica festival.

Two weeks of Latin American film and video screenings.

Late Oct-early Nov
Buenos Aires Photo
Palais de Glace, Recoleta
www.buenosairesphoto.com
Five-day art fair dedicated entirely to photography.

Late Oct-mid Nov **Ciclo de Música Contemporánea**
Teatro San Martín, Microcentro
www.teatrosanmartin.com.ar
Cycle of contemporary music, with concerts spread out over the month.

Late Oct-early Nov **Buenos Aires Rojo Sangre**
Complejo Monumental Lavalle, Microcentro
http://rojosangre.quintadimension.com
Week-long festival for bizarre low-budget, independent horror films.

End Oct-early Nov **Personal Fest**
Club Ciudad de Buenos Aires, Nuñez
www.personal.com.ar/personalfest
Two-day international music festival.

End Oct-first Sat of Nov
Semana del Orgullo
Various venues
www.marchadelorgullo.org.ar

Mid Nov **Diversa Festival Internacional de Cine Gay, Lésbico, Trans de Argentina**
Various venues
www.diversa.com.ar
Ten-day international LGBT film festival.

Mid Nov **Gran Premio Nacional**
Hipódromo Argentino de Palermo
www.palermo.com.ar
One of the most important derbies of the year.

Mid Nov **La Noche de los Museos**
Various venues
www.lanochedelosmuseos.com.ar
Free entrance to the city's museums throughout the night.

Mid Nov-early Dec **Campeonato Argentino Abierto de Polo**
Hipódromo Argentino de Palermo
www.aapolo.com
The world's fifth oldest polo competition takes place over the course of a month.

Late Nov **Lucha de Almohadas**
Plaza Dr. Benjamín Gould, Palermo
www.luchadealmohadas.blogspot.com
Flash mob pillow fight.

Late Nov-early Dec **Festival Internacional de Tango Queer**
Various venues
www.festivaltangoqueer.com.ar

It's all about same-sex dance partners at this week-long tango fest.

December

Ongoing **Torneo Apertura** (see Aug); **Campeonato Argentino Abierto de Polo** (see Nov); **Festival Internacional de Tango Queer** (see Nov)

Early Dec **Buenos Aires Jazz Festival Internacional**
Various venues
www.buenosairesjazz.gov.ar
Five-day international jazz festival.

Early Dec **Festival Buenos Aires Danza Contemporánea**
Various venues
www.buenosairesdanza.gov.ar
Week-long contemporary dance festival.

Early Dec **Copa Peugeot Argentina de Tenis**
Buenos Aires Lawn Tennis Club
www.copapeugeotdetenis.com.ar
Male tennis stars duke it out over four days for a cup title.

Mid Dec **Gran Premio Internacional Carlos Pellegrini**
Hipódromo de San Isidro
www.hipodromosanisidro.com.ar
The biggest event of the year at the only grass horse-racing track in Argentina.

BA Fashion Week p33

Between friends

Here's one more reason to get the party started in BA: *el Día del Amigo*. It may not be an official bank holiday or as A-list as *Navidad* (Christmas) or *el Año Nuevo* (New Year's), but it's no Groundhog Day either. It gives BA's friendship-worshipping *porteños* one state-sanctioned day, 20 July, to obsess over their social lives and tie up telecommunication lines while helping to boost the economy by exchanging small gifts and hitting the town with gusto.

The roots of Friends' Day are humble indeed. Argentinian professor and two-time Nobel Peace Prize nominee Enrique Febbraro successfully lobbied the government in 1969 to establish a day that encourages peace and harmony while celebrating good mates. That year's moon landing – an event that brought people together in front of their TV sets worldwide – further inspired his effort. Although the U.S. Congress had instituted Friendship Day nationally in 1935, the first Sunday in August (as it is celebrated in North America and India) never really caught on, unlike Argentina's Friends' Day, which *porteños* take very seriously. You will likely find restaurants and nightspots in BA packed with friends gathering to celebrate one another. So take advantage of the great specials on offer, and the opportunity to spread a little love – and don't forget to make your reservations at least a week in advance.

Itineraries

Reserva Ecológica p147

BA on a Budget

Any serious traveller knows the best way to experience a new place is to submerge oneself in the culture and live as the locals do. The secret to seeing the capital through *porteño* eyes? Spend as little money as possible. The average BA citizen doesn't have tons of pesos to fritter away on expensive wine tastings and over-priced tango dinner shows, nor do they feel the pull of the typical overcrowded tourist hotspots.

But buying quality experiences with as few pesos as possible doesn't mean you have to skimp on fun. For less than US$20 (AR$68, give or take a few pesos), you can easily take on the city as locals do, with an entertaining, activity-filled day. So skip those usual visitor haunts and play *porteño* for the day – just make sure you have plenty of coins on hand as BA *colectivos* (buses) don't accept bills. And remember, prices are always subject to change.

START :
Your hotel

Rise and shine to take advantage of the continental breakfast that is typically included in BA hotel room rates. With eggs, bacon and potatoes often on the menu, it's a lot more satisfying than the standard coffee and *facturas* (pastries) that you are likely to find at most cafés. After filling up, get ready to work it off. Head to San Telmo via *colectivo* (Nos. 9, 10, 20, 24, 28, 29, 45, 86, 195, AR$1.25) and rent a bicycle from **La Bicicleta Naranja** (Pasaje Giuffra 308, 4362 1104, www.labicicletanaranja.com. ar). The cost is AR$8 per hour, and be sure to bring some sort of identification to leave as collateral.

From there, coast down the hill and veer right onto Paseo Colón. Watch out for ruthless drivers and fellow bike riders alike. Pass the Facultad de Ingeniería on your left and take the first left onto Estados Unidos. Two blocks later, crossing

or this winter

beat the winter blues is by embracing
the colors of the rainbow. We're hot
from a single vivid item as an accent
rth of tones at once. Our advice: Start
own table, and if you're giving
k a peek in the giftee's cabinet so
ent what's already there. DANA DICKEY

Avenida Ingeniero Huergo, the street becomes Rosario Vera Peñaloza. Continue straight ahead and pedal past Puerto Madero to the **Reserva Ecológica** (p147).

Located on the far side of the docks near the city center, the reserve offers a one-of-a-kind wildlife experience along the coast of the Rio de la Plata. Travel by bike on the 'Camino de los Lagartos' (Path of the Lizards) or lock up your wheels at the park entrance and set off on foot on one of the many trails. Keep an eye out for ceibo trees, iguanas and more than 200 bird species. For a more structured approach, guided tours are available weekends at 10.30am free of charge, and moonlight tours once a month, with a reservation.

If the nature loving – and pedalling – has made you a little hungry, ride down *calle* del Canal, which runs parallel to the reserve and is teeming with food vendors. Nab a *choripán* (baguette sandwich with grilled sausage) and a cold Coke for AR$9. Spread on some *chimichurri* (a traditional Argentine sauce made from chopped parsley, garlic, onion and other spices) or select from the medley of available condiments used to spice up local meat dishes.

Browse the stalls at the fair in **Plazoleta Haroldo Conti** across from the entrance to Reserva Ecológica, before hopping back on the bike and heading to Giuffra. Once you're on your own two feet again, walk back down to Paseo Colón. Cross the avenue to the bus stop at the steps of the Facultad de Ingenieria and catch bus No. 33 to Costanera Norte (AR$1.25).

The 20- to 30-minute bus ride will give you ample time to rest up if you're lucky enough to claim a seat. Just past the Port of Buenos Aires on your right, the Costa Salguero Complex will come into view. Prepare to get off at the following traffic light, when Punta Carrasco appears on your right. Cross *calle* Rafael Obligado and look for the light blue fence on your left which will take you to the entrance of **Parque Manuel Belgrano** (Salguero 3450, 4807 7700), which is open 10am daily from January to March. AR$7 will gain you access to the pool, and although you won't be able to build a sand castle, make believe you're at the beach and join a pick-up game of volleyball or relax in the shade under the park's trees.

After a refreshing dip and some rest and relaxation, it's time to move on. A short walk to your left along Avenida Sarmiento will take you to nearby **Parque Tres de Febrero**. To get there, follow Sarmiento past the planetarium to Avenida Figueroa Alcorta, where you'll find Plaza Holanda on the right and Tres de Febrero on the left. Families come to enjoy the park's open space while couples spend quality romantic time lounging on the grass. Join the exercise enthusiasts and rent a pair of rollerblades (AR$8 for 30min), or a *carrito*, a small cart with bicycle pedals (AR$15 for 30 min for two riders), and circle the track while people watch.

After you've had your fill of park life, return to Sarmiento and turn left onto Avenida del Libertador. Cross the street and wait for bus No.130 near the corner of Libertador and Republica de la India (AR$1.25). The bus travels along Libertador, which eventually becomes Avenida Leandro Alem. Disembark at Corrientes and find the subway entrance. Walk underground and board Line B going to Los Incas (AR$1.10) At peak hours (morning, lunch and after work) seats are scarce, so squeeze into any open space or grab a pole and hang on.

Any *Subte* ride isn't complete without people peddling things from ripped DVDs and *trucho* (fake) Nike socks to markers and electrical adapters, all usually for less than AR$10. If you're lucky, you might find yourself entertained by improv actors, musicians and even underage jugglers. Don't let yourself get too distracted though, or you'll miss your exit at the Federico Lacroze station.

Once you've climbed back above ground, you won't miss the **Cementerio de la Chacarita** (p140) – just look for the huge wall. Opened in the early 1870s to house the casualties of a yellow fever epidemic, this lesser-known cemetery receives far fewer visitors than its more popular, older sister, Cementerio de la Recoleta. But don't hold that against it. The Chacarita cemetery is more than ten times the size of the Recoleta graveyard, and one of the biggest in the world.

The tall columns of the entryway lead to a web of streets, which in turn, lead to vaults and mausoleums with underground galleries and typical graveyards with headstones and wooden crosses. Though it's not as exclusive as the Recoleta necropolis, Chacarita is not without its 'star' residents, which include tango singing legend Carlos Gardel and Argentinian poet Alfonsina Storni. Cover as much ground as your legs can stand – seeing everything could take hours – and if you've got the time (and the energy) check out the adjoining British and German cemeteries.

Hungry yet? By now it's probably around sunset, so head back to the subway, pay AR$1.10, and board a train going to LN Alem. Exit at the Uruguay station, and just above ground you'll find an Avenida Corrientes classic, **Guerrín** (Corrientes 1368, 4371 8141), where you can get some of the tastiest pizza in town. Order two slices with your choice of toppings and a soft drink or cold beer for AR$10.50, and squeeze into a spot on one of the long counters.

After eating, return to Corrientes and enjoy the night air. It's happy hour somewhere (or, as they call it in BA, 'after office'), and you've only spent around AR$60, so you've probably got enough cash left for a few cheap drinks to cap off your adventure or maybe even for a taxi back to your hotel. If you go for the former option, pick a bar, any bar, and let the good times roll.

Cementerio de la Chacarita p140

Parque Tres de Febrero

The Love Tour

We often hear it said: 'I've fallen in love with Buenos Aires!' Which is fine – until you actually think about it. What good is a city as a lover? Can you take it home to meet your parents? Will it share its headphones with you on the subway? Will it get down on its knees and forage for stray aspirin when you're hungover?

Better, surely, to fall in love with another human being using Buenos Aires as a backdrop for your passion. It's a city that offers a rich array of possibilities for a romantic day out. What follows is an itinerary that will keep you snared in the tender trap from midday through the wee small hours of the *madrugada* (early morning).

START:
Palermo Viejo

Leave dawn to the larks, and start your day with lunch. Take your date to **Il Ballo del Mattone** (p102), a family-run trattoria in Palermo Viejo that unites a modish junk-shop aesthetic with good homemade pasta and puds. The romance lies in the bohemian, early 1960s Roman vibe; if you've always wanted to channel Marcello Mastroianni or Anita Ekberg in *La Dolce Vita* (later in this tour, there's even a chance to go stand in a fountain), now's your chance. Dodge the bald mannequins and Fellini posters and slide into one of the banquettes.

After you've enjoyed your pasta specials seated side by side, settle up and head out onto Gorriti Street, into the startling mix of traditional middle-class barrio and bohemian-bourgeois trendsetter that is contemporary Palermo Viejo. Take the first left and then the first right onto Honduras, cross the railway line several blocks ahead and stroll along to the intersection with Gurruchaga, where you then take a left. One block away on the corner of El Salvador is **Amor Latino** (p115) one of the city's premier peddlers of sexy undies. Grab a white-hot bra, panties and mask combo for you or your date (or for both of you – you're not in Kansas anymore), and stash it away for later.

There's a fair chance you might want to call off the tour right now and head straight back to your suite. So it goes. Otherwise, continue along Gurruchaga until you hit Santa Fe. Take a left, and then a right on to Sarmiento, skirting the botanical gardens and the zoo until you reach the entrance to the **Rosedal**, at Iraola and Sarmiento.

The Rose Garden is the gorgeous and immensely popular nucleus of Parque Tres de Febrero, and will likely be packed with trysting couples like yourselves. Stop and smell the roses; there are more than 12,000 different bushes to choose from.

Continue towards the heart of the park and you'll find yourself in the **Jardín de los Poetas** (Poets' Garden), with its fountains and busts of famous rhymers. Among the dead heads are Argentinian poets Alfonsina Storni and Jorge Luis Borges and world literary greats such as Dante Alighieri and Federico Garciá Lorca. Impress your date by standing in front of Shakespeare's bust and reciting the imperishable lines from the bard's 116th sonnet: 'Love alters not with his brief hours and weeks/But bears it out even to the edge of doom/If this by error and upon me proved/I never writ, nor no man ever loved'.

Now for something even cheesier. Just beyond the Poet's Garden you'll see a white bridge crossing the lake that surrounds the Rosedal. This is the **Puente de los Enamorados** or Bridge of the

Lovers. According to legend, couples should step on to the bridge hand in hand, right foot first, and proceed half way across before stopping for a kiss. Apparently this will guarantee a successful relationship (though a pleasing personality, a steady job and a daily personal hygiene regime will probably help too).

The park may be romantic, but it's also crowded. What you need now is some quality time *à deux* – and what could be better than a sunset river cruise you booked ahead of time with **Smile on Sea** (www.smileonsea.com). Depending on the season, your boat will depart from the Yacht Club Buenos Aires in Puerto Madero (take a taxi from Palermo) sometime between 5pm and 7pm (be sure to confirm the timing in advance). For US$200, you'll be piloted out into the Río de la Plata, plied with champagne, and afforded a unique view of the city as it recedes into the distance.

Gran Bar Danzón p86

ITINERARIES

Regardless of what time you glide back into port, the night, as they say around here, will still be in nappies. Linger awhile in Puerto Madero, perhaps taking a romantic stroll across the sinuous Puente de la Mujer, before hailing a taxi. If you're not in the mood for a pre-dinner cocktail by now, you haven't been trying hard enough.

Your destination is **Gran Bar Danzón** (p86), a long-established wine bar that continues to outstrip the competition. Ascend the candle-lit stairway and grab a couple of pews at the long bar. Here, you can either put the award-winning wine list (most labels are available by the glass) through its paces or sip on one of star mixologist Norman Barone's cocktails of the week.

The gorgeously dim and perfectly calibrated lighting is what makes this venue so popular with couples. Regardless of how many other flirting twosomes are

crammed into the room, it always feels intimate and cosy.

It will take something special to make you want to leave Danzón – which is why you made a reservation at **Nectarine** (p86), BA's best French restaurant. Even the walk there is aphrodisiacal as it takes you through upscale Recoleta, where the broad boulevards and mansard-roofed palaces look more like Paris than Paris ever did.

The restaurant itself, sheltered from the general hubbub in an alleyway close to the intersection of Vicente López and Montevideo, is a continuation on this old-world theme. Nectarine is the acme of fine dining, offering formal – but not overly solemn – service. A range of beautifully sculptured and richly flavoured dishes are available either a la carte or on an eight-course tasting menu, and the wine list is a labyrinth of possibilities; let the experienced sommelier be your guide. Duck confit and cabernet by candlelight – are you and your *amor* in the mood yet?

Once you've polished off the coffee and *petit fours*, and emerged blinking into the silvery city light, several options are available. You can call it a night and slink back to your hotel room (ten points for lust, zero for stamina); you can go on to one of BA's nightclubs and dance till dawn (five and five); or you can book yourselves a two- or three-hour stint at a *telo*, (love motel) easily recognised by the blinking neon sign that reads *albergue transitorio* (ten out of ten on both counts). The Arab-styled boudoirs of **Rampa Car** in Palermo Viejo (Angel J Carranza 1347, 4773 6964, www.hotelrampacar.com) are perfect in-the-mood enhancers. What next? Well, that's hopefully something you don't need a guidebook for.

BA After Sunset

Night-owl *porteños* are notoriously tardy, and perhaps it's because the later, the better. The setting sun marks the point where play replaces work, and the farther night falls, the deeper the beauty of the capital. Take a four-to-six-hour sundown walk around the architectural highlights of downtown Buenos Aires, and you'll surely encounter a surplus of unique visual stimulation.

START:
Puerto Madero

When the rays of light from the receding sun turn the colour of chilled Quilmes, make your way to the water's edge. Constructed between 1998 and 2001 by Spanish architect Santiago Calatrava, the **Puente de la Mujer** (Bridge of the Lady, Juana Manuela Gorriti and C. Lorenzini) anchors Puerto Madero to mainland Buenos Aires and offers sweeping views of the area's glass skyscrapers.

After lingering for a while in the dying light, start off your night-time expedition by following the arrow-shaped span of the bridge towards the city centre. Move up the hill to the **Casa Rosada** (Balcarce 50) and **Plaza de Mayo**, where floodlights illuminate the facades of historic buildings around the square: the **Cabildo** (p51), the **Catedral Metropolitana** (p51) and the **Banco de la Nación**.

Next, walk up **Avenida de Mayo**. On your right, check out the ornate **Casa de la Cultura** (p51), which was constructed in 1896 and was once the former headquarters of Argentina's daily newspaper *La Prensa*. Look out for the stencil art and spray-painted slogans adorning the walls along the *avenida*; many of them voice the latest opinions about social injustices and other issues both at home and abroad.

Take a right on Esmeralda and walk two blocks to the **Continental Hotel** (Saenz Peña 725). Located in a restored building designed by architect Alejandro Bustillo, the hotel is an excellent example of 1940s BA architecture. In the ground-floor bar Cetrino, order a café *cortado*, or make it

Puerto Madero

un doble to boost your energy and propel you into the nightlife.

Two other interesting drinking and eating options can be found along Sarmiento, the next *calle* down. **Brighton** (Sarmiento 645, 4322 1515) is a bar with acres of polished wood and brass that exudes an old-world British feel, while next door **Café Paulin** (Sarmiento 635, 4325 2280), sports a circular bar that creates a convivial *Cheers*-like atmosphere.

Continue along Sarmiento and make a right on Suipacha; the *fleur de lys* logo hanging in front of **Confitería Ideal** (p65) is hard to miss. From 9.30pm, seven days a week, you can take tango classes inside this former sweet shop. A *milonga* tango party follows most nights. Even if you don't feel like dancing, peek inside at the Parisian-style elevator and dusty, antique mirrors lining the walls of this turn-of-the-century building.

Next up, walk a few steps down to Avenida Corrientes, turn right, and head a few short blocks to the impossibly wide **Avenida 9 de Julio**, where the impressively phallic Washington Monument look-alike **Obelisco** (p54) is lit up at night along with the buildings and ever-changing array of billboard advertisements that surround this iconic intersection.

Walking south on Avenida 9 de Julio, re-enter Avenida de Mayo five blocks up to the right, and continue straight to **Plaza del Congreso**, some half dozen blocks ahead. Admire the sodium lights that splash the *avenida* in pools of yellow and soak the ornate facades of these Parisian-inspired buildings in a faded sepia tone straight out of a 1930s film noir.

Even after dark, the area is buzzing with people walking their dogs (be careful not to step in any poop) or chatting on park benches and exchanging lingering glances with strangers. If you're feeling a little competitive, step into **36 Billares** (Avenida de Mayo1259) for a game of pool, or check out one of the tango shows that take place here nightly.

The area around Plaza del Congreso is a mixed bag of bland apartment blocks and official-looking residences. In the leafy park in front of the Palacio de Congreso, look for the **The Thinker**, a sculpture created from Rodin's original mould. To the right of the Palacio is the **Confitería del Molino** (Rivadavia 1801), a 150-year-old building with

Plaza de Mayo

a rather Dutch-looking windmill on its facade. The *confitería* (café), closed in 1997, was once a meeting point for Argentinian politicans.

Hail a radio taxi out front and head to **Plaza San Martín** in Retiro. Amidst stately trees, gorgeous buildings and impressive statues, amorous couples engage in steamy make-out sessions. If you're in the right company, this is the perfect place for a kiss.

From San Martín, take Avenida Sante Fe less than one block to Esmeralda, turn right, and follow the *calle* as it turns into Arroyo and eventually Alvear, BA's most exclusive *avenida*. After passing the **Park Hyatt Buenos Aires** (p177), admire the darkly gothic **Maguire House** (Avenida Alvear 1683). Although it's not lit up at night, enough illumination from the nearby street lamps will reveal the creepy details on the mansion's exterior and intertwined in the massive wrought-iron gates. If the Addams Family had set up house in Buenos Aires, this would have been their first choice.

Ready for a change of night-time scenery? Make Palermo your next destination and get there *porteño*-style by bus. While the *subte* (BA's subway) may need its beauty sleep

(trains run between 5am and 10.45 pm daily), *colectivos* (BA buses) run all night long. From the Maguire House, U-turn back to Montevideo, take a right and walk towards the intersection of Juncal and Vicente Lopez at Plaza Vicente Lopez. There you can hop on the No. 110 bus to Palermo Soho which will leave you a few blocks from **Plazoleta Cortázar** (otherwise known as Plaza Serrano). The bar possibilities lining the blocks on *calles* Costa Rica, Gorriti, Godoy Cruz and Avenida Scalabrini Ortiz, are endless. Pick a watering-hole and pull up a stool. **Crónico** (Jorge Luis Borges 1646, 4833 0708) is open 24 hours, and expats flock to **Sugar** (p128). And because weekends in BA officially begin on Monday night, any day of the week you'll find a club offering a musical menu ranging from electronica to retro 1980s pop. Time flies when you're having fun, especially in BA, and before you know it, it'll be closing time.

Still not ready for bed? Fortunately, in a sleepless city of residents that see night as a mere extension of the day, another bar, a café, a *telo* (love hotel), or whatever you happen to be looking for, is never far away.

Buenos Aires by Area

Palacio Barolo

The Centre

Every metropolis has one: a bustling hub of commerce and tourism, inundated with traffic, noise and various life forms. Welcome to BA's El Centro district. Monday to Friday, the Microcentro grid, with its narrow and overflowing pavements, is strictly business, while neighbouring Retiro emphasises both high-traffic (a massive transport hub with three train stations and a bus terminal littered with run-down stalls) and high class (the majestic **Plaza San Martín**). For Europhiles, there's the 12-lane-wide Avenida 9 de Julio and Avenida de Mayo, a boulevard of restaurants, cafés, shops and grand office buildings that resembles both Barcelona's La Rambla and Rome's Via Veneto. Plaza de Mayo lies at one end of Avenida de Mayo and has long been the site of weekly protests. The Barrios of Congreso and Tribunales are less politcally and significant but are nonetheless lively and picturesque.

Plaza de Mayo

No serious tourist visits BA without making at least one pilgrimage to Plaza de Mayo, the city's political centre. The highlight: the **Casa Rosada**, the famously pink presidential palace (though not the one where the head of state actually lives; that's located in the suburb of Olivos) in front of which the Madres de Plaza de Mayo gather every Thursday at 3.30pm to protest about the disappearance of their loved ones during the military government of the 1970s. Other points of interest include the **Banco de la Nación,**

Argentina's state bank; the **Cabildo**, former headquarters of the city council; and **Pirámide de Mayo**, an obelisk that was raised in 1811 for the first anniversary of the May Revolution.

Sights & museums

Catedral Metropolitana

Avenida Rivadavia, y San Martín (4331 2845). Subte A, Plaza de Mayo or D, Catedral or E, Bolívar. **Open** 8am-7pm Mon-Fri; 9am-7.30pm Sat, Sun. **Admission** free. **Map** p52 B3 **❶**

On the western side of the plaza is this neo-classical cathedral. The plan for the cream-coloured building, the sixth cathedral on this site, was hatched in 1753; the first façade was blessed in 1791, and the final touches were added in 1910. The right-hand nave houses a mausoleum for the remains of José de San Martín, Argentina's 'liberator'.

Museo Histórico Nacional del Cabildo

Bolívar 65, entre Avenida de Mayo e Hipólito Yrigoyen (4334 1782/4342 6729). Subte A, Plaza de Mayo or D, Catedral or E, Bolívar. **Open** 11.30am-6pm Tue-Fri; 2-6pm Sat, Sun. **Admission** AR$1. No credit cards. **Map** p52 B3 **❷**

The Cabildo was the HQ of the city council between 1580 and 1821. The museum comprises a number of austere rooms in which you'll find valuable items such as a magnificent gold and silver piece from Oruro (Bolivia); one of the country's first printing presses; and a number of items relating to the English invasions of the early 19th century.

Avenida de Mayo

Shamelessly European in its slightly faded glamour, Avenida de Mayo is a free-for-all of commercial enterprises: shops, restaurants and cafés line both sides of its blocks. Ornamental architectural attractions abound, from the **Palacio Barolo**

to the double-domed **Edificio de la Inmobiliaria.** Visitors who come at the right – or wrong, depending on how one looks at it – time are likely to see protestors in the street en route to the **Casa Rosada**.

Sights & museums

Casa de la Cultura

Avenida de Mayo 575, entre Perú y Bolívar (4323 9669). Subte A, Perú or D, Catedral or E, Bolívar. **Open** Feb-Dec 8am-8pm Mon-Fri; by tour Sat, Sun. Closed Jan. **Admission** free. **Map** p52 B3 **❸**

Built in 1896, this building was once the headquarters of the *La Prensa* newspaper but now belongs to the city government. Its French feel goes beyond the façades: the impressive Salón Dorado, inspired by the Palace of Versailles, hosts chamber music concerts each Friday at 7pm.

Palacio Barolo

Avenida de Mayo 1370, entre San José y Santiago del Estero. Subte A, Saénz Peña. **Map** p52 C1 **❹**

One of the city's most emblematic buildings, this 1923 construction is a neo-gothic allegorical tribute to the 100 cantos of Dante's *Divine Comedy*. Hell is on the ground floor: Latin inscriptions taken from nine literary works represent the nine infernal circles and are engraved on the entrance hall's nine vaults. The first 14 floors comprise Purgatory, while Paradise can be found in the upper reaches. At the top is a domed lighthouse, representing God. Guided tours are available for AR$20.

Eating & drinking

Café Tortoni

Avenida de Mayo 829, entre Piedras y Tacuarí (4342 4328/www.cafetortoni. com.ar). Subte A, Piedras. **Open** 7.30am-2am Mon-Thur; 7.30am-3am Fri, Sat; 9am-1am Sun. **$**. **Café.** **Map** p52 B2 **❺**

Argentina's oldest café is everything you would expect it to be: grand and

BUENOS AIRES BY AREA

The Centre

A **B** **C**

1

Independencia

Bernardo de Irigoyen

Museo del Traje

Moreno

CONGRESO

Departamento
Central de
Policía

Plaza del
Congre

Palacio Barolo

Saenz Peña

Centro
San

2

MONSERRAT

Belgrano

Lima

Avenida de Mayo

AVENIDA DE MAYO

AVENIDA 9 DE JULIO

Café Tortoni

Piedras

Diagonal Norte

Obelisco

9 de Julio
Carlos
Pellegrini

3

Manzana de las Luces

Legislatura

Museo de
la Ciudad
Museo Etnográfico

San Francisco

Bolívar

ROQUE SAENZ PEÑA

Casa de la Cultura

Palacio de Gobierno de la Ciudad

Museo
del Cabildo

Catedral

CORRIENTES

Lavalle

Aduana

Santo Domingo

Catedral
Metropolitana

Banco Nación

Museo Numismático

MICROCE

4

Museo de la
Casa Rosada

Casa Rosada

Parque
Colón

Museo
del Banco
Nación

Catedral Anglicana

Convento
San Ramón

Museo de la Policía

Florida

Museo Mitre

Plaza de
Mayo

Museo del
Banco Provincia

Centro
Cultural
Borges

Galerías
Pacífico

PUERTO
MADERO

Puente de la Mujer
Fragata
Sarmiento

Correo
Central

Leandro Alem

AVENIDA CÓRDOBA

Harr

Plaza
Roma

Luna Park

AVENIDA LEANDRO ALE

5

Corbeta
Uruguay

DIQUE 4

AVENIDA MADERO

Buquebus
Terminal

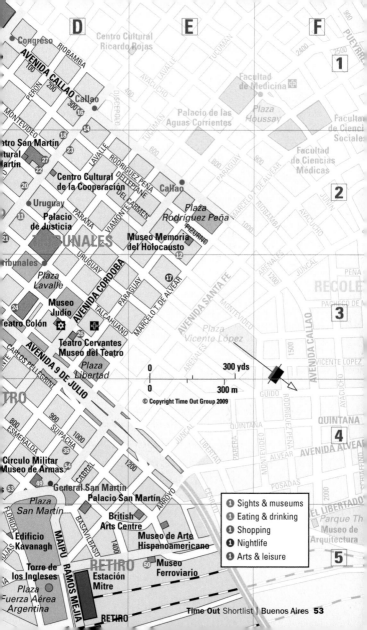

D | **E** | **F**

Congreso
Centro Cultural
Ricardo Rojas

AVENIDA CALLAO
100
PERÓN 200
Callao
300 16
14

RIOBAMBA

TUCUMÁN

LAVALLE

AYACUCHO

Facultad
de Medicina

2400
2500
PUEYRRL...
900

1

MONTEVIDEO
18
ntro San Martín
ultural
artín
23
27
22
20
Uruguay
11
Palacio
de Justicia
21

DISCÉPOLO

Centro Cultural
de la Cooperación

PARANÁ

LAVALLE

RODRÍGUEZ PEÑA

DELLEPIANE

DEL CARMEN

VIAMONTE

Callao

Palacio de las
Aguas Corrientes

Plaza
Houssay

Plaza
Rodríguez Peña

PARAGUAY

Facultad
de Ciencias
Médicas

Facultar
de Cienci
Sociales

TUCUMÁN

600

800

900

1000

MARCELO T DE ALVEAR

RIOBAMBA

AYACUCHO

JUNÍN

2

TRIBUNALES

Tribunales

Plaza
Lavalle

24

AVENIDA CÓRDOBA

Museo
Judío

Teatro Colón

URUGUAY

PARAGUAY

TALCAHUANO

Museo Memoria
del Holocausto
12

17

MARCELO T DE ALVEAR

AVENIDA SANTA FE

MONTEVIDEO

ARENALES 1200

JUNCAL

PEÑA

RECOLE

PACHECO DE M

1500

3

26
Teatro Cervantes
Museo del Teatro
Plaza
Libertad

0   300 yds

0   300 m
© Copyright Time Out Group 2009

Plaza
Vicente López

ARENALES

AVENIDA CALLAO

VICENTE LÓPEZ

AYACUCHO

GUIDO

AVENIDA 9 DE JULIO

TRO

ESMERALDA
800

SUIPACHA
900

1000

35

CARLOS PELLEGRINI

CABRAL

QUINTANA

AVENIDA ALVEAR

LIBERTAD

MONTEVIDEO

PARERA

ALVEAR

RODRÍGUEZ PEÑA

QUINTANA

4

2000

Círculo Militar
Museo de Armas
53
49
54
General San Martín
Palacio San Martín

Plaza
San Martín

Edificio
Kavanagh

Torre de
los Ingleses

Plaza
Fuerza Aérea
Argentina

FLORIDA

MAIPÚ

RAMOS MEJÍA

BASAVILBASO

British
Arts Centre

Museo de Arte
Hispanoamericano

RETIRO

Estación
Mitre

RETIRO

ARROYO

CERRITO

POSADAS

Museo
Ferroviario

50

EL LIBERTAD
Parque Th
Museo de
Arquitectura

CHACABUCO

5

❶ Sights & museums
❶ Eating & drinking
❶ Shopping
❶ Nightlife
❶ Arts & leisure

Café Tortoni p51

charmingly ceremonial. Since 1858, it's played host to a stellar cast, from the depths of bohemia to the heights of the literati and across the political spectrum. Beyond the wooden tables and marble floor a popular salon hosts jazz and tango shows.

Plaza Asturias

Avenida de Mayo 1199, y Salta (4382 7334). Subte A, Lima. **Open** 11.30am-3am daily. **$$.** No credit cards. **Spanish**. Map p52 C2 ⑥

The AR$26 lunch here kicks off with a complimentary pre-prandial sherry and a plate of tapas on the house – zingingly tasty anchovies or soft white octopus tentacles. Pick a main course from a set of six – the *favada asturiana*, a savoury butterbean stew served with a *chorizo* (spicy sausage), a *morcilla* (blood sausage), bacon and a thick piece of pork belly is particularly tasty. Dessert, a soft drink or a small bottle of wine, and a final shot of limoncello are included.

Congreso & Tribunales

All roads in this part of El Centro lead to the once-controversial **Obelisco**, part Washington

Monument, part phallic symbol. At the time of writing Tribunales's **Teatro Colón,** BA's world-renowned opera house and one of the area's most important buildings, was set to be closed until at least 2010. Otherwise, these barrios are best known for their government buildings, such as **Palacio del Congreso**, a dome-and-column structure that mimics the US Capitol building and was the site of the first constitutional assembly in 1813, and **Palacio de Justicia,** seat of the Supreme Court.

Sights & museums

El Obelisco

Avenida 9 de Julio, y Corrientes, Tribunales. Subte B, Carlos Pellegrini or C, Diagonal Norte, Tribunales. Map p52 C3 ⑦

The 223-foot (68-metre) Obelisco was built to mark four historical events: the first and the final foundation of Buenos Aires; the 1880 declaration of the city as the country's federal capital; and the site of the demolished church of San Nicolás, where the national flag was first flown.

Palacio del Congreso

*Hipólito Yrigoyen 1849, entre Entre
Ríos y Combate de los Pozos (4370
7100). Subte A, Congreso.* Closed Jan.
Admission free. **Map** p53 C1 ⑧

Argentina's constitution was inspired
by the US model; and likewise, the
Palacio del Congreso resembles
Washington's bicameral legislature.
Completed in 1906, the Congress building's extravagant interior is open for
guided tours.

Eating & drinking

Banchero

*Corrientes 1300 y Talcahuano,
Tribunales (4382 4669/www.
bancheropizzerias.com.ar).
Subte B, Uruguay.* **$**. **Pizzeria**.
Map p53 D2 ⑨

The Banchero family has three restaurants and has been in the food business
since the late 1800s, giving them plenty
of time to perfect their craft. Though
pizza is their specialty – they invented
the 'fugazzeta' by adding mozzarella to
the Genovese *fugazza* (a sauceless
pizza topped with caramelised onions,
oregano and seasonings) – they also
serve traditional Argentinian cuisine,
from pastas and empanadas to *milane-
sas* (breaded cutlets) and steak.

Chan Chan

*Hipólito Yrigoyen 1390, entre San José
y Santiago del Estero, Congreso (4382
8492). Subte A, Sáenz Peña.* **Open**
noon-4pm, 8pm-12.30am Tue-Sun.
$. No credit cards. **Peruvian**.
Map p52 C1 ⑩

Among a long list of Peruvian dishes
here are the *chicharrón de pescado*
(deep-fried fish balls), the generous
mixed *ceviche* (raw fish marinated in
lime), *papas a la Huancaina* (spicy
spuds slathered in a cream sauce),
and the *seco de carne* (tender beef
with rice and beans). Also popular are
daily specials such as *pulpo en aceite*
(octopus) and *anticuchos de salmon*
(pink salmon served on kebab sticks).

Los Inmortales

*Corrientes 1369, entre Talcahuano y
Uruguay, Tribunales (4373 5303/0800
999 5674/www.losinmortales.net).
Subte B, Uruguay.* **Open** noon-2am
Mon-Fri, Sun; noon-4am Sat. **$$**.
Pizzeria. **Map** p53 D2 ⑪

In a city overflowing with pizzerias,
this BA stalwart holds its own. Most
come for *pizza a la piedra* (thin and
baked in a stone oven), but the cal-
zones, pasta, *empanadas* (Argentinian
pasties) and fish don't disappoint.
There are three other locations in BA.

Restó

*Montevideo 938, entre Marcelo T de
Alvear y Paraguay, Tribunales (4816
6711). Subte D, Callao.* **Open** noon-
3pm Mon-Fri; 8.30-11pm Thur, Fri.
$$. No credit cards. **Argentinian**.
Map p53 E2 ⑫

The 'slow food' credentials of this
petite restaurant on the ground floor of
the Central Architect's Society don't
translate, thankfully, into slow service,
which is attentive and knowledgeable.
On Thursday and Friday nights, by
reservation only, there's a choice of
four set menus at AR$70, AR$80,
AR$90 or AR$100 – an excellent way
to go –- plus a five-course tasting
menu. Vegetarians will be in their ele-
ment with a meat-free menu that might
include tabbouleh followed by a pro-
volone cheese and sun-dried tomato

tart, or a fresh salad of watermelon, tomato and buffalo mozzarella.

Status

Virrey Cavellos 178, entre Hipólito Yrigoyen y Alsina, Congreso (4382 8531/www.restaurantstatus.com.ar). Subte A, Sáenz Peña. **Open** noon-4pm, 8pm-midnight Mon-Sun. **$. Peruvian**. **Map** p52 C1 ⑬

This cantina serves abundant platters of *ceviche* (raw fish 'cooked' in citrus juices) and lamb, as well as nicely spicy starters. Busy during the day, the restaurant is usually packed by 9pm (expect to queue) with a chatty crowd of discerning backpackers, businessmen, artists and members of the local Peruvian community.

Shopping

Gandhi Galerna

Avenida Corrientes 1743, entre Callao y Rodríguez Peña, Tribunales (4374 7501). Subte B, Callao. **Open** 10am-10pm Mon-Thur; 10am-midnight Fri, Sat; 4-10pm Sun. **Map** p53 D1 ⑭

Gandhi has long been the place where Buenos Aires thinkers and talkers gather. It has an unrivalled selection of local journals and magazines.

Wildlife

Hipólito Yrigoyen 1133, entre Salta y Lima, Congreso (4381 1040). Subte A, Lima. **Open** 10am-8pm Mon-Fri; 10am-1pm Sat. **Map** p52 B2 ⑮

Camping, outdoor and extreme sports gear, new and secondhand, is sold here. Climbers, anglers, campers and parachutists come here in droves to get kitted out.

Zivals

Avenida Callao 395, y Corrientes, Tribunales (4371 7500/www. zivals.com). Subte B, Callao. **Open** 9.30am-10pm Mon-Sat. **Map** p53 D1 ⑯

Claiming to stock the widest selection of music in South America, Zivals (also an excellent bookshop) has all genres but specialises in classical, jazz, folk, tango and hard-to-find independent local recordings.

Chan Chan p55

Age of reconstruction

Some of BA's top tourist attractions get a makeover just in time for Argentina's 200th birthday.

Palacio de Correos y Telecomunicaciones

To help mark Argentina's 2010 bicentenary, government agencies have launched a series of special renovation projects. Century-old buildings, monuments and public spaces have been under the scaffolding, among them the Casa Rosada, Teatro Colón and Museo Nacional de la Inmigración.

The focus at the Casa Rosada has been on the restoration of a mural in an underground part of the Museo de la Casa Rosada. Mexican master David Alfaro Siqueiros's *Artistic Exercise* will be unveiled in 2010 as part of the bicentennial celebration.

The city's biggest project, however, is the refurbishment and conversion of the Palacio de Correos y Telecomunicaciones on downtown Avenida Corrientes into one of the largest cultural centres in the world. Originally designed in 1889 to house Argentina's central post office, it has been vacant since 2003. The newly remodelled building will be renamed Centro Cultural del Bicentenario (www.proyectoccb.com.ar).

The project, which claimed first prize in an international competition to decide the fate of the National Historic Monument, introduces experimental architectural elements into the building's restoration and provides for the addition of concert halls, exhibition rooms and auditoriums. The groundbreaking architectural elements include a cage-like series of metal columns; a suspended glass structure, referred to as the 'chandelier', which will host temporary exhibitions; and a symphony hall dubbed the 'blue whale' for its massive whale-like shape.

The Centro Cultural del Bicentenario, which is due to open on 25 May 2010, is set to be the principal site for commemorative activities related to the bicentenary.

Palacio del Congreso p55

BUENOS AIRES BY AREA

Nightlife

El Living

Marcelo T de Alvear 1540, entre Montevideo y Paraná, Tribunales (4811 4730/4815 6574/ www.living. com.ar). **Open** 7pm-3am Thur; 10pm-6am Fri, Sat, and bank holidays.
Map p53 E3 ⓱

El Living is a two-room chill-out nightclub-lounge for the indie-geek scene. Get there around 10pm, and you can enjoy a decent dinner for AR$40 – an aperitif, main course, dessert and a drink – and stay on for an evening of quirky, unpredictable tunes.

Arts & leisure

Belisario Club de Cultura

Avenida Corrientes 1624, entre Rodríguez Peña y Montevideo, Tribunales (4373 3465). Subte B, Callao. **Shows** *Jan-Feb* Fri, Sat. *Mar-Dec* Thur-Sun. No credit cards.
Map p53 D1 ⓲

A small but interesting venue, this is home to some of the best experimental theatre around as well as a regular programme of circus-influenced performances and antics.

Espacio INCAA KM 0 – Gaumont Rivadavia

Rivadavia 1635, entre Rodríguez Peña y Montevideo, Congreso (4371 3050). Subte A, Congreso. **Open** from noon daily. No credit cards.
Map p52 C1 ⓳

This excellent, cheap three-screen cinema is supported by INCAA, the national film board, and only shows new Argentinian releases.

Lorca

Avenida Corrientes 1428, entre Paraná y Uruguay, Tribunales (4371 5017). Subte B, Uruguay. **Open** from 1.45pm daily. No credit cards.
Map p53 D2 ⓴

One of the most traditional cinemas on Corrientes, Lorca also is one of BA's best options for independent film, showing a good pick of local and foreign non-mainstream movies.

Multiteatro

Avenida Corrientes 1283, y Talcahuano, Tribunales (4382 9140/ tickets 5236 3000/www.multiteatro. com.ar). Subte B, Uruguay. **Shows** 9pm Wed-Sun. **Map** p52 D2 ㉑

With its three versatile, smallish auditoriums, Multiteatro has a reputation for putting on provocative one-person shows as well as local adaptations of contemporary classics.

Sala Leopoldo Lugones

10th floor, Avenida Corrientes 1530, entre Paraná y Montevideo, Tribunales (0800 333 5254/www.teatrosanmartin. com.ar). Subte B, Uruguay. **Map** p53 D2 ㉒

This cinema is located within the San Martín theatre complex and mostly screens leftfield arthouse flicks.

Teatro Astral

Avenida Corrientes 1639, entre Montevideo y Rodriguez Peña, Tribunales (4374 5707/9964/ www.teatroastral.com.ar). Subte A, Congreso or Subte B or D, Callao. **Map** p53 D2 ㉓

Argentina's most famous feather-clad showgirls have swayed their hips on the stage of the Astral, the main revue theatre on Corrientes, which hosts mainstream hits like *Hairspray*.

Teatro Colón

Cerrito 618, entre Tucuman y Viamonte, Tribunales (4378 7344/ www.teatrocolon.org.ar). Subte D, Tribunales. **Map** p53 D3 ㉔

This stunning opera house closed for a quick facelift in 2006 and hasn't opened since. It's now scheduled to reopen in 2010, but you can still peek inside at its baroque glory.

Teatro Liceo

Avenida Rivadavia 1499, entre Paraná y Uruguay, Congreso (4381 5745/ www.multiteatro.com.ar). Subte A, Sáenz Peña. No credit cards. **Map** p52 C1 ㉕

Part of the same group as Multiteatro, this 700-seater, 140-year-old venue is the oldest of its kind in the capital, and it's still going strong.

Teatro Nacional Cervantes

Avenida Córdoba 1155, entre Libertad y Cerrito, Tribunales (4816 4224/ www.teatrocervantes.gov.ar). Subte D, Tribunales. No credit cards. **Map** p53 D3 ㉖

This 80-year-old, state-run theatre seats 1,000 people in two auditoriums and stages Latin American and Spanish plays as well as some dance events. It also holds regular film cycles of mainly Argentinian classics.

Teatro San Martín

Avenida Corrientes 1530, entre Paraná y Montevideo, Tribunales (information 4371 0111/tickets 0800 333 5254/ www.teatrosanmartin.com.ar). Subte B, Uruguay. **Shows** *Mar-Dec* Wed-Sun. **Map** p53 D2 ㉗

Renowned for the quality and eclecticism of its programmes, ranging from cast-iron classics to avant-garde experiments, the San Martín incorporates three auditoriums with a combined capacity of 1,700 in a building that is a hymn to 1970s design.

Microcentro

Mind the gaps! The downtown pavements (as in so much of BA) are as uneven as they are packed and narrow. The main points of interest – the pedestrian shopping calles Florida and Lavalle, and the strip of banks and cafés on the west side of Avenida Leandro N Alem, down one of the few slopes in the flat capital – are not for the claustrophobic, the agoraphobic or the unsteady of feet. During regular business hours, everything here moves at a brisk pace, with honking cars whizzing by and people rushing in all directions; but come happy hour, the streets empty and take on a sort of ghost-town feel. That said, there's still plenty of fun to be had here. Microcentro nightlife is a work in progress, with

Music for the masses

Hundreds of thousands of devoted pop and rock fans make BA the hottest South American destination for superstars on tour. Madonna, Robbie, Kylie, Liza and Alanis – meet some of your biggest fans. In the past few years, Argentinians, with more financial clout to shell out their pesos for a few good tunes, have flocked to the shows of the aforementioned pop icons, putting BA back on the hot list of international tour stops. So rapturously are acts received here that the appreciation flows both ways: U2 has passed through several times and used a show here as part of its 2008 concert film, *U2 3D*, praising the crowd as any act's dream audience, thanks to an unusually high level of enthusiasm. The spectator experience is well worth sharing, especially since ticket prices are still relatively low.

A-list acts draw crowds here as large as in other major international cities, and there are a number of venues massive enough to contain them all. The Estadio Monumental (p156), just north of town in Núñez, isn't only for flare-shooting football fans. Madonna's sold-out multi-night tour stop in late 2008 took up residence at the gargantuan stadium. Big names like Cyndi Lauper and Arctic Monkeys have graced the historic boxing ring-cum-concert hall Luna Park (p63), where the acoustics score low but the bouncing crowds keep spirits high. The Microcentro's Teatro Gran Rex (p64) is a more intimate space that draws the seat-friendly likes of Coldplay and Björk, while

Madonna

San Telmo's La Trastienda (p72) recently hosted the smart kid's indie hero Bright Eyes and soulful Irish songwriter Damien Rice. Meanwhile, Argentina's music festivals now have the commercial clout to draw the biggest acts. The annual Quilmes Rock takes place over ten days every March and draws more than 200,000 attendees, thanks to headliners such as Radiohead, Kraftwerk and the Wailers. Early summer has the smaller but equally popular Personal Fest, host to Blondie, Morrissey, Duran Duran and Snoop Dogg in past years. Add the various musical flavours of the B-52s, Black Sabbath, Elton John, Lenny Kravitz, R.E.M. and Peter Gabriel (as well as unexpected entries like Michael Bolton, Dionne Warwick and Boy George) to the BA live-music mix, and you've got the recipe for South America's best concert scene.

new places popping up monthly. All you need are a few pointers and an ear to the ground.

Sights & museums

Museo Histórico y Numismático del Banco de la Nación Argentina

First floor, Bartolomé Mitre 326, entre 25 de Mayo y Reconquista (4347 6277). Subte B, Florida. **Open** 10am-3pm Mon-Fri. **Admission** free. **Map** p52 B4 ㉘

A real mouthful of a museum, this one is mainly of interest to anthropologists and those who enjoy staring at money they'll never be able to spend. It exhibits exotic early bank notes (in circulation since 1820) featuring dogs, goats, cows and even a kangaroo, as well as gold and silver coins.

Museo Mitre

San Martín 336, entre Corrientes y Sarmiento (4394 7659/www.museo mitre.gov.ar). Subte B, Florida. **Open** 1-6pm Mon-Fri. **Admission** AR$1. **Map** p52 B4 ㉙

This colonial mansion dating from 1785 was, between 1860 and 1906, the home of former president and founder of *La Nación* newspaper, Bartolomé Mitre. The library is the main attraction: it holds some of the region's most important books, as well as documents on Latin American history and some unique photographic exhibits.

Eating & drinking

Le Bar

Tucumán 422, entre Reconquista y San Martín (5219 0858/www.lebar buenosaires.blogspot.com). Subte B, Florida. **Open** from noon Mon-Fri; from 9pm Sat. **$$**. **Cocktail bar**. **Map** p52 C4 ㉚

This classy cocktail joint has a cutting-edge interior design that contrasts exquisitely with the old-time look of the building. Go upstairs to the top bar, where punters sit in circular dug-out seating. On the menu, exotic world flavours spice up some of the best finger food in town.

CBC – California Burrito Co.

Lavalle 441, entre San Martín y Reconquista (4328 3056/3057/ www.californiaburritoco.com) Subte B, Florida. **Open** noon-11pm Mon-Fri. **$$**. No credit cards. **Mexican**. **Map** p52 B4 ㉛

With an assembly-line model in which you point out your fillings as you move along the line, CBC claims to offer over 15,000 possible burrito combinations. Less dubious than this marketing claim are the quality and freshness of the food and the size of the portions. Add to that friendly service and a clean-lined decor, and you'll understand why lunchtime here means queues out the door.

Empire Thai

Tres Sargentos 427, entre San Martín y Reconquista (4312 5706). Subte C, San Martín. **Open** noon-midnight Mon-Fri; 7pm-2am Sat. **$$**. **Southeast Asian**. **Map** p52 C5 ㉜

Meshing a sleek New York sensibility with a more colourful Asian aesthetic, Empire's fashionable interior is reason enough to swing by for chicken satay and an excellent Thai curry. The Thai crackers served with tangy sauce before the meal make a welcome change from the usual bread basket, as do the authentic salty-sweet Thai flavours in the mouth-burning green curry and crunchy pad thai.

Pura Vida

Reconquista 516, entre Lavalle y Tucumán (4393 0093/www.puravida buenosaires.com). Subte B, LN Alem. **Open** 9am-6pm Mon-Fri. **$**. No credit cards. **Health food**. **Map** p52 B4 ㉝

When the steak, *empanada* (pasties) and wine diet begins to take its toll, refreshing relief beckons at Pura Vida juice bar. Creatively conceived dishes such as the delicious corn and coconut soup, chunky doorstep sandwiches and bulging wraps prove that healthy does not have to mean hungry. If elbowing your way through the downtown lunch

Retiro p65

rush isn't your thing, try the Recoleta location at Uriburu 1489.

Tomo I

Hotel Panamericano, Carlos Pellegrini 521, entre Lavalle y Tucumán (4326 6695/www.tomo1.com.ar). Subte B, Carlos Pellegrini. **Open** noon-3pm Mon-Fri; 7.30pm-1am Mon-Sat. **$$$**. **Argentinian**. Map p52 C3 ㉞

Tomo I sets the scene with glowing lighting, warm tans and spotlessly white tables. Your amuse-bouche might be a sip of tomato soup or a tiny brioche with peppers or pâté; and the home-made *ñandú* (ostrich) raviolis in mango sauce are a revelation of sweetly spiced meat inside won ton-like wrappers.

Shopping

Autoría BsAs

Suipacha 1025, Microcentro (5252 2474/www.autoriabsas.com.ar). **Open** 9am-8pm Mon-Fri; 10am-2pm, 4-8pm Sat. Map p53 D4 ㉟

This multi-space design boutique houses a varied array of clothing and objects created by talented local designers. Flip through carefully selected garments from clothing designers Vicki Otero, Spina, Vero Ivaldi and Min Agostini, and accessories and home decor items from Nobrand, Guiño, Móviles and Andrea Cavaganaro, among others. A gallery section includes works from recognised artists as well as novices, and features not only paintings and photos, but also sculptures and installments. Great for a browse, Autoría is a well-executed fusion of art and design.

La Botica del Vino

Galería Larreta, unit 12, Florida 971 (4894 2054/www.bdv.com.ar) Subte C, San Martín. **Open** 10am-8pm Mon-Fri. Map p52 C4 ㊱

The friendly and knowledgeable staff at this calle Florida store will be able to suggest a great wine for you, whatever your budget. Check the websites for special offers.

Galerías Pacífico

Florida 737, entre Viamonte y Córdoba (5555 5100/www.galerias pacifico.com.ar). Subte B, Florida. **Open** 10am-9pm Mon-Sat; noon-9pm Sun. Map p52 C4 ㊲

This mall is housed in a turn-of-the-century building with superb frescoes painted by five Argentinian muralists. You'll find famous brand names such as Christian Dior and Lacoste here, as well as dozens of local retail stars like Sibyl Vane and Vitamina.

Kelly's

Paraguay 521, entre San Martín y Florida (4311 5712/www.kellys.com.ar). Subte C, San Martín. **Open** 10am-8pm Mon-Fri; 10am-3pm Sat. Map p52 C4 ㊳

From small trinkets with images of the Obelisco to leather items and beautiful hand-woven blankets from the north of the country, there's something here for every taste and budget – and that includes cheap and cheerful fridge magnets and all manner of knick-knacks in the little Aladdin's cave at the back.

Nightlife

Bahrein

Lavalle 343, y Reconquista (4315 2403/www.bahreinba.com). **Open** from 12.30am Wed, Fri, Sat; 10pm-4am Sun. Map p52 B4 ㊴

The boys are finally outnumbering the girls on some nights, so the recent push to gay up the disco seems to be working. For a reasonable price (the cover charge ranges from AR$10 to AR$20), you get decent electro DJs and a perfect view of beautiful people on two dancefloors, but an extra-strength caipirinha will now set you back a cool AR$25.

La Cigale

25 de Mayo 722, entre Viamonte y Córdoba (4312 8275). Subte B, LN Alem. **Open** from 6pm Mon-Fri; from 8pm Sat and bank holidays. No credit cards. Map p52 C5 ㊵

At La Cigale, you're as likely to find the *Pink Panther* being shown on a

Dadá p66

giant screen as you are live music on the tiny stage or a minimal DJ. The four happy hours, from 6pm to 10pm, are some of BA's most impressive and well priced, with white Russians, mojitos, blue lagoons and pints of Heineken all two-for-one, at prices from AR$16 to AR$20.

Cocoliche
Rivadavia 878 (4331 6413/www. *cocoliche.net). Subte A, Piedras.* **Open** from 11pm Tue-Sun. **Map** p52 B3 ㊶
Intimate, uncommercial and low-key, this ice-cool downtown nightspot has a rotating programme with pricey cocktails (over AR$20) and a generally avant-garde vibe that pulls in a slightly left-of-centre crowd. This is the most underground of BA's main clubs, and it has been known to stay open well into the morning on Saturdays and Sundays.

Luna Park
Bouchard 465, entre Corrientes y *Lavalle (5279 5279/5353 0606/* *www.lunapark.com.ar). Subte B,* *LN Alem.* **Map** p52 B5 ㊷
Lily Allen, Cyndi Lauper and Arctic Monkeys are among the stars to have recently graced the stage of this large boxing arena. It's a great space, but there are drawbacks: thick columns can block views, and the dodgy sound system can make top acts sound like shambling amateurs.

Teatro Gran Rex
Avenida Corrientes 857, entre Suipacha *y Esmeralda (4322 8000). Subte B,* *Carlos Pellegrini or C, Diagonal Norte* *or D, 9 de Julio.* No credit cards. **Map** p52 C3 ㊸
The Gran Rex is ideal for those artists (like Björk) who require the attention of a comfortably seated audience. The

theatre holds 3,500, and punters can choose between the stalls (*platea*), the mezzanine (*super pullman*) or the dress circle (*pullman* – cheap seats, worse sound).

Arts & leisure

Atlas Lavalle

Lavalle 869, entre Suipacha y Esmeralda (5032 8527/www.atlascines.com.ar). Subte C, Lavalle. **Open** from noon daily. No credit cards. **Map** p52 C3 ❹

This once-historic cinema has been split up into five smaller screens featuring mostly new releases.

Centro Cultural Borges

Galerías Pacífico, Viamonte y San Martín (5555 5449/www.ccborges. org.ar). Subte C, San Martín. **Open** 10am-9pm Mon-Sat; noon-9pm Sun. **Map** p52 C4 ❹

With an eclectic events programme that includes flamenco, ballet, postmodern tango, independent cinema and experimental theatre, the Centro Cultural Borges has hosted many of the must-see shows of recent years, including the annual travelling World Press Photo exhibition.

Confitería Ideal

1st floor, Suipacha 380, y Corrientes (5265 8069/4328 7750/www. confiteriaideal.com). Subte C, Diagonal Norte. **Open** Milonga 10.30pm-4am Tue-Sun. No credit cards. **Map** p52 C3 ❹

This busy tango spot has a full schedule of classes by day but really comes alive at night with the *milonga* and live orchestra. Particularly good is Thursday night's Tangoideal bash (www.tangoideal.com.ar) and Unitango Club's Tuesday and Friday night affairs (www.unitango.com).

La Marshall

Maipú 444, y Corrientes (4912 9043/ mobile 15 5458 3423/www.lamarshall. com.ar). Subte B, Florida. **Open** Classes 10.30pm Wed. *Milonga* 11.30pm Wed. No credit cards. **Map** p52 C3 ❹

Small, relaxed and welcoming, this very modern (and very gay-friendly) *milonga* has an open-minded musical programme featuring ethnic, contemporary and electronic tango as well as more traditional sounds.

Teatro Opera

Avenida Corrientes 860, entre Suipacha y Esmeralda (4326 1335). Subte B, Carlos Pellegrini or C, Diagonal Norte or D, 9 de Julio. **Map** p52 C3 ❹

Since Teatro Opera opened in 1872, many great local artists have performed here. Jazz greats such as Louis Armstrong and Ella Fitzgerald have also graced its stage.

Retiro

There are basically two reasons to go to Retiro – to catch a train or a bus out of town at one of the terminals along Avenida Ramos Mejía or to spend quality down time in **Plaza San Martín**, arguably the most beautiful spot in town. It's surrounded by **Palacio Paz**, the largest private residence in Argentina; **Palacio San Martín**, home of the filthy rich Anchorena clan; and the **Edificio Kavanagh**, an art deco landmark that was South America's tallest building when it was inaugurated in 1935. The neighbouring **Marriott Plaza Hotel** and **Torre Monumental**, a Big Ben lookalike that everyone calls Torre de los Ingleses, round out the area's visual appeal.

Sights & museums

Museo de Armas de la Nación

Avenida Santa Fe 750, entre Maipú y Esmeralda (4311 1071). Subte C, San Martín. **Open** 1-7pm Mon-Fri. Closed Jan, Feb. **Admission** AR$4. **Map** p53 D4 ❹

This well-curated weapons museum in the Palacio Retiro houses a sizeable collection of arms and army uniforms, some dating from the 12th century and some contemporary, in 17 rooms.

Museo Nacional Ferroviario

Avenida del Libertador 405, y Suipacha (4318 3343). Subte C, Retiro. **Open** 10.30am-4pm Mon-Fri. **Admission** free. **Map** p53 E5 ㊿

Housed in an ageing railway building, this tribute to the age of the train covers two floors and comprises exhibits from a railway era that puts recent car-obsessed governments to shame.

Eating & drinking

Dadá

San Martín 941, entre Marcelo T de Alvear y Paraguay (4314 4787/ www.dadabistro.com). Subte C, San Martín. **Open** noon-2am Mon-Sat. **$$. Argentinian**. **Map** p52 C5 ㉛

Inside this tiny space, owner Paulo and his family serve a menu as colourful and imaginative as the lighting and furnishings that adorn the restaurant. The Lomo Dadá fillet steak, the *ojo de bife* (ribeye steak), the salmon with polenta and the houmous and guacamole dips stand out.

Filo

San Martín 975, entre Marcelo T de Alvear y Paraguay (4311 0312/1871/ www.filo-ristorante.com). Subte C, San Martín. **Open** noon-midnight daily. **$$. Italian**. **Map** p52 C5 ㉜

At this hip pizzeria, one of the most popular in all of BA, come 1pm, even the bar stools are packed with rows of financial advisors chowing down on focaccia chips and grilled vegetables. With a cool, urbane interior accented by splashes of red and yellow, a lengthy menu stocked with authentic Italian pastas as well as over 100 types of gourmet pizza, Filo's an obvious con-

Plaza San Martín p50

tender for the best place to grab a bite downtown. There are oversized fresh bread baskets on every table and a traditional brick oven keeps the room toasty. There is a good selection of pasta dishes too, while the more health-conscious will want to pair their pizza with a salad made from steamed vegetables that are so ripe they hardly need seasoning.

Shopping

Casa López

Marcelo T de Alvear 640, entre Florida y Maipú (4894 8520/8521/ www.casalopez.com.ar). Subte C, San Martín. **Open** 9am-8pm Mon-Fri; 10am-6pm Sat, Sun. **Map** p53 D4 ⓺⓷
Founded in 1943, this fashionable leather goods shop situated near Plaza San Martín specialises in handcrafted products, including wallets, tote bags, clutches and luggage. The leather jack-

ets are stylish, and the briefcases are sleek and professional. Quality and attention to detail account for the slightly higher prices.

Ligier

Avenida Santa Fe 800, y Esmeralda (4515 0126/www.ligier.com.ar). Subte C, San Martín. **Open** 9.30am-8pm Mon-Fri; 10am-2pm, 4-8pm Sat. **Map** p53 D4 ⓹⓸
Catering mostly to tourists and offering personalised attention, delivery and packaging, Ligier has cannily placed its branches close to many of the big hotels in BA.

Plata Nativa

Unit 41, Galería del Sol, Florida 860, entre Córdoba y Paraguay (4312 1398/ www.platanativa.com). Subte C, San Martín. **Open** 10am-7.30pm Mon-Fri; 10am-2pm Sat. **Map** p52 C4 ⓹⓹
This small, hidden treasure trove of indigenous and Latin American art and textiles also sells antique silver and contemporary ethnic accessories. But it's the necklaces woven in agate and turquoise, inspired by Mapuche jewellery, that have attracted loyal fans around the world.

Nightlife

The Kilkenny

Marcelo T de Alvear 399, y Reconquista (4312 7291). Subte C, San Martín. **Open** from noon Mon-Fri; from 8pm Sat, Sun. **Map** p52 C5 ⓹⓺
The good old Kilkenny remains as packed as ever, especially at weekends, when the tourist set pour in. Young and frisky Argentinians frequent this Irish pub, often looking to pull more than a Guinness.

Zanzibar

San Martín 986, entre Marcelo T de Alvear y Paraguay (4312 9636). Subte C, San Martín. **Open** from noon Mon-Fri; from 10pm Sat. No credit cards. **Map** p52 C5 ⓹⓻
An unpretentious, low-lit bar dedicated to rum and reggae and at times soul or hip hop, with a handful of tables and chairs offering varying degrees of comfort.

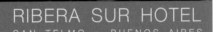

San Telmo p72

South of the Centre

Here is where it all began. Tango, that is. In the mid 19th century, gypsies, tramps and thieves congregated on the fringes of BA society, creating a music and dance form that has come to define the barrio where it all started: La Boca. Today, neighbouring San Telmo is the place to find the most authentic tango shows and while Monserrat (one barrio towards the centre) has begun its march toward modern times, Constitución and Barracas remain decades behind. Tourist-heavy San Telmo aside, these barrios are among the handful that represent the 'real' BA and not the postcard version. But the authenticity could be costly, so be aware after dark: when the sun goes down, so does the level of safety in the deep south.

Monserrat & Constitución

Monserrat is San Telmo before gentrification set in. Vintage-looking buildings and simple but beautiful colonial-era churches such as the **Iglesia de San Ignacio**, the **Iglesia de San Francisco** and the **Basílica de Santo Domingo** dot the turf, particularly on the **Manzana de las Luces** (Block of Enlightenment) along calles Alsina, Bolivar, Moreno and Perú. God is in the architectural details – not just in the houses of worship – so pray to Him that you don't trip over the cracks and potholes in the pavements or step on dog faeces while you stroll around admiring the scenery.

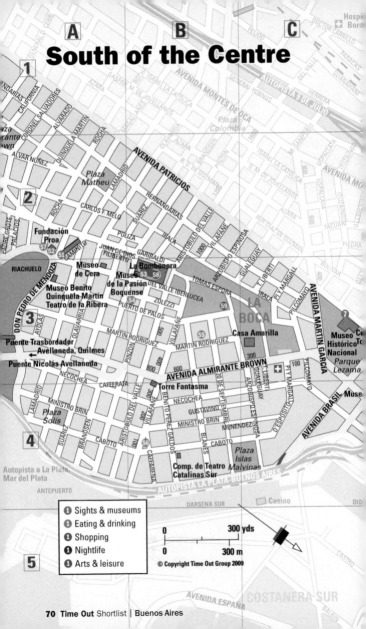

South of the Centre

A B C

1

2

Fundación Proa 57 52 51

Museo de Cera

Museo Benito Quinquela Martín
Teatro de la Ribera

3

RIACHUELO

Puente Trasbordador
Avellaneda, Quilmes

Puente Nicolás Avellaneda

4

Plaza Solís

Comp. de Teatro Catalinas Sur

5

La Bombonera 53 58

Museo de la Pasión Boquense 54

LA BOCA

Casa Amarilla

Torre Fantasma

Plaza Islas Malvinas

Museo Histórico Nacional 7

Parque Lezama

Museo Ce To

CALIFORNIA
ALVARADO
CORONEL SALVADORES
QUINQUELA MARTIN
ROCHA
LAMADRID
ALVAR NUÑEZ
Plaza Matheu
AVENIDA PATRICIOS
CARLOS F MELO
SUAREZ
HERNANDARIAS
IRALA
POLIZA
JUAN DE DIOS FILIBERTO
GARIBALDI
MINITO
DEL VALLE IBERLUCEA
ZOLEZZI
PUERTO DE PALOS
MARTIN RODRIGUEZ
OLAVARRIA
AVOLA
PINZON
CAFFERATA
NECOCHEA
MINISTRO BRIN
SUAREZ
BRANDSEN
CABOTO
CAFFERERA
ARISTOBULO DEL VALLE
BENITO PEREZ GALDOS
VILLAFANE
AVENIDA ALMIRANTE BROWN
NECOCHEA
GUSTAVINO
MINISTRO BRIN
BLANES
CABOTO
MENENDEZ
20 DE SEPTIEMBRE
GUALEGUAY
ARZOBISPO ESPINOSA
D ESPOSITO
PI Y MARGALL
PICHINCHA
AVENIDA MARTIN GARCIA
AVENIDA BRASIL

AVENIDA MONTES DE OCA
GENERAL HORNOS
Plaza Colombia
ISABEL LA CATOLICA
AZARA
R DE GUZMAN
ARZOBISPO ESPINOSA
GUALEGUAY
LIBERT
IRALA
TOMAS ESPORA
PILCOMAYO

AUTOPISTA 9 DE JULIO
DEL VALLE
HERRERA
GUANITANT
AVENIDA MO
TUZAINGO
TACUARI
PIEDRA
BOLIVAR
Hospi Boro
DOCTOR CARRILLO
PARACAS

Autopista a La Plata, Mar del Plata

ANTEPUERTO

AUTOPISTA LA PLATA-BUENOS AIRES

DARSENA SUR
Casino
DI

AVENIDA ESPAÑA

COSTANERA SUR
BALBIN

0 Sights & museums
0 Eating & drinking
0 Shopping
0 Nightlife
0 Arts & leisure

0 — 300 yds
0 — 300 m

© Copyright Time Out Group 2009

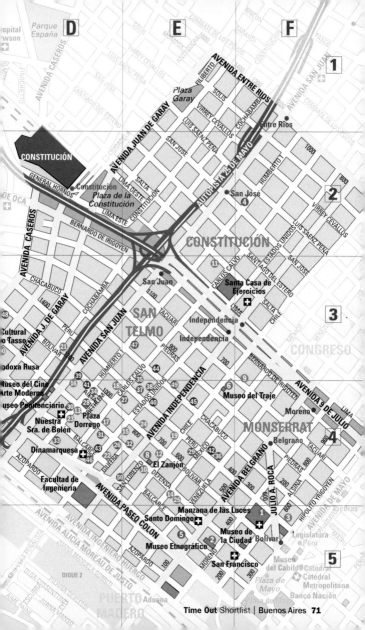

D Parque España E F

Hospital Dowson

1

AVENIDA ENTRE RIOS
AVENIDA 25 DE MAYO
AUTOPISTA 25 DE MAYO

Plaza Garay

AVENIDA JUAN DE GARAY

Entre Ríos

CONSTITUCIÓN

Constitución
Plaza de la
Constitución

2

San José 4

AVENIDA CASEROS

BERNARDO DE IRIGOYEN

CONSTITUCIÓN

CHACABUCO

11

San Juan

Santa Casa de
Ejercicios

AVENIDA J. DE GARAY

SAN
TELMO

Independencia

Independencia

3

CONGRESO

Centro
Cultural
Torquato Tasso

48

AVENIDA SAN JUAN

Orthodoxa Rusa

Museo del Cine

Arte Moderno

Museo Penitenciario

Nuestra
Sra. de Belén

Dinamarquesa

Facultad de
Ingeniería

AVENIDA PASEO COLON

39
16
41
34
28
30
23
33

Plaza
Dorrego

BERNARDO DE IRIGOYEN

AVENIDA 9 DE JULIO

9

6

Museo del Traje

Moreno

MONSERRAT

Belgrano

AVENIDA INDEPENDENCIA

AVENIDA BELGRANO

45

JULIO A. ROCA

Legislatura
Perú

4

8 12
El Zanjón

Santo Domingo

Manzana de las Luces 1

Museo
Etnográfico

2
Museo de
la Ciudad

Bolívar

San Francisco

del Cabildo
Plaza de
Mayo

Museo
Catedral
Metropolitana
Banco Nación

5

DIQUE 2

PUERTO
MADERO Aduana

Time Out Shortlist | Buenos Aires 71

Sights & museums

Manzana de las Luces

Perú 272, entre Moreno y Alsina (4342 3964/www.manzanadelasluces. gov.ar). Subte A, Plaza de Mayo or D, Catedral or E, Bolívar. **Open** noon-3pm Tue, Wed, Fri; 3-7pm Sat, Sun. **Admission** free; guided tours AR$5. **Map** p71 F5 ❶

The 'Block of Enlightenment' is a complex of historical buildings that occupies an entire city block (*manzana* can mean 'block' as well as 'apple'). You can tour the semi-circular chamber, the patios and a series of 18th-century tunnels that used to link the building to the coast behind what is now Plaza de Mayo, several hundred metres away. The block's Iglesia de San Ignacio dates from 1734.

Museo Etnográfico

Moreno 350, entre Balcarce y Defensa (4331 7788/www.museoetnografico. filo.uba.ar). Subte A, Plaza de Mayo or D, Catedral or E, Bolívar. **Open** 3-7pm Wed-Sun. Closed Jan. **Admission** AR$2. **Map** p71 E5 ❷

This museum's small, fascinating collection includes headdresses, masks and cooking implements as well as panels describing Argentina's indigenous tribes, including the Yamanas of Tierra del Fuego, region by region. A carved wooden Japanese Buddhist altarpiece is the museum's most valuable object.

Eating & drinking

D'Oro

Perú 159, entre Hipólito Yrigoyen y Adolfo Alsina (4342 6959/1871/ www.doro-resto.com.ar). Subte A, Perú or D, Catedral or E, Bolívar. **Open** 9am-12.30am Mon-Fri; 7pm-1am Sat. **$$. Italian. Map** p71 E5 ❸

A simple formula – classic risottos and pastas whipped up in an open kitchen, a jovial sommelier decanting Italian imports, and a downtown location with foot traffic galore on weekday afternoons – works for D'Oro, one of the best lunch spots in the area. Pull up a tall stool at the attractive tiled bar and order some crisp focaccia, washing it down with sauvignon blanc; or settle down for an entrée like meat-stuffed ravioli in malbec sauce, or fig and cognac penne – a savoury treat prepared as you watch.

Arts & leisure

Centro Región la Leonesa

Humberto 1° 1462, y San José (4304 5595). Subte E, San José. **Open** *Milonga* 6pm-12.30am Mon; 6pm-midnight Wed; 11pm-4am Thur; 6pm-2am Fri; 4-10.30pm, 11pm-4am Sat; 4pm Sun. Classes daily. No credit cards. **Map** p71 F2 ❹

This superb hall with one of the best *pistas* (dancefloors) in the city hosts excellent *milongas* (tango dance parties). Reservations are essential for the hugely popular Niño Bien event on Thursday nights.

La Trastienda

Balcarce 460, entre Belgrano y Venezuela (4342 7650/ www.latrastienda.com). Subte A, Plaza de Mayo or D, Catedral, or E, Bolívar. **Map** p71 E5 ❺

In the ruins of an old mansion dating from 1895, the Trastienda holds 400 people seated at small tables and another 1,000 standing. A mecca for serious musicians and discerning fans, it attracts cutting-edge local bands, established Latin American talent and international artists such as Damien Rice.

San Telmo

Just a few years ago, San Telmo was BA's countercultural bohemian centerpiece. Today, however, a still-in-progress makeover similar to NYC's revival of Brooklyn has transformed San Telmo into one of BA's trendiest barrios, second only to Palermo in that regard. It still maintains old-world charm thanks to ornate Parisian-style buildings (some of which recall New Orleans's French Quarter) and its

BA's mystery meat

Pinchos de yacaré

Looking for a new taste sensation? Nowadays, there's more to the Buenos Aires meat scene than one hundred different ways to cook a cow or roast a pig. Eager to branch out from traditional parrilla cuisine, several top chefs and fine-dining restaurants around town are experimenting with some of Argentina's indigenous meats. Among the up-and-coming menu offerings emerging from BA's five-star kitchens on white plates drizzled with reductions and atop fancy confits: *yacaré*, a species of caiman, a reptile related to the alligator, found in northern Argentina; *vizcacha*, a rodent related to the chinchilla, found in northern Argentina and in the Pampas; *ñandú*, a large bird similar to an ostrich; and *jabalí*, a wild boar.

These exotic meats, or *carnes autóctonas*, were eaten by indigenous people centuries ago and are still widely consumed in their respective regions. Only recently have they begun to migrate to Buenos Aires's gourmet restaurants. Some eateries, like the Palermo and San Telmo branches of Divina Patagonia (p107), which has wild boar in stout beer, honey and star anise sauce, and La Boca's Patagonia Sur (p82), which has tender braised Patagonian lamb and goat from Cuyanos, aren't exclusively devoted to the alternative meat movement. Others, like Palermo's Oro y Cándido (p111) and San Telmo's El Baqueano (p74), exclusively showcase *carnes autóctonas*.

Indigenous carnivore cuisine isn't always so exotic sounding (case in point: Argentinian *búfalo*) – and it doesn't only refer to meat. *Surubí*, *dorado* and *pacú*, river fish from north-eastern Argentina, are making it onto more BA menus, as is *perdiz*, a type of Argentinian quail. While none of these will likely ever replace the supremacy of the cow in BA's kitchens, perhaps one day *vizcacha* will be to the Argentinian parrilla what escargot is to the French bistro.

Sunday fixtures: the antiques market on Plaza Dorrego and the street peddlers along calle Defensa. Locals tend to be more immune to San Telmo's charm than tourists, but it gives BA an individual, unforgettable identity.

Sights & museums

Museo del Traje

Chile 832, entre Tacuarí y Piedras (4343 8427/www.funmuseodeltraje. com.ar). Subte C, Independencia. **Open** 11am-5pm Mon-Fri (tours on the hour). **Admission** AR$20. **Map** p71 E4 ⑥

Appreciate some of BA's design history at this small, entertaining museum. The bald, black-and-white mannequins posed like cocktail partygoers are a bit on the creepy side, but the intricately crafted dresses they're wearing are gorgeous and well preserved.

Museo Histórico Nacional

Defensa 1600, y Caseros (4307 1182). **Open** 11am-5pm Tue-Fri; 3-6pm Sat; 2-6pm Sun. Closed Jan. **Admission** AR$2. **Map** p70 C3 ⑦

This useful introduction to the city's history includes exhibits from the pre-Columbian, conquest and post-independence periods, plus countless photographs of military men with drooping moustaches.

El Zanjón de Granados

Defensa 755, entre Chile e Independencia (4361 3002). **Open** 11am-5pm Mon-Fri (tours on the hour). **Admission** AR$20. **Map** p71 E4 ⑧

Part archaeological museum, part event space, El Zanjón is a beautifully restored residence encapsulating three centuries of urban living. Although the façade dates from 1830, traces from an earlier patrician home – an open-air cistern, a lookout tower and a 1740s wall comprised of seashell mortaring – serve to transport you to the era of Spanish settlement. In 1985, the crumbling wreck was rescued by amateur historian, Jorge Eckstein, who started dredging the 545 feet (166 metres) of tunnels

Sagardi p77

beneath his property. Seventeen years and 139 truckloads of debris later, he'd unearthed a treasure trove of workaday and eclectic objects – French tiles, African pipes, and English china.

Eating & drinking

647 Dinner Club

Tacuarí 647, entre México y Chile (4331 2950/www.club647.com). **Open** from 8pm daily. **$$$**. **Argentinian**. **Map** p71 F3 ⑨

The dazzling interior design here is all 1940s Shanghai, with dripping chandeliers, floor-to-ceiling French smoked mirrors and velvet chaise longues and booths. The lights are seductively low, better to impress your date while sipping on the signature 647 (sake, grapes with mirin and champagne). The food options are as varied as the cocktails.

70 Living

NEW *Defensa 714, entre Chile e Independencia (4362 2340).* **Open** from noon Mon-Fri, Sun; from 6pm Sat. $$. **Lounge**. Map p71 E4 ⑩
This new resto-lounge has everything you might need for a perfect evening out in BA, including a terrace, great cocktails, candlelit ambiance and tasty appetisers. Sit by the windows looking out on San Telmo's main street, or head upstairs to the outdoor terrace to listen to trip hop and bossa nova under umbrellas and stars.

Aramburu

Salta 1050, entre Humberto 1° y Carlos Calvo (4305 0439/www.arambururesto. com). Subte C, San Juan or E, San José. **Open** 8-11pm Tue-Sat. $$. No credit cards. **Argentinian**. Map p71 E3 ⑪
Creativity abounds in every dish here, from the maize chips and garlic cream spread to the complimentary starter flight of radish and cream foam, rabbit paté with a candied apple sliver, and melon dipped in smoked prosciutto flakes. Creativity takes wing with the endive-wrapped blue cheese custard, and soars with the seared scallops and arugula salad. Main dishes like baked salmon and beef filets over fennel purée stimulate the taste buds, as do the apple raviolis with merlot sauce on the dessert menu.

El Baqueano

NEW *Chile 495, y Bolívar (4342 0802).* **Open** noon-3pm, from 8pm Tue-Sun. $$$. **Argentinian**. Map p71 E4 ⑫
This newly-opened San Telmo restaurant specialises in regional Argentine meat – but not the traditional kind. Menu staples include wild boar (*jabalí*), ostrich (*ñandú*), hare (*liebre*), and alligator (*yacaré*), served up in dishes like alligator brochettes, lamb meatballs and llama carpaccio.

Bar Plaza Dorrego

Defensa 1098, y Humberto 1° (4361 0141). **Open** 8am-3am daily. No credit cards. **Bar**. Map p71 D4 ⑬
Inside this century-old watering hole, a pale lemon hue is cast over the dusty bottles and etched walls, while tango crackles out over black-and-white images of Carlos Gardel.

Brasserie Petanque

Defensa 596, y México (4342 7930/www.brasseriepetanque.com). **Open** noon-3.30pm Mon-Fri, Sun; from 8.30pm Tue-Sat. $$$. **French**. Map p71 E4 ⑭
Everything you would expect from a French menu makes an appearance, including an exceptional bœuf bourguignon, foie gras, steak tartare and, of course, escargot, all served in a light, wide-open space. The crêpes and salad deal is good value, allowing you to splurge on delicious Kir Royals.

La Brigada

Estados Unidos 465, entre Bolívar y Defensa (4361 4685). **Open** noon-3pm, 8pm-midnight Sun, Tue-Thur; noon-4pm, 8pm-1am Fri, Sat. $$. **Argentinian**. Map p71 E4 ⑮
This San Telmo favourite is a refined version of the traditional parilla serving excellent cuts of meat, alongside spicy chorizo, grilled provoleta cheese, crispy vegetable fritters and various salads. The crispy kid *chinchulines* (chitterlings) and the *molleja* (sweetbread) are highly recommended, as is the excellent range of malbecs.

Café San Juan

San Juan 450, entre Bolívar y Defensa (4300 1112). Subte C, San Juan. **Open** noon-4pm, 8.30pm-midnight Tue-Sun. $$$. No credit cards. **Spanish**. Map p71 D4 ⑯
The kitchen staff here builds the tapas menu and generously sized pasta dishes around hand-picked seasonal vegetables. The cured ham with mushrooms or the zucchini-rich fettucine are ideal for sharing. The dinner menu comprises more substantial fare like *bife de chorizo* (sirloin), salmon and pork loins in cream sauce.

Chez

Defensa 1000, y Carlos Calvo (4361 4338/www.che-z.com.ar). **Open** from 10am Tue-Sun. $$$. **French**. Map p71 D4 ⑰

La Trastienda p72

This authentic French restaurant invites you to sip a glass of complimentary champagne any time you like. The catch: you have to unclasp the paper napkin holder that says 'Chez' and turn it over to read the invitation to the bubbly, then hand it to your waitress. Couple your flute with the salade cigogne with green leaves, tomato, gruyère cheese, boiled egg and bacon; or the house salad of red and green lettuce, tomato and bacon, topped with a poached egg. The platter of assorted charcuterie and cheeses is another winner – follow it with the ossobuco ravioli.

El Federal
*Carlos Calvo 599, y Perú
(4300 4313).* **Open** 8am-2am Mon-Thur, Sun; 8am-4am Fri-Sun. **Bar.**
Map p71 D4 ⑱
Built in 1864, El Federal is one of BA's most historic bars. There's a standard set of coffees, beers and spirits and a long list of snacks and sandwiches – the *lomo completo* beef sandwich comes with all the trimmings.

Gran Parilla del Plata
Chile 594, y Perú (4300 8858). **Open** noon-4pm, from 8pm Mon-Sat; from noon Sun. **$$. Argentinian.**
Map p71 E4 ⑲
All the cuts of meat here are exquisite; but most nights, it's the *ojo de bife*

(rib-eye) and *entraña* (skirt steak – a novelty to most foreigners) that are recommended by the waiters. Combine any of them with the baked potatoes with bacon and Philadelphia cheese and a fresh salad. Classy but affordable, this one's always reliable.

Lezama
Brasil 359, entre Defensa y Balcarce (4361 0114). **Open** noon-4.30pm, from 8pm Tue-Sat; noon-2am Sun. **$$.**
Argentinian. **Map** p70 D3 ⑳
Though it has a menu with an impressive range of sauced-up dinners, Lezama's forte tends to be the simpler dishes, so pick one of the standards– tortillas, salads, pastas, steaks. The *lomo* (tenderloin) with a fresh rocket and tomato salad is a top choice.

Manolo
Bolívar 1299, y Cochabamba (4307 8743/www.restaurantmanolo. com.ar). **Open** noon-1am Tue-Sun. **$.**
Argentinian. **Map** p71 D3 ㉑
Manolo is buzzing most nights with a loyal clientele who come to feast on the excellent parrilla standards. There's a sprinkling of traditional criollo cuisine, such as the *locro* (a stew of pork, beans and spices) as well as chicken prepared in a dozen different ways. The suprema Gran Manolo, a breaded chicken breast topped with ham, egg, cheese and olives, is a sure bet.

Pride Café

*Balcarce 869, y Pasaje Giuffra,
San Telmo (4300 6435).* **Open** 9am-
9pm Mon-Fri; 11am-8pm Sat; 10am-
10pm Sun. **$**. No credit cards. **Café.**
Map p71 D4 ㉒

This gay-friendly San Telmo meeting
point has cute young waiters, a good
early crowd, and a decent music mix.
Best food choice: *café cortado* and a
slice of pie.

Sagardi

NEW *Humberto Iº 319, entre Defensa y
Balcarce (4361 2538/www.sagardi.
com.ar).* **Open** *Bar* noon-midnight
Mon-Sat; 9am-midnight Sun.
Restaurant 1-4pm, 8pm-midnight daily.
$$$. **Basque.** Map p71 D4 ㉓

This gleaming new Basque *pintxos*
joint cuts a splendid figure from the
outside, with its glassed-in open
kitchen. Tiny sandwiches, portions of
Spanish omelette and savoury cro-
quettes are set out on the bar, while
the sit-down restaurant at the back
offers grilled sausages, cod and *txule-
ton* (fat beef steaks).

La Vinería de Gualterio Bolívar

*Bolivar 865, entre Independencia
y Estados Unidos (4361 4709/
www.lavineriadegualteriobolivar.com).
Subte C, Independencia.* **Open** 12.30-
4pm, 9pm-midnight Tue-Sun. **$$$**
No credit cards. **Argentinian.**
Map p71 E4 ㉔

Light molecular touches like potato
foams appear on the menu here, as do
scallops with stewed lamb's tongue
and vanilla squash mash with a citrus
vinaigrette. The slow-cooked egg dish
is heated at 62ºC for 50 minutes and
served with white truffle, lamb stock
and goat-cheese foam. There's also a
40-vegetable salad containing cooked
and raw ingredients, flowers, roots,
germinated seeds and shoots. Only set
menus are available in the evening.

Vintage Bar

NEW *Defensa 588, entre México y
Venezuela (4342 4464/www.vintage-
bar.com.ar).* **Open** noon-late Mon-Fri,
8pm-late Sat, 10am-10pm Sun. **$$$**.
Bar. Map p71 E4 ㉕

This joint has an appealingly lofty
interior and a low-key atmosphere.
Litre jugs of Warsteiner are an excel-
lent AR$20 for one and AR$30 for two
during happy hours that stretch, unin-
terrupted, from Monday to Saturday.
The seafood platters and grilled
steaks are worth sticking around for.

Shopping

El Buen Orden

*Defensa 894, y Estados Unidos
(mobile 15 5936 2820/www.elbuen
orden.com.ar).* **Open** 11am-7pm
daily. No credit cards.
Map p71 D4 ㉖

New items appear daily and stock is
constantly rotated in this antique store
that's more like a museum to all things
retro than a shop. There's everything
from clothing and bags to period piece
jewellery, hats and eyewear. Pick up a
vintage pill box or a powder compact,
or browse through the buttons, buck-
les and lace trims.

Fedro San Telmo

*Carlos Calvo 578, entre Bolívar y Perú
(4300 7551/www.fedrosantelmo.
com.ar).* **Open** 11am-10pm Mon-Sat;
3-9pm Sun. Map p71 E4 ㉗

Specialising in foreign language publi-
cations, this excellent shop stocks new
books in English, French, Portuguese
and Italian. Picture books, magazines
and music CDs are also sold. The Wi-Fi
and coffee is on the house, as are the reg-
ular talks and readings. Enquire here
about local history courses, also given in
English and French.

Feria San Pedro Telmo

Plaza Dorrego. **Open** 10am-5pm Sun.
Map p71 D4 ㉘

For a lighthearted browse, go to San
Telmo's central square, Plaza Dorrego,
on a Sunday. Around 270 stalls sell
antique dolls, soda siphons, jewellery,
tango memorabilia and other col-
lectibles. Despite the hordes of curious
tourists browsing through the wares,

Plaza Dorrego still evokes something of the spirit of old Buenos Aires.

Ffiocca

Perú 599, y México (4331 4585/ www.ffiocca.com). Subte E, Belgrano. **Open** 10.30am-7.30pm Mon-Fri; 10.30am-3pm Sat. **Map** p71 E4 ㉙
This multibrand, retro-style boutique offers the best of avant-garde fashion. Florencia Fiocca's own line shares hanging space with those of fellow designers Cora Groppo, Benedit Bis and Marina Massone, among others. The eponymous label features high-tech microfibres and decorative pleating and stitching used on dresses, skirts and coats in colours ranging from coral and petrol blue to classic black and chalk white.

Gil Antigüedades

Humberto 1° 412, y Defensa (4361 5019/www.gilantiguedades.com.ar). **Open** 11am-1pm, 3-7pm Tue-Sun. **Map** p71 D4 ㉚
Amidst the enormous collection of vintage fashion, there's something to suit almost every taste and pocket. With 25 years in business and more than 6,000 pieces, including clothing, jewellery, footwear, fans, parasols and figurines, this store emphasises quality and variety.

L'ago

Defensa 919 and Defensa 970, entre Estados Unidos y Carlos Calvo (4362 3641/www.lagosantelmo.com). **Open** 10am-8pm daily. **Map** p71 D4 ㉛
Modern, retro and handmade are all under one roof (well, two, technically) at L'ago, named after the Italian hometown of co-owner Luis Ricci's parents. Enter and lose yourself in a world of eclectic objects: retro furniture, lighting fixtures, creative toys, dolls and art by young Argentinian artists.

Un Lugar en el Mundo

Defensa 891, entre Estados Unidos e Independencia (4362 3836). **Open** 10.30am-8pm daily. **Map** p71 E4 ㉜
The creative fruits of Argentinian designers on the rise fill the racks of this funky multi-brand San Telmo store with clothing and accessories for both sexes. Before you get too excited, the original Pucci dresses are not for sale.

La Maja Remates

Humberto 1° 236/238, entre Paseo Colón y Balcarce (4361 6097/ www.lamajaremates.com.ar). **Open** 10.30am-6.30pm daily, auctions 8pm Thur (no auctions Jan-Feb). **Map** p71 D4 ㉝
A world of wonder for those who like their antiques piled high and browsable, La Maja contains a fair amount of bric-a-brac as well as some truly marvelous pieces, including a range of chandeliers that span the ages.

Marcelo Toledo

Humberto 1° 462, entre Defensa y Bolívar (4362 0841/www.marcelotoledo. net). Subte C, San Juan. **Open** 10.30am-6pm Mon-Fri, Sun. **Map** p71 D4 ㉞
Marcelo Toledo counts ex-US President Bill Clinton, singer Robbie Williams and the Spanish royal family among his VIP clients. His 120-piece collection entitled 'Evita' has been presented around the world, and it features necklaces in silver, gold and precious stones inspired by Argentina's former first lady, Eva Perón. Toledo's more recent creations include handworked silver daisies, jasmines, magnolias and pansies with embossing and chiseling detail.

María Rojo

Carlos Calvo 618, entre Perú y Chacabuco (4362 3340). **Open** 11am-8pm Tue-Sun. **Map** p71 E3 ㉟
Wander through the rooms of María Rojo, a clothing store in a beautiful old San Telmo house, to find womenswear, shoes, accessories and creations like those of Disparatada Belleza, which fuse antique fabrics and odd pieces to create unique dresses, skirts and jackets.

Pablo Ramírez

Perú 587, entre Venezuela y México (4342 7154/www.pabloramirez.com.ar). **Open** 10.30am-7.30pm Mon-Fri; 10.30am-3pm Sat. **Map** p71 E4 ㊱
Ramírez complements his sailor necklines, wide-legged trousers and

cinch-waisted dresses with textural details such as openwork and subtle transparencies. Black, white and polka-dot motifs abound, and accessories like huge white sunglasses or feather hairpieces complete the look of chic sophistication.

Puntos en el Espacio

Perú 979, entre Estados Unidos y Carlos Calvo (4307 1742/ www.puntoseneleespacio.com.ar). **Open** 11am-8pm Mon-Sun. **Map** p71 E4 ③⑦
Visit this ample, well-displayed space for a huge selection of clothing for guys and girls, plus bags, accessories, footwear and decorative household items, all from dozens of talented young designers.
Other location Independencia 402, San Telmo (4307 5665).

Walrus Books

Estados Unidos 617, entre Perú y Chacabuco (4300 7135/www. walrus-books.com.ar). Subte C, Independencia. **Open** 10am-8pm Tue-Sun. **Map** p71 E4 ③⑧
There are over 4,000 titles in this shop's eclectic range of used but good quality English books. If you're a reader, you're almost guaranteed to find something of interest, whether it's classic or modern literature or non-fiction.

Nightlife

Fugees 99

Bolívar 1190, y San Juan (no phone). **Open** 2-7am Fri, Sat. **Map** p71 D3 ③⑨
If breakdance circles and spontaneous rap battles inspire you, and if you like your hip hop without the velvet rope and bling, Fugees is the place. Locals and global travellers mix it up to Biggie and Daddy Yankee.

Gibraltar

Perú 895, y Estados Unidos (4362 5310). **Open** 6pm-4am Mon-Fri; noon-4am Sat, Sun. No credit cards. **Map** p71 E4 ④⓪
Well-priced beer in pint glasses, genuinely spicy curries, an exhaustive

Creative comeback

La Boca is back on BA's cultural map. The reopening of the art institution **Fundación Proa** (p82) in November 2008 after 18 months of renovations has returned a dose of panache to the barrio, and has added another venue to the capital's art scene. Milanese architecture firm Caruso-Torricella directed the 138% expansion, appropriating the two adjacent buildings into the 19th-century structure and blowing up Proa's size to an enormous 2,300 square metres, spaced out over two floors of exhibition and educational space and topped off by an airy, minimalist gourmet café overlooking the harbour of the Riachuelo River.

So the digs look dandy, but what about the art? The grand reopening kicked off with the South American premier of French found-object conceptualist Marcel Duchamp's 'Readymade' works, followed by a treasure trove of contemporary photographs from Germany's Düsseldorf School; a comprehensive glimpse at Futurism; and 'Art in the Auditorium', premiering a collaborative new media project showcasing emerging film and video artists conceived by London's Whitechapel Gallery. An ongoing cycle of smaller-scale performances, installations, and art-video and independent-film screenings is held in the library, restaurant and brand-new auditorium.

Caminito

collection of whiskies, and the friendliest bar owners in the city all help to explain why you'll find so many expat elbows on the bar here.

Mitos Argentinos
Humberto 1º 489, entre Bolívar y Defensa (4362 7810/www. mitosargentinos.com.ar). **Open** from 8pm Fri, Sat. **Map** p71 D4 ㊶

Local rock and blues bands play in this charming old San Telmo house, and though most are not well known, they're wisely selected, so it's worth the experience. Dinner is available on Fridays and Saturdays, while on Sundays lunch is served during tango classes and shows. After hours, the dancing continues until way after sunrise.

Museum
Perú 535, entre México y Venezuela (4771 9628/www.museumclub.com.ar). **Open** 8pm-2am Wed; from 10pm Fri-Sun. **Map** p71 E4 ㊷

Wednesday's 'after office' (that's happy hour in BA lingo) parties

remain Museum's biggest draw. This is the place for anyone after heaving crowds, cheap booze, occasional live music and a record collection that resembles a full-on cheeseboard. Women get in for free, but ladies beware: the guys at this meet market are even less subtle than usual in making their moves.

Nacional
Estados Unidos 308, y Balcarce (4307 4913/www.myspace.com/ barelnacional) **Open** from 9pm Thu-Sun. **Map** p71 D4 ㊸

Located in an antique house above the restaurant Los Loros, this cabaret-style bar is an intimate affair. It hosts local talent, and bands frequently sign on for old-fashioned month-long runs, playing once a week during that time.

La Preciosa
NEW *Chacabuco 947, entre Estados Unidos y Carlos Calvo (www.lapreciosaclub.com.ar).* **Open** from midnight Fri. **Map** p71 E3 ㊹

You won't find anything in La Preciosa at Club 947 that you wouldn't spot in any other B-list mainstream gay disco. Hot boys? Check. Horny guys? Check. A comfortable space to sit and take it all in? Not here, folks. The ambience is a tad grubby, but judging from the packed house during the inaugural season, no one seems to care. Check out the website for information on how to get on the list for free entry before 3am.

La Puerta Roja

Chacabuco 733, entre Chile e Independencia (4362 5649/ www.lapuertaroja.com.ar). Subte E, Independencia. **Open** 6pm-6am daily. **Map** p71 E4 45

La Puerta Roja ('the red door', which is all that marks the spot) is a rare breed: a real bar. There isn't a cocktail umbrella in sight, the space is large, the music eclectic, the decor simple, and the prices and menu firmly set to attract the youngsters, backpackers and resident foreigners who pack the bar. The cheap, tasty and filling menu includes meatball subs, croquettes with clams, and pretzels with spicy mustard or houmous.

Arts & leisure

Bar Sur

Estados Unidos 299, y Balcarce (4362 6086/www.bar-sur.com.ar). **Open** 8pm-2am daily. Show every 2hrs. **Map** p71 D4 46

The tango show here is fairly fancy, but the intimate bar and emphasis on participation makes this a fun and friendly little joint.

Espacio Ecléctico

Humberto Iº 730, entre Chacabuco y Piedras (4307 1966/www.espacio eclectico.com.ar). **Open** 3-8pm Tue-Fri; 5-10pm Sat, Sun. Closed Jan, Feb. **Map** p71 E3 47

An intimate space featuring theatre, music and film, Espacio Ecléctico also presents regular art exhibitions which range between the traditional and the unconventional.

La Manufactura Papelera

Bolívar 1582, entre Brasil y Caseros (4307 9167/www.papeleracultural. 8m.com). **Shows** 6pm and 8.30pm Tue-Sun. Closed Jan. No credit cards. **Map** p70 D3 48

Enjoy a more intimate operatic experience in this former paper factory, where groups stage little-performed classical works.

Teatro Margarita Xirgú

Chacabuco 875, entre Independencia y Estados Unidos (4307 0066/ www.margaritaxirgu.com). Subte C or E, Independencia. **Map** p71 E4 49

This stunning example of Catalonian architecture is a treat for your eyes as well as your ears, with its carefully preserved interior and superb acoustics perfect for high-decibel classical performances.

El Viejo Almacén

Avenida Independencia 300, y Balcarce (4307 7388/www.viejoalmacen.com). **Open** 8am-12pm daily. **Dinner** 8pm. **Show** 10pm. **Map** p71 D4 50

In 1968 singer Edmundo Rivero took over this venue as a refuge for musicians and, as a plaque on the doorway states, 'those who have lost their faith'.

La Boca

Everybody knows La Boca for its colourful, corrugated iron shacks and as the home base of the local football team Boca Juniors. Some areas are dicey, and the barrio's location at the mouth (which, incidentally, translates as 'la boca' in Spanish) of the Riachuelo makes the one-time main BA port inconvenient to get to, but worth the trip.

Sights & museums

Caminito

Map p70 A2 51

This street's name literally means 'little walkway'. These days, the street is thronged with tango dancers, artisans and tourists.

Fundación Proa

Avenida Pedro de Mendoza 1929, entre Magallanes y Rocha (4104 1000/www. proa.org). **Open** 11am-8pm Tue-Sun. **Admission** AR$10; AR$6 students; AR$3 pensioners. **Map** p70 A2 ⬤52
See box p79.

Museo de la Pasión Boquense

Brandsen 805, y Del Valle Iberlucea (4362 1100/www.museoboquense.com). **Open** 10am-7pm daily (closed on match days). **Admission** AR$12 museum only; AR$22 museum & tour; half-price concessions.
Map p70 B3 ⬤53
Stop by this museum adjacent to La Bombonera stadium for all things Boca Juniors. There are loads of audiovisual gadgets, mountains of facts and figures and, of course, tributes to Boca legend Diego Maradona.

Eating & drinking

Don Carlos

Brandsen 699, y Zolezzi (4362 2433). **Open** noon-3pm, 8-11.30pm Mon-Sat. **$$**. No credit cards. **Argentinian**. **Map** p70 B3 ⬤54
Five 'P's – '*picadas* (tapas), pizza, pasta, *pescado* (fish), *parrilla* (grill)?' – is the question with which Don Carlos himself greets every table. The parade of small dishes – from fresh home-made mozzarella to *fainá* (a dense, flat chick-pea bread) to whatever is on the grill – continues until you ask it to stop, at which point a sixth 'P', *postres* (desserts), will be offered, along with coffee.

Il Matterello

Martín Rodríguez 517, y 20th de Septiembre (4307 0529). **Open** 12.30-3pm, 8.30pm-midnight Tue-Sat; 12.30-3pm Sun. Closed Jan. **$**. **Italian**. **Map** p70 B3 ⬤55
A crisp, clean, cantina-style La Boca eaterie where a mixed plate of warm and cold antipasti serves to enliven the taste buds in preparation for an excellent al dente tagliatelle with a puttanesca sauce or a truly sumptuous *fazzoletti alla carbonara* (wide pasta

with an eggs, cream, cheese and bacon sauce).

El Obrero

Agustín Caffarena 64, entre Ministro Brin y Caboto (4362 9912). **Open** noon-4pm, from 8pm Mon-Sat. **$**. No credit cards. **Argentinian**. **Map** p70 B4 ⬤56
El Obrero, literally 'the worker,' is one of the most famous restaurants in BA. Most people choose from the parrilla items listed on the chalkboard, but there are also pastas and fish dishes and a selection of old-style desserts such as *sopa inglesa* (like trifle).

Patagonia Sur

Rocha 803, y Pedro de Mendoza (4303 5917/www.restaurantepatagoniasur. com). **Open** noon-4pm, 7.30pm-midnight Thur-Sat; noon-4pm Sun. **$$$**. **Argentinan**. **Map** p70 A2 ⬤57
Here's an anomaly: an exclusive restaurant in one of BA's poorest neighbourhoods serving Argentinian comfort food like *choripanes* (sausage sandwiches) and empanadas at haute cuisine prices (AR$310 for a three-course set menu). Incongruities aside, every item is of the highest quality.

Arts & leisure

Estadio Alberto J Armando (La Bombonera)

Brandsen 805, y la Vía (4309 4700/ www.bocajuniors.com.ar). **Map** p70 B3 ⬤58
Watching a game here is a unique and vertiginous experience: the concrete stands vibrate, and at the higher levels, you feel a wrong move might tip you out onto the pitch itself. The *platea baja* in the stands area is your recommended (and safer) vantage point.

Estadio Luis Conde (La Bombonerita)

Arzobispo Espinoza 600, y Palos (4309 4748/www.bocajuniors.com.ar). **Tickets** AR$10-$20. No credit cards. **Map** p70 B3 ⬤59
Home base of Argentina's Boca Junior's basketball team.

Floralis Genérica p84

North of the Centre

The barrios to the north of the centre are why BA is often called the Paris of South America. It may be part shrewd marketing plan and part wishful thinking, but the sentiment is based on more than a small dose of reality. The tree-lined streets of Recoleta, which in spots recall Le Marais in the city of lights, are some of the most spectacular in town, and the real estate – though not quite as exclusive as the famous cemetery for which the barrio is perhaps best known – is among the priciest. Barrio Norte, the Recoleta sub-barrio where both the buildings and the money are newer, has fewer tourist attractions but a lively drinking and dining scene. And Palermo, home to the city's trendiest restaurants, bars and hotels, contributes greatly to BA's reputation as the party capital of South America. The less hedonistic generally gravitate towards the many parks and gardens that make Palermo the city's greenest, as well as its largest barrio. The construction boom that continues to dominate the area suggests that the best might be yet to come.

Recoleta & Barrio Norte

If it's good enough for Evita, whose final resting place is in the cemetery that bears the barrio's namea… The jewel in BA's crown, Recoleta has shops, restaurants, wide open grassy spaces and a grand hotel (the **Alvear Palace**) to rival those in any first-world urban centre. The **Village Recoleta**, across from the cemetery on Vicente López, is a strip-mall-style complex with

Cementerio de la Recoleta

restaurants, a bookstore, several fast food outlets and one of the city's best cineplexes. Classier Avenida Alvear is where the label-obsessed squeeze in their retail therapy. Tired of being surrounded by people who are more rich and fabulous than you are? Head to Barrio Norte, a more middle-class Recoleta sub-barrio that brings the splendour down several notches to the level of mere mortals.

Sights & museums

Cementerio de la Recoleta

Junín 1760, entre Guido y Vicente López, Recoleta (4803 1594).
Open 7am-5.45pm daily. **Admission** free to the living. **Map** p85 B4 ❶
The cemetery, opened in 1822, is home to hundreds of illustrious corpses, laid out in a compact yet very extensive maze of granite, marble and bronze mausoleums. Originally a public cemetery, it is now even harder to get into than the posh flats that surround it.

Many Argentinian presidents are entombed here, but most of the cemetery's visitors probably come to see the resting place of María Eva Duarte de Perón, aka Evita.

Floralis Genérica

Avenida Figueroa Alcorta, y Austria, Recoleta. **Map** p85 C5 ❷
Designed by Argentine architect Eduardo Catalano, the Floralis Genérica lies in the Plaza de las Naciones Unidas. A steel and aluminum flower sculpture whose petals open and close with the sun, this was Catalano's gift to his natal city. At night, with petals closed, a red light shines from the flower's interior.

Museo Nacional de Bellas Artes

Avenida del Libertador 1473, y Pueyrredón, Recoleta (4803 8814/ 4691/www.mnba.org.ar). **Open** 12.30-7.30pm Tue-Fri; 9.30am-7.30pm Sat, Sun. **Admission** free. **Map** p85 B5 ❸
The MNBA is home to 32 rooms, sculpture patios, an architecture display, studios, a library and an auditorium. The country's biggest collection

Recoleta & Barrio Norte

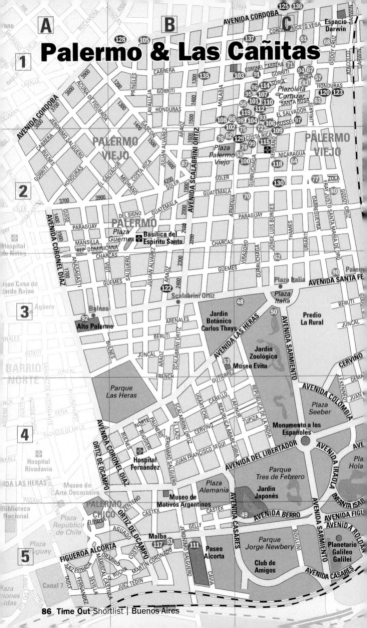

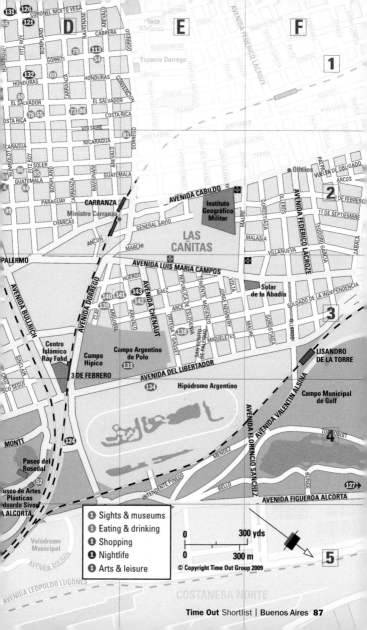

of 19th- and 20th-century Argentinian art is on permanent display here. The international collection on the ground floor includes works by El Greco, Rubens, Rembrandt and Goya.

Palais de Glace

Posadas 1725, y Schiaffino, Recoleta (4804 1163/www.palaisdeglace.org). **Open** 2-8pm Tue-Sun. **Admission** free. **Map** p85 B5 ❹

Palais de Glace, which opened its doors to skaters in 1910, means 'ice palace'. The grand circular structure also housed a landmark tango salon before being declared a National Monument in 2004. Today, the renovated palace hosts major exhibitions in fashion and the visual arts. Free tours in English are held every Saturday and Sunday at 5pm by appointment.

Eating & drinking

788 Food Bar

Arenales 1877, entre Riobamba y Callao, Barrio Norte (4814 4788/ www.788foodbar.com.ar). Subte D, Callao. **Open** 10am-5am Mon-Sat. **$$**. **Argentinian**. **Map** p85 A4 ❺

In this beautifully appointed room, the gracious service – with elegant touches like a warmed, covered bread box on your table – make dining a pleasure. The food is also among the most creative in BA, with a menu that changes regularly – try the 'don't miss' dishes when they are on offer – the brown-sugar braised pork, for instance, and the tomato-cardamom flan.

El Alamo

Uruguay 1175, entre Santa Fe y Arenales, Recoleta (4813 7324/ www.elalamobar.com). **Open** 4pm-4am Mon-Wed; 10am-4am Thur-Sat; noon-4am Sun. **Pub**. **Map** p85 A4 ❻

More expats than Argentinians fill this gritty American pub, but what really gets the crowd rolling in is the free beer and free selected drinks for ladies from 6pm-midnight (with a food purchase of AR$15). Take advantage of the pub fare and mega breakfast deals, and kick back – if you are able to find an empty seat – and watch big-screen sports games while you drink your heart out.

La Bourgogne

Alvear Palace Hotel, Avenida Alvear 1891, entre Callao y Ayacucho, Recoleta (4808 2100/www.alvearpalace.com). **Open** noon-3.30pm Mon-Fri; 7.30pm-midnight Mon-Sat. **$$$$**. **French**. **Map** p85 B5 ❼

This is a French restaurant with a French chef, housed in a French-style building and located in the area of Buenos Aires that is the most flagrantly Parisian. In other words, don't yell for ketchup. Do, however, order the sea bream with butter sauce and caviar or the grilled veal with thyme flowers or the rabbit 'crunch' with mustard sauce. The service is formal and near flawless.

La Cabaña

Rodríguez Peña 1967, entre Posadas y Alvear, Recoleta (4814 0001/ www.lacabanabuenosaires.com. ar). **Open** noon-4pm, 7pm-midnight daily. **$$$**. **Argentinian**. **Map** p85 A5 ❽

This legendary supper club of BA's old-time oligarchy has stuffed cows, rustic decor, and elaborate woodwork on its four floors, and the roof terrace is a great spot for a pre-prandial cocktail. La Cabaña is as much a museum as a steakhouse, with one vital difference: the meat is good.

Casa Bar

Rodríquez Peña 1150, y Santa Fe, Recoleta (4816 2712/www.casabar buenosaires.com). Subte D, Callao. **Open** from 5pm Mon-Fri; from 9pm Sat; from 7pm Sun. **Bar**. **Map** p85 A4 ❾

The outsized bar flanked by two flatscreen TVs fits in well with the modern decor of this restored French mansion, and it's a good spot to watch local soccer or American football matches with other foreign fans. There are penny-pinching deals as well as quality liquors and beers from all over the world, and occasional live music might be anything from jazz, blues and rock to the sweet sounds of country music.

Casa SaltShaker

Address provided when you reserve,
Barrio Norte (www.casasaltshaker.com).
Open from 9pm Fri, Sat. **$$$**. No
credit cards. **Eclectic**.
See box p143.

Cumaná

Rodríguez Peña 1149, entre Santa
Fe y Arenales, Recoleta (4813 9207).
Open noon-1am daily. **$**. No credit
cards. **Argentinian**. Map p85 A4 ⑩
You'll be hungry as soon as you walk
through the door here. Surrender to the
onslaught of tantalising aromas and
settle at one of the rustic tables and
order some *locro* (a thick corn and meat
stew) and home-made empanadas
(Argentina's version of the Cornish
pasty). Popularity like this comes at a
cost: be prepared to queue for around
an hour at weekends, when the place is
jumping with a young, fun crowd.

Fervor

🆕 *Posadas 1519, y Callao, Recoleta*
(4804 4944). **Open** noon-4pm, from
8pm daily. **$$**. **Argentinian**.
Map p85 B5 ⑪
This trendy restaurant is a hot spot for
locals and tourists alike. Traditional
picks like *ojo de bife* (rib-eye steak)
and *tortilla de papas* (fried potato
omelette) are quality choices, but the
real star here is the seafood: calamari,
cuttlefish, shrimp, scallops, and
salmon grilled to perfection. In a city
where top-notch seafood is rare, Fervor
stands out for its plentiful portions,
warm atmosphere and highly
commendable service.

Gran Bar Danzón

Libertad 1161, entre Santa Fe y
Arenales, Recoleta (4811 1108/
www.granbardanzon.com.ar). Subte D,
Tribunales. **Open** from 7pm Mon-Fri;
from 8pm Sat, Sun **$$**. **Argentinian**.
Map p85 A4 ⑫
The 'gran' is merited: this is a truly
great wine bar and restaurant and a
banquet for the senses from the
moment you climb up the candlelit and
incense-scented stairwell. The main
menu roams freely between Europe

and Latin America, offering flawless
fusion dishes like confit of duck
perched atop a banana blini, veal
braised in port with potatoes and
caramelised onions, and red salmon in
a brioche crust served with a fig and
tomato chutney. Or, if you think East
is best, try the superb sushi. A wine list
of over 200 labels and great promotions
make this an exceptional place for a
drink, for dinner or both.

Milion

Paraná 1048, entre Marcelo T de
Alvear y Santa Fe, Recoleta (4815
9925/www.milion.com.ar). **Open** noon-
2am Mon-Wed; noon-3am Thur; noon-
4am Fri; 8pm-4am Sat; 8pm-2am Sun.
$$. **Argentinian**. Map p85 A4 ⑬
This elegant mansion is as popular as
ever, with classical architecture that's
offset by dim lighting, cutting-edge art
displays, projected visuals and art-
house movies. Milion's high-ceilinged
rooms are often littered with reservation cards, making it a nightmare to
find a seat. But somewhere between the
first floor terrace, the lovely garden and
the marble staircase you're bound to
find a spot. Dinner is served in the
restaurant downstairs.

Nectarine

Vicente López 1661, entre Montevideo
y Rodríguez Peña, Recoleta (4813
6993). **Open** noon-3pm, 8pm-midnight
Mon-Fri; 8pm-midnight Sat. **$$$**.
French. Map p85 A4 ⑭
Hidden up a small pedestrian alley,
Nectarine has a small interior that's
sophisticated without being formal, and
provides the perfect setting for a
romantic tryst. Both the wine list and
the menu at this, one of the most exclu-
sive restaurants in BA, are rich in
options and flavours.

Oviedo

Beruti 2602, y Ecuador, Barrio Norte
(4822 5415/www.oviedoresto.com.ar).
Subte D, Pueyrredón. **Open** noon-
3.30pm, 8pm-1am daily. **$$$**.
Spanish. Map p85 B3 ⑮
Oviedo has a clubbish atmosphere
and is a favourite with businessmen
and political hacks; but never mind

CHOCOLATE

the clientele, feel the quality. Here, classic Iberian dishes are prepared with great care and attention to detail. *Tortilla a la española*, goat's cheese croquettes, grilled *chipirones*, baked clams, and oven-baked white fish and potatoes are savoury reminders of the old country. Choose from *lenguado* (sole) or *bacalao* (cod), caught fresh in Mar del Plata, or pick from an abundant selection of shellfish. Steak, rabbit, and lamb with mushrooms are staples here, as are home-made pastas, which round out a very complete menu.

Piegari

Posadas 1042, y La Recova, Recoleta (4326 9654/9430). **Open** noon-3.30pm, from 7.30pm daily. **$$**. **Italian**. **Map** p85 A5 ⑯
From pasta to meat, risotto, seafood and pizza – all delicious, high-quality and abundant – you're sure to find something to satisfy your every craving at Piegari. Worth mentioning from the dessert menu are the home-made cakes, prepared with fresh ingredients from local markets.

Piola Pizzerie Italiane

Libertad 1078, entre Santa Fe y Marcelo T de Alvear, Recoleta (4812 0690/www.piola.it). **Open** noon-2am Mon-Wed; noon-3am Thur, Fri; from 7pm Sat, Sun. **$$**. **Italian**. **Map** p85 A4 ⑰
With locations scattered across both the Americas, this pizzeria chain has got gourmet pie-tossing down to a science: roll the dough to make the thinnest crust possible, top it with fresh greens and sharp cheeses, and serve it up in a slick space lit by vibrantly coloured lanterns. Salads and pasta are on the menu too, but the best bet is one of Piola's signature pizzas, like the smoked salmon and ricotta-topped Rimini or the leafy Praga, a white pizza piled high with various toppings.

Sirop & Sirop Folie

Units 11 & 12, Vicente López 1661, entre Montevideo y Rodríguez Peña, *Recoleta (4813 5900).* **Open** *Sirop* noon-3.30pm, from 8pm Mon-Fri; from 8pm Sat. *Sirop Folie* from 11am Tue-Sun. **$$**. **Argentinian**. **Map** p85 A4 ⑱
The alley on which Sirop is located is very Parisian: a fantastic place to eat outside on a warm spring day. Across the passageway, Sirop Folie is a more relaxed version of sister Sirop, with charming interior touches and plenty of light. Just as impressive as the decor are the fantastic brunches that include salmon, excellent cheeses, scrambled eggs with bacon and home-made chips.

Sorrento

Posadas 1053, La Recova, Recoleta (4326 0532/www.sorrentorestaurant. com.ar). **Open** noon-1.30am daily. **$$$**. **Italian**. **Map** p85 A5 ⑲
The first branch of Sorrento was opened in 1876, and a time traveller from Sorrento's salad days would feel comfortable browsing through the current menu, which is devoted to Italian classics like *sorrentino alla bivonesa* (stuffed ravioli in a mushroom sauce) and *risotto lamesiana* (saffron risotto with prawns). Sorrento is also one of the few BA restaurants to specialise in fresh fish: *abadejo* (pollock), *lenguado* (sole) and *merluza* (hake) – among many others – are cooked to order when in season.

Tandoor

Laprida 1293, y Charcas, Barrio Norte (4821 3676/www.tandoor.com.ar). Subte D, Agüero. **Open** noon-4pm, from 8pm daily. **$$**. **Indian**. **Map** p85 C3 ⑳
If you're familiar with the traditional, kitsch Indian restaurant – at least in its Western incarnation – bedecked with moving waterfall pictures, low lighting and an unsightly carpet, you'll be surprised that the bright and airy Tandoor is anything but. Your deliciously light fish curry with Bengal yoghurt and tomatoes will have been prepared under three pairs of expert eyes. As well as curry classics like chicken tikka masala, the menu includes several very good lamb dishes.

Shopping

Ateneo Grand Splendid

Avenida Santa Fe 1860, entre Callao y Riobamba, Barrio Norte (4811 6104/4813 6052). Subte D, Callao. **Open** 9am-10pm Mon-Thur; 9am-midnight Fri, Sat; noon-10pm Sun. **Map** p85 A3 ㉑

Bag a comfy chair and spend an afternoon browsing the wide selection of books in this grand renovated theatre, or have a drink in the on-stage café. CDs and DVDs are also sold.

Benedit Bis

Unit 13, Galeria Promenade, Avenida Alvear 1883, Recoleta (4806 0985). **Open** 10.30am-8pm Mon-Fri; 10.30am-2pm Sat. **Map** p85 B5 ㉒

Sisters Rosa and Juana Benedit make clothes for elegant women who like to stand out. They include multicoloured dresses, blouses and camisoles in chiffon or cotton jacquard-style fabrics, and puffball shorts are combined with colourful patchwork tops – ideal for the playful and uninhibited.

Cardón

Avenida Santa Fe 1399, entre Uruguay y Talcahuano, Recoleta (4813 8983/ www.cardon.com.ar). **Open** 9.30am-8pm Mon-Sat; 11am-6pm Sun. **Map** p85 A4 ㉓

Escape the city in Cardón's top-drawer collection of men's, women's and children's casual clothing. The wool sweaters, cotton shirts, and alpaca scarves are all well made and comfy. The knitted shawls contain ethnic touches, and a new line of accessories features belts and horn bracelets. Fine, durable leather goods such as wallets and men's boots are also available at the various branches.

Carolina Hansen

Terrazas Buenos Aires Design, Pueyrredón 2501, Recoleta (5777 6119/www.carolinahansen.com.ar). **Open** 10am-9pm daily. **Map** p85 B5 ㉔

The use of woven textiles made in Humahuaca, in the north-western border province of Jujuy, means that Carolina's clothes possess a natural

and unique quality. Sheep, llama wool and fine silk threads are combined to produce elegant womenswear.

Celedonio Lohidoy

Unit 39, Galeria Promenade, Avenida Alvear 1883, entre Ayacucho y Callao, Recoleta (4809 0046/www.celedonio. net). **Open** 10am-8pm Mon-Fri; 10am-2pm Sat. **Map** p85 B5 ㉕

Lohidoy has collaborated with international fashion houses Kenzo and Ungaro, and his jewellery even featured in *Sex and the City*. His signature pieces are baroque necklaces with semi-precious stones and pearls, and the line has recently been expanded to include scarab brooches containing gems from the north of Argentina, along with butterfly forms adorned with Swarovski crystal details.

Chocolate

Patio Bullrich shopping centre, Avenida del Libertador 750, entre Montevideo y Libertad, Recoleta (4815 9530/ www.chocolateargentina.com.ar). **Open** 10am-9pm daily. **Map** p85 A5 ㉖

A favourite on the high street, with branches in most of the city's shopping centres, Chocolate has now been a player in the fashion game for a quarter of century. The Recoleta branch continues to offer good quality essentials such as modal tops and classic cotton jackets as well as the batik T-shirt dress in silk and the mini-dress with lantern sleeves.

Comme Il Faut

Rue des Artisans, apartamento M, Arenales 1239, entre Libertad y Talcahuano, Recoleta (4815 5690/ www.commeilfaut.com.ar). **Open** 11am-7pm Mon-Fri; 11am-3pm Sat. **Map** p85 A4 ㉗

Hidden away in a peaceful lane off one of Recoleta's swanky streets, Comme Il Faut offers beautifully made tango shoes for *milongas* and more. It is also, in case a wedding is in the offing, perfect for brides-to-be.

Desiderata

Avenida Santa Fe 1801, y Callao, Barrio Norte (4816 5380/

Recoleta p83

Benedit Bis p92

www.desiderata.com.ar). **Open** 9am-8.30pm Mon-Sat. **Map** p85 A4 ㉘
A black and white check top with an enormous bow is a typically playful Desiderata garment. Modern, feminine options for daywear as well as for an evening out are accessorised with clutch bags in complementary colours.

La Dolfina
Avenida Alvear 1315, entre Cerrito y Libertad, Recoleta (4815 2698/ www.ladolfina.com). **Open** 10am-8pm Mon-Sat. **Map** p85 A5 ㉙
Perfect for polo lovers, this brand's ambassador is star player Adolfo Cambiaso. The cotton polo shirts with La Dolfina's logo are a solid investment, and the khaki trousers have a flattering fit. Sweaters and soft

leather jackets complete the look. The stylish leather bags are ideal for a weekend break.

Feria Plaza Francia
Plaza Francia y Plaza Alvear, Avenida del Libertador y Pueyrredón, Recoleta. **Open** 9am-7pm Sat, Sun. **Map** p85 B5 ㉚
Handbags, handcrafted kitchen utensils, mate gourds and mufflers – you name it, you can buy it at Feria Plaza Francia. Top-quality arts and crafts are the specialty at this weekend fair.

Galería Bond Street
Avenida Santa Fe 1670, entre Montevideo y Rodríguez Peña, Recoleta (www.xbondstreet.com.ar). Subte D, Callao. **Open** 10am-10pm Mon-Sat. **Map** p85 A4 ㉛

Ateneo Grand Splendid p92

Alternative teens flock here for the latest punk fashions, while hip twenty-somethings dig the colourful trainers and trendy urban wear. Lucky Seven and American Tattoo, a favourite of Diego Maradona, are just some of the parlours that will thrill the piercing and body-art inclined.

Galería 5ta Avenida

Avenida Santa Fe 1270, entre Libertad y Talcahuano, Recoleta (4816 0451/ www.galeria5taavenida.com.ar). **Open** 10am-9pm Mon-Sat. **Map** p85 A4 **32**
It's not all about vintage at Galería 5ta (short for 'quinta' – fifth) Avenida, but that's one of the things this grungey and fab mini-mall does best. Here, persistence pays off: for those prepared to rummage about, there are great pieces to be found, from tooled leather bags and vintage sportswear to interesting conversation piece jewellery. For vintage eyewear, visit Óptica Nahuel at store number 38 (4811 2837).

Legacy

Avenida Santa Fe 1571, entre Montevideo y Paraná, Recoleta (4815 4012/www.legacy.com.ar). **Open** 9am-8pm Mon-Sat. **Map** p85 A4 **33**
This chain offers preppy clothes for men and women who enjoy the great outdoors. Fine cotton shirts, rugby tops, khakis, tartan flannels, wool sweaters, Argyle cardigans and men's sports jackets are as comfortable as they are well made. Legacy also stocks its own fragrance line and accessories such as baseball caps, leather belts and wallets.

Ona Sáez

Avenida Santa Fe 1609, entre Montevideo y Rodríguez Peña, Recoleta (4815 0029/www.onasaez.com). **Open** 10am-8.30pm Mon-Sat. **Map** p85 A4 **34**
Ona Sáez's Pop collection pays tribute to Pac-Man culture, comic books and designer Paco Rabanne. Technicolour denim, micro dresses and pin-up style shoes are for brave types, while Oxford style denims and heart print or Liberty patchwork

T-shirts are the brand's more wearable alternatives. Known for its variety of well-fitting jeans for both sexes, this, one of numerous BA branches, is a great place to include in the search for your ideal pair.

Patio Bullrich

Avenida del Libertador 750, entre Montevideo y Libertad, Recoleta (4814 7400/www.shoppingbullrich.com.ar). **Open** *Shops* 10am-9pm daily. *Restaurants* 10am-midnight daily. **Map** p85 A5 **35**
This, the oldest and most luxurious of all BA's malls, was once the city's meat auction house. The elegance it now displays extends from the shiny marble floors to the smartly uniformed lift operators, and the many top-end boutiques include Trosman, Etiqueta Negra and Jazmín Chebar.

Peter Kent

Arenales 1210, y Libertad, Recoleta (4804 7264/www.peterkent.com.ar). Subte C, San Martín. **Open** 10am-8pm Mon-Sat. **Map** p85 A4 **36**
Founded in 1972, Peter Kent has since established itself as one of the best luxury brands in BA. Using quality leathers and suedes and employing local craftsman, it specialises in classic designs with a modern twist. You'll find shelves stacked with sheep skin purses, colourful wallets, passport holders, change purses and jewellery boxes.
Other location Avenida Alvear 1820 (4804 7264).

Posse

Juncal 1309, y Parera, Recoleta (4813 6185/www.posseonline.com). **Open** 10am-8pm Mon-Fri; 11am-3pm Sat. **Map** p85 A4 **37**
When designing for their label, sisters Pilar and Guadalupe picture a feminine, sexy woman who knows what she wants. Garments inspired by fairies and rock 'n' roll glamour are perfect for romantic rebels. Figure-hugging trousers and tops join dresses with bold prints and a '70s touch – all emphasising the best of the female form.

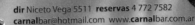
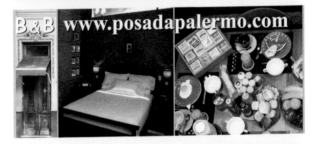

Rossi & Caruso

Posadas 1387, entre Rodríguez Peña y Montevideo, Recoleta (4811 1538/ www.rossicaruso.com). **Open** 9.30am-8.30pm Mon-Fri; 10am-7pm Sat. **Map** p85 A5 ③⑧

Visit this shop on the elegant calle Posadas for classically chic women's handbags, men's briefcases, and a wide variety of leather jackets for him and her. There are also traditional, equestrian-inspired silver accessories including bracelets, key rings and cufflinks, and high-quality gift items like silver gaucho knives and *mate* gourds. **Other location** Avenida Santa Fe 1377 (4814 4774).

Tramando, Martín Churba

Rodríguez Peña 1973, entre Posadas y Avenida Alvear, Recoleta (4811 0465/ www.tramando.com). **Open** 10.30am-8.30pm Mon-Fri; 11am-7pm Sat. **Map** p85 A5 ③⑨

Churba's signature silhouettes are loose and labyrinthine. Voluminous pleated trousers in silk reflect a mix of oriental and art deco influences, and the characteristic intertwining, fusing and wonky weaving feature on necklines and accessories. The hand-worked dresses in chalky tones are a highlight, but if you can't work up the nerve to don such daring designs, try some of the accessories or homeware items.

Varanasi

Libertad 1696, entre Posadas y Avenida Libertador, Recoleta (4815 4326/www.varanasi-online.com). **Open** 10am-8pm Mon-Fri; 10am-6pm Sat. **Map** p85 A5 ④⓪

Design duo Mario Buraglio and Victor Delgrosso's collection includes both casual and cocktail wear; there are flattering, muted tones of cream and beige combined with classic navy, as well as livelier shades like yellow, coral and red, meshed in intriguing forms that are undoubtedly influenced by both designers' backgrounds in architecture. These items are versatile enough to take you effortlessly from boardroom to bar and, if necessary, back again.

Nightlife

The Basement Club

The Shamrock, Rodríguez Peña 1220, entre Juncal y Arenales, Recoleta (4812 3584, www.theshamrockbar.com). **Open** from 9pm Thur; from 1am Fri, Sat. **Map** p85 A4 ④①

This Recoleta classic benefits from plugged-in promoters who consistently bring in some of BA's best DJs in an ever-changing line-up that focuses on electronica and deep house. It's a great joint that's always full, and is one of the few clubs that gets busy earlier on, especially on Thursdays. It's also one of the best places in BA to be during the key nightlife hours of 3am to 7am, when the place is rocking with a mix of locals, tourists and some of the most up-for-it clubbers in BA.

Glam

Cabrera 3046, entre Laprida y Agüero, Barrio Norte (4963 2521/www. glambsas.com.ar). **Open** from 1am Thur-Sat. **Map** p85 B2 ④②

A good two years past its prime, Glam still packs lots of beautiful gay guys in on Thursdays (AR$25; AR$15 with a pass) and Saturdays (AR$30; AR$20 with a pass), with expatriates, tourists (you'll hear as much English as Spanish) and *porteños* of all ages rounding out the crowd. Pick your cruising spot – two bars, several lounge areas or one packed dancefloor – and let the fun and games begin.

Arts & leisure

Galería Isabel Anchorena

Unit 4H, Arenales 1239, entre Libertad y Talcahuano, Recoleta (4811 5335/www.galeriaisabelanchorena. sion.com). **Open** 11am-8pm Mon-Fri; 11am-4pm Sat. **Map** p85 A4 ④③

This superbly curated Recoleta gallery, which unlike many galleries is open throughout the summer, displays the two- and three-dimensional works of 30 solid contemporary artists. In late 2008, Miguel Darienzo's phantasmal mixed-media works were presented at this, one of the most consistently interesting galleries in the city.

Markus Day Spa

Ground floor, Callao 1046, entre Santa Fe y Marcelo T de Alvear, Barrio Norte (4811 0058/4814 0494/www.markus formen.com). Subte D, Callao. **Open** 11am-11pm Mon-Fri; 11am-10pm Sat. **Map** p85 A3 ㊹

The first integral spa exclusively for men in Latin America, Markus offers killer services, including a fantastic three-hour pampering called Enjoy Life; another called Adore Me comes with a bowl of fruit, tea and juices, and a tantric massage. There are also skin treatments, manicures, pedicures, botox, a decent barber and, with some notice, minor plastic surgery (this is BA, after all).

Megatlón

Rodriguez Peña 1062, entre Marcelo T de Alvear y Santa Fe, Recoleta (4816 7009/www.megatlon.com). Subte D, Callao. **Open** 24hrs 7am Mon-8pm Sat; 10am-6pm Sun. **Map** p85 A4 ㊺

Slick, clean and busy, the Megatlón chain has all the latest exercise devices and hamster wheels. It also offers a range of classes.

Museo Participativo de Ciencias

1st floor, Centro Cultural Recoleta, Junín 1930, y Quintana, Recoleta (4807 3260/www.mpc.org.ar). **Open** 10am-5pm Mon-Fri; 3.30-7.30pm Sat, Sun. Closed Mon in summer. No credit cards. **Map** p85 B5 ㊻

'Prohibido no tocar' (it's forbidden not to touch) is the endearing motto of this science museum in the Recoleta cultural centre, where kids can explore the mysteries of the natural sciences. For art-loving parents, the art gallery housed in the same building is well worth a visit, and if you come at the weekend, you'll have the added benefit of a visit to the crafts fair in the green space outside at Plaza Francia.

Village Recoleta

Vicente López 2050, entre Junín y Uriburu, Recoleta (0810 810 2463

with credit card booking/www.village cines.com). **Map** p85 B4 ㊼

This huge complex located right across the street from Recoleta Cemetery includes a 16-screen cinema with the latest releases, and it's surrounded by numerous bars, eateries and shops.

Palermo & Palermo Viejo

The various Palermo subdivisions – Viejo, Chico, Soho, Hollywood – are basically real-estate jargon. In general, Palermo is less about sightseeing and more about good times. Both drinking spots and rolling greens are in bountiful supply here, and the barrio includes the city's coolest restaurants, its best clothing stores, its nicest boutique hotels, one of BA's hippest plazas (**Plazoleta Cortázar**), one of its most traffic-congested (**Plaza Italia**), various embassies, film production companies (in so-called Palermo Hollywood, natch) and excellent people-watching. In fact, Palermo is similar in look and feel to the Soho sections of both London and New York, with a touch of NYC's West Village thrown in.

Sights & Museums

Jardín Botánico Carlos Thays

Avenida Santa Fe 3951, Palermo (4831 4527). Subte D, Plaza Italia. **Open** *Nov-Mar* 8am-8pm daily; *Apr-Oct* 9am-6pm daily. **Admission** free. **Map** p86 C3 ㊸

Designed by celebrated French landscaper Charles Thays and inaugurated in 1898, BA's botanical garden is slightly shabby but nonetheless tranquil and full of fascinating flora. Thousands of species (and feral cats) flourish here, and fountains, orchids, cacti, ferns and spectacular trees make

Jardín Japonés

this a paradise for anyone who likes pottering around in the garden.

Jardín Japonés

Avenida Berro, y Casares, Palermo (4804 4922). Subte D, Scalabrini Ortiz. **Open** 10am-6pm daily. **Admission** AR$3 Mon-Fri; AR$4 Sat, Sun. **Map** p86 C5 ㊾

Created in 1967 as a gift from the local Japanese community, BA's Japanese garden is one of the largest in the world outside of Japan. You'll find over 150 species of flora here, many brought specially from the mother country, with some on sale at the small shop next to the entrance. There's also a great Japanese restaurant.

Jardín Zoológico

Avenida Santa Fe, y Las Heras, Palermo (4011 9900/www.zoobuenosaires.com.ar). Subte D, Plaza Italia. **Open** 10am-6pm Tue-Sun. **Admission** AR$12.50; free under-12s. **Map** p86 C3 ㊿

BA's city zoo is one of those interesting but discomfiting attractions that many animal lovers will prefer to shun. Of more general interest are the buildings, constructed between 1888 and 1904, which copy the architecture of the animals' native countries. Of the beasts themselves, the polar bears are glum but stoical, the monkeys are cheeky and permanently horny and a baby giraffe is the latest 'guest' to wow the crowds. There are now night openings.

MALBA: Colección Costantini

Avenida Figueroa Alcorta 3415, entre Salguero y San Martín de Tours, Palermo (4808 6500/www.malba.org.ar). **Open** noon-8pm Mon, Thur-Sun; noon-9pm Wed. **Admission** AR$10; AR$5 reductions. Free Wed. **Map** p86 B5 (51)

At MALBA, Frida Kahlo and Diego Rivera, Tarsila do Amaral and other ground-breaking painters share the walls with Argentinian modern masters such as Antonio Berni and Jorge de la Vega. There's also a good café and terrace restaurant, plus a small cinema specialising in cult and art-house retrospectives.

Museo de Artes Plásticas Eduardo Sívori

Avenida Infanta Isabel 555, y Libertador, Palermo (4774 9452/ www.museosivori.org. **Open** *Dec-Apr* noon-8pm Tue-Fri; 10am-8pm Sat, Sun. *May-Nov* noon-6pm Tue-Fri; 10am-6pm Sat, Sun. **Admission** AR$3; free under-12s. Free Wed. **Map** p87 D4 ⓺②

Located in Parque Tres de Febrero, this excellent museum houses a major collection of Argentinian paintings and sculpture that spans the 19th century to the present day.

Museo Evita

Lafinur 2988, entre Gutiérrez y Las Heras, Palermo (4807 9433/0306). Subte D, Plaza Italia. **Open** 1-7pm Tue-Sun. **Admission** AR$5. **Map** p86 B3 ⓺③

Opened in 2001, this museum is housed in an aristocratic residence that Juan Perón expropriated; he converted it into a women's shelter for his wife's quasi-statal welfare agency. Paintings, posters and busts are displayed alongside the outfits Eva wore on tours of Europe, with the star exhibits being two dresses designed by Paco Jamandreu, which she wore for her audiences with the Pope, and her *libreta cívica* (ID card): number 0.000.001. Arguably better than the museum itself is the newly refurbished restaurant and outdoor terrace.

Eating & drinking

Il Ballo del Mattone

Gorriti 5936, entre Ravignani y Arévalo, Palermo Viejo (4776 4247/ www.ilballo.com.ar). **Open** noon-5pm, from 7.30pm daily. **$$**. **Italian**. **Map** p87 D1 ⓺④

In true trattoria fashion, only a few dishes are on offer each night in this family-run restaurant, and your best bet is pasta – on a recent visit, twisted homemade noodles in scarparo sauce, amply portioned and perfectly al dente, were the hands-down winner against a comparatively bland salmon. Cousins are in the kitchen, uncles take orders, a teenage niece clears the table… and the hodge-podge ornamentation creates an informal atmosphere in which local families and trendies feel equally at home.

Bangalore Pub & Curry House

Humboldt 1416, y Niceto Vega (4779 2621), Palermo Viejo. **Open** 6pm-4am daily. No credit cards. **Pub**. **Map** p87 D1 ⓺⑤

Another winner from the team behind Gibraltar, Bangalore is BA's first pub and curry house, and it performs both functions with aplomb. Downstairs, there's comfy seating and jugs of gin and tonic, while the upstairs dining area is an intimate hideaway in which to sample the sub-continental cuisine. Get there unfashionably early if you want to snag a seat.

Bar 6

Armenia 1676, entre El Salvador y Honduras, Palermo Viejo (4833 6807/www.barseis.com). **Open** from 8am Mon-Sat. **$$**. **Argentinian**. **Map** p86 C1 ⓺⑥

The ambience includes a cool Scandinavian interior, mood lighting and dark velvet couches, not to mention good-looking twenty- and thirtysomethings occupying them. The fusion menu offers reliable crowd-pleasers like vegetable wok, coriander and chilli quesadillas, and grilled salmon, as well as more exotic fare like pan-seared rabbit and coconut vermicelli with clams and cuttlefish.

Bar Uriarte

Uriarte 1572, entre Honduras y Gorriti, Palermo Viejo (4834 6004/ www.baruriarte.com.ar). **Open** from noon daily. *Restaurant* noon-4.30pm, 8pm-12.30am daily. **$$**. **Argentinian**. **Map** p86 C1 ⓺⑦

Casa Cruz p105

Bar Uriarte's kitchen turns out food that could simply be termed 'classic'. Grilled asparagus with prosciutto and quail's eggs fly from this station here; pizzas slide bubbling from that oven, and pastas emerge cooked to perfection from another station along the line. The home-made ñoquis, sweetbreads and steaks off the grill are particularly tasty.

Bereber

Armenia 1880, entre Nicaragua y Costa Rica, Palermo Viejo (4833 5662). **Open** from 8pm Tue-Sun. **$$**. **Middle Eastern**. Map p86 C2 ⓾
This fashionable restaurant has the twin distinction of being the sole Moroccan spot in town and of offering one of the loveliest spaces for dining. Treat yourself to the salad sampler featuring mini cubes of nutmeg squash, almond chickpeas, pineapple carrots, yogurt and garlic cucumbers,

and coriander tomatoes. Or skip the starter and go straight to the *habra* – a large dish of lamb, vegetables and piquant goats cheese.

Bio

Humboldt 2199, y Guatemala, Palermo Viejo (4774 3880). Subte D, Palermo. **Open** 10.30am-5pm Mon; from 10.30am Tue-Sun. **$$**. **Vegetarian**. Map p87 D2 ⓾
Feeling guilty after a week-long gorge-fest of chorizo and fried cheese? There's hardly a finer locale for detoxifying than this hip organic bistro. Start your atonement with a steaming pot of green tea and complimentary chunks of heart-healthy brown bread, then choose an entrée suited to the season: quinoa risotto with seasonal vegetables and goat's cheese, tofu in a mustard reduction, and mushroom-topped bruschetta are just a few specialties of the house.

Green Bamboo p107

Las Cabras

Fitz Roy 1795, y El Salvador, Palermo Viejo (5197 5301). Subte D, Palermo. **Open** noon-1am daily. **$$**. No credit cards. **Argentinian**. Map p87 D1 ⑥

Meat lovers have been queueing up to get tables at this parrilla since it opened in early 2008. The secret recipe? Cheap, good quality food. It doesn't stray from the pasta and parrilla formula, but a mixed grill (enough for at least three), including two types of chorizo and all the offal you can think of, is great value at AR$44. The wine list ticks the value-for-money box too, with very little mark-up from supermarket prices. Arrive early to avoid a long wait.

La Cabrera

Cabrera 5127 y 5099, y Thames, Palermo Viejo (4832 5754/ www.parrillalacabrera.com.ar). **Open** 8pm-1am Mon; 12.30-4pm, from 8pm Tue-Sun. **$$$**. **Argentinian**. Map p86 C1 ⑥

This parrilla is possibly the most popular restaurant in BA right now. Professional staff serve extra-large portions of expertly prepared beef, grilled with a few sprigs of rosemary or sage. The steak-size *mollejas* (sweetbreads) are the best in the city. Half portions will be fine for even the hungriest, especially as 10-12 interesting side plates land on your table. The sister restaurant, La Cabrera Norte, half a block away, has helped cut waiting times, but a reservation made in advance is essential.

Casa Coupage

First floor, Guemes 4382, y Jorge Luis Borges (4833 6354/www.casacoupage. com.ar). **Open** from 8pm Thur, Fri by reservation only. **$$$**. No credit cards. **Argentinian**. Map p86 C3 ⑥

See box p143.

Casa Cruz

Uriarte 1658, entre El Salvador y Honduras, Palermo Viejo (4833 1112/www.casacruz.com). **Open** from 8.30pm daily. **$$$. Argentinian.** Map p86 C1 ⑥

For BA's most striking dining experience, pass through a pair of 16-foot brass doors and enter the surreal land of Casa Cruz. There's a sleek oval bar, an oversized Chesterfield sofa and a spot-lit, redwood-panelled dining area. The menu offers 'modern urban Argentinian' cuisine, but for those not hungry or arriving late, the bar is a lively nexus of local celebrities and upscale tourists.

Casa Rica

Nicaragua 4817, y Thames, Palermo Viejo (4775 9861). **Open** from 7pm Tue-Thur; from 12.30pm Fri-Sun. **Bar.** Map p86 C2 ⑥

With a unique mix of Moroccan and Latin design, colourful rooms, multilevel terraces and great house music mixed by DJs on the first floor, newbie Casa Rica is making a name for itself. Call ahead for reservations on the terraces, which fill up quickly on weekends with large groups dining on *picadas* (meat and cheese platters).

Ceviche

Costa Rica 5644, entre Bonpland y Fitz Roy, Palermo Viejo (4776 7373/www.ceviche.com.ar). **Open** 12.30-3pm Mon-Fri; 8pm-1am Mon-Sat. **$$$. Peruvian.** Map p87 D1 ⑥

It might not be Argentinian, but ceviche should nevertheless near the top of every traveller's 'to eat' list in BA. Ceviche restaurant has mastered the simple art of preparing this emblematic Peruvian dish – essentially raw fish 'cooked' in citrus juice. Other dishes, including meat, seafood and Peruvian classics, are accompanied by a very impressive selection of wine.

Cluny

El Salvador 4618/22, entre Malabia y Armenia, Palermo Viejo (4831 7176/www.cluny.com.ar). **Open** from noon Mon-Sat. **$$$. Argentinian.** Map p86 B1 ⑥

The menu here is studded with standouts like the excellent grilled octopus starter – crisp on the outside and deliciously tender on the inside; or the parmesan risotto with mushrooms topped with a seemingly melting chunk of beef, cooked for hours on end in red wine. The rather expensive wine list leans towards the usual suspects (the larger bodegas from Mendoza), but a glass of sweet Santa Julia *tardío* (late harvest) makes a nice accompaniment to the passionfruit parfait dessert.

Crizia

Gorriti 5143, entre Uriarte y Thames, Palermo Viejo (4831 4979/5105/www.crizia.com.ar). **Open** from 6.30pm Mon-Sat. **$$$. Argentinian.** Map p86 C1 ⑥

On a menu speckled with surprises are comparative rarities like fresh swordfish and red tuna. Every dish looks and tastes great, not least the house speciality: oysters, fat and fresh and best accompanied by chilled vodka. The risotto with prawns and mascarpone cheese or crab cakes with guacamole and Philadelphia cheese are fit for seafood lovers, while the meatobsessed will adore the slow-cooked Patagonian lamb and the *bondiola* (pork tenderloin) served with pears.

La Cupertina

Cabrera 5296, y Godoy Cruz, Palermo Viejo (4777 3711). **Open** 11.30am-3.30pm, 8-11.30pm Tue-Sat. **$. No credit cards. Argentinian.** Map p86 C1 ⑥

When it comes to making *empanadas* (Argentina's version of the Cornish pasty) and *locro* (South American meat and corn stew), most Argentinians will tell you that grandma is in a class of her own. Battling for second place is Tucumán-born Cecilia Hermann, owner and cook at La Cupertina. The menu includes dishes like *chivitos*, the Uruguayan take on the transport caff 'full monty' sandwich; and *tamales* (corn meal dough stuffed with meat), a dish characteristic of Argentina's northern provinces.

Divina Patagonia

Honduras 5710, y Bonpland, Palermo Viejo (4771 6864/www.divina patagonia.com). **Open** from 6pm Mon-Sat. $$. **Patagonian.**
Map p87 D1 ⑥⑨

Argentina's south is the source of many of the country's best ingredients, among them the famed *cordero* (lamb), *centolla* (king crab) and all kinds of game and wild fruits and vegetables. These are all served at Divina Patagonia as main courses (wild boar in raspberry sauce, say) or *tablas* (platters) to mix and match.

Don Julio

Guatemala 4691, y Gurruchaga, Palermo Viejo (4831 9564/4832 6058). **Open** noon-4pm, 8pm-midnight daily. $$. **Argentinian.** Map p86 C2 ⑦⓪

Don Julio knows meat. And thanks to owner Pablo, who sends his waiters to wine school, your server will know just how to help you choose the cabernet that best complements your *bife de chorizo* (sirloin steak). Beef lovers order hot-off-the-grill classics, while veggies like the *soufflé de calabaza y espinaca con crema de verdeo* – a crisy and savoury squash and spinach creation.

La Fabrica del Taco

Gorriti 5062, entre Thames y Serrano, Palermo Viejo (4833 3534/www. lafabricadeltaco.com). **Open** from 8pm Tue-Thur; from 1pm Fri-Sun. $.
Mexican. Map p86 C1 ⑦①

An authentic Mexican *taqueria*, this laidback Palermo joint serves up cheesy tacos, quesadillas, hamburgers *a la Mexicana*, buckets of Corona and fresh fruit drinks, plus spicy salsas. There's also a kitsch bar in the rear courtyard.

Freud y Fahler

Gurruchaga 1750, entre El Salvador y Costa Rica, Palermo Viejo (4833 2153). **Open** 12.30-3.30pm, 8.30pm-midnight Mon-Sat. $$. **Argentinian.** Map p86 C2 ⑦②

The light and breezy atmosphere makes this a lovely spot for a solo lunch, and chef-owner Pablo Lykan ramps it up a notch at night-time,

when the sketched-out dishes – hand-drawn on the menu – bloosom into a more complex cuisine that includes dishes like two-textured rabbit salad, twice-cooked chicken and dual-temperature soup.

Green Bamboo

Costa Rica 5802, y Carranza, Palermo Viejo (4775 7050/www.green-bamboo.com.ar). **Open** from 8.30pm daily. $$. **Southeast Asian.** Map p87 D1 ⑦③

This well-established and popular Vietnamese restaurant combines the five essential taste elements of sweet, salty, bitter, spicy and acidic. Begin with a seafood-based menu of starters including prawns fried in sesame seeds and curry, ginger and sweet chilli squid tentacles, then move on to the fish of the day marinated with tamarind, basil and shallots, wrapped up in a bamboo leaf and barbecued. For a refreshing aperitif to bring your mouth back to life, give the green grass cocktail a go.

Limbo

Armenia 1820, entre Costa Rica y Nicaragua, Palermo Viejo (4831 4040/www.limborestaurant.com). **Open** from 9am daily. $$. **Bar.** Map p86 C2 ⑦④

Limbo has the right balance of style and substance. Out front, there's a small patio for those who want to see and be seen, and inside, there's a comfortable bar as well as sofas, sculptures and paintings on the wall. The star attraction is the rooftop terrace. Overlooking Plaza Palermo Viejo, this hidden sun trap is a perfect way to relax with tapas and one of more than 100 types of wine on offer.

Mark's Deli & Coffee House

El Salvador 4701, y Armenia, Palermo Viejo (4832 6244/www.markspalermo. com). **Open** 8.30am-9.30pm Mon-Sat; 10.30am-9pm Sun. $. No credit cards. **Café.** Map p86 C2 ⑦⑤

Mark's is modelled on the hip New York deli, and the scenario is similar:

Cluny p105

fashion identicats – mostly young, female and leaning towards the uppermost end of the beauty spectrum – whiling away their time. Also on hand are plenty of Macbook-owning foreigners tuning in to the free Wi-Fi.

Minga

Costa Rica 4528, entre Armenia y Malabia, Palermo Viejo (4833 5775). **Open** from noon daily. **$$**. **Argentinian**. Map p86 B2 ⑦⑥

With its beige, glass, and distressed wood furnishings, Minga doesn't look like your average neighbourhood steak-house – nor does it act like one. Your *bife de lomo* isn't just plopped down in front of you, but presented on an elegant cutting board with tiny saucers of *chimichurri* (herb and chilli sauce) and garlic. *Papas fritas* are available, sure,

but they're hard to justify when grilled pumpkin and buttery sweet potatoes baked in foil are on the menu. As for the desserts, grapefruit sorbet, sesame seed gelato and a swizzle stick fashioned out of honey and cashews definitely are not run-of-the-mill.

Mira Vida Soho Wine Bar

Darragueyra 2050, entre Guatemala y Soler, Palermo Viejo (4774 6433/ www.miravidasoho.com). **Open** noon-midnight Mon-Thur; noon-1am Fri-Sun. **Wine bar**. Map p86 C2 ⑦⑦

This boutique hotel bar has a large selection of fine wines by the glass, from a cellar stocked with a healthy selection of bottles from various, often small, bodegas. Excellent tapas are available, and tasting sessions and private events can be arranged.

Meet… Germán Martitegui

One of the city's leading restaurateurs, Germán Martitegui helped kick-start modern haute cuisine in Buenos Aires. In December 2008, the chef-owner of Olsen (p111) and Casa Cruz (p105), opened Tegui (p115), hidden behind a graffitied wall in Palermo Viejo. Here he talks about his latest venture – and the state of Argentinian gastronomy.

What inspired you to open Tegui?

My other restaurants are big, and I can't have much personal contact with people. I wanted a place that's hidden, that's difficult to find, where the only people who come are people who like what I do. I wanted to do something much more personal.

How would you characterise the menu at Tegui?

It's experimental because we prepare a small number of dishes and keep changing them. We try to use things in a different, surprising way. To integrate classic ingredients with things that aren't classic. We also send out a lot of *entremedios* between courses. We want people to feel like they're being taken care of.

What are the current restaurant trends in Buenos Aires?

With the economic crisis, the only restaurants that are going to stay open are the good ones. So restaurants are starting to be more careful about service and how they treat people. It's going to be a little more humane. Besides that, I'm seeing new Argentinian chefs take Argentinian food and reformulate it.

Is there an identifiable Argentinian cuisine?

The Italian influence is very important. That mixed with something Spanish is what we call *porteño* food. Then there's northern Argentinian food, which has Spanish, Arabic and indigenous influences.

Is there anything about Argentinian food culture that you'd like to improve?

I'd like it if Buenos Aires weren't the only city in the country with good restaurants. The difference between Buenos Aires and the rest of the country is huge.

Where do you like to go for a cheap bite?

There's a pizza chain called Ugi's that I really like. The pizza costs ten pesos. And it's always good.

If you were leaving Buenos Aires tomorrow, where would you go for your last meal?

Maybe Uruguay (www.pablo massey.com), Pablo Massey's restaurant. Or Standard (p112). I'd eat a *milanesa* — the *milanesa napolitana* there is my favourite.

La Cabrera p104

Miranda

Costa Rica 5602, y Fitz Roy, Palermo Viejo (4771 4255). **Open** from 9am daily. **$$. Argentinian.** Map p87 D1 ⓐ

This fashionable contemporary parrilla is enough to make vegetarians throw out their principles. Miranda is a steakhouse for trend-conscious carnivores – instead of fries or mashed potatoes, the *solomillo de cerdo* (pork loin) and thick-cut *lomo* are presented with caramelised vegetables and fruits. The jacinta salad, with grilled chicken and squash, is one of the huge, highly recommendable side dishes on offer.

Olsen

Gorriti 5870, entre Carranza y Ravignani, Palermo Viejo (4776 7677). **Open** from noon Tue-Sat; from 10.30am Sun. **$$$. Scandinavian.** Map p87 D1 ⓐ

If your aim is to take on the 60-plus vodka shots on offer, you would be doing an injustice to Olsen's excellent cured meat and fish menu. Lunchtime snacks include a modern Scandinavian smorgasbord comprising smoked salmon, trout and blinis, while dinner

delicacies of red tuna (practically impossible to get hold of in BA), slow-cooked lamb and smoked pork may actually distract you from the stylish, fabulous surroundings.

Oro y Cándido

Guatemala 5099, y Fray Justo Santa María de Oro, Palermo Viejo (4772 0656/www.oroycandido.com). Subte D, Palermo. **Open** 9am-11.30pm Mon-Sat. **$$. Argentinian.** Map p86 C2 ⓐ

Inspired by New York-style delis, Oro y Cándido is part general store, part deli, part gourmet restaurant. Based entirely on regional, Argentinian products, the menu benefits from Sabores de Argentina, a company that supplies artisan food products from the interior provinces to Buenos Aires. Featured items include native river fish, llama, wild boar, ostrich and water buffalo, some of which are used in the pastas and deli-style sandwiches, along with artisan breads and cheeses.

Oui Oui

Nicaragua 6068, entre Arévalo y Dorrego, Palermo Viejo (4778 9614). **Open** 8am-8pm Tue-Fri; 10am-8pm

BUENOS AIRES BY AREA

Sat, Sun. **$$**. No credit cards. **French**.
Map p87 E2 ⑥

Oui Oui offers honest, down-to-earth Gallic fare of the kind the French actually eat rather than just talk about. Thirty-year-old Rocío García Orza works wonders in the kitchen with filled croissants, fresh baguettes, vichyssoise and pain au chocolat, which is all spelled out on chalkboards amid a colourful environment of dried flowers and rosewood tables.

Quimbombó

Costa Rica 4562, entre Malabia y Armenia, Palermo Viejo (4831 5556/ www.quimbombo.com.ar). Subte D, Scalabrini Ortiz. **Open** from 8am daily. **$$**. **Eclectic**. Map p86 B2 ⑥

Focusing on natural gourmet food, Quimbombó adjusts its menu according to the season. Main courses might include a papaya quesadilla with guacamole and sweet potato; teriyaki chicken with caramelised onion and peppers; or a bit-of-everything thali (a sampler plate of various Indian dishes). Finish with kulfi for dessert – Indian ice-cream, made with condensed milk, yogurt, pistachios and rose water.

Social Paraíso

Honduras 5182, entre Thames y Uriarte, Palermo Viejo (4831 4556/ www.socialparaiso.com.ar). **Open** 12.30-3.30pm, 8.30pm-midnight Tue-Sat; 12.30-4pm Sun. **$$**. **Argentinian**. Map p86 C1 ⑥

Chef-owner Federico Simoes's Syrian-Lebanese roots are reflected in an ever-changing, highly eclectic menu that includes various meat and seafood dishes. But the *maracuyá* (passion fruit) mousse and Szechwan-pepper ice-cream wedged between caramelised apple slices have become something of a staple by popular acclaim.

Standard

Fitz Roy 2203, y Guatemala, Palermo Viejo (4779 2774). **Open** from 8pm Mon-Sat. **$$$**. **Argentinian**. Map p87 D2 ⑥

Standard manages to pull off the impressive feat of seeming both stripped-down, plain and classic, and thrillingly modern. You can't go wrong with a *milanesa napolitana* (veal fried in breadcrumbs, topped with tomato sauce, ham and melted cheese) or the fish of the day, but consider branching out a little: though the idea of *raviolis de seso y espinaca* (calves brain and spinach raviolis) might be a little rich for some, they are polished off with enormous gusto by the loyal local clientele.

Sudestada

Guatemala 5602, y Fitz Roy, Palermo Viejo (4776 3777). **Open** noon-3.30pm, from 8pm Mon-Sat. **$$**. **Southeast Asian**. Map p87 D2 ⑥

At this small but always packed eaterie, main courses with names like *tho boc* (grilled rabbit), *siap mepanggang* (barbecued pork with pungent sauce) and *ping kay* (grilled corn-fed chicken with vegetables) are as elaborate as the interior design – which takes minimalism to the extreme – is not. For dessert, the semolina cake with raisins and the chocolate overdose will test your willpower. Give in.

Taco Box

Soler 5581, entre Humboldt y Fitz Roy (4776 2613/www.tacobox.com.ar). **Open** 8pm-12.30am Mon-Thur; 8pm-1.30am Fri-Sun. **$$**. No credit cards. **Mexican**. Map p87 D2 ⑥

The Taco Box ignores the nation's inclination to spice-dodge and goes all out to bring Mexican food (as served in the US) to the masses. Grab one of the elevated booths and start with a Coupette – a fishbowl-sized glass of frozen margarita. The fajitas are great and big enough for two or more.

Taj Mahal

Nicaragua 4345, entre Aráoz y Scalabrini Ortiz, Palermo Viejo (4831 5716/www.tajmahalbuenosaires.com.ar). **Open** from 8.30pm Mon-Sat. **$$**. **Indian**. Map p86 B2 ⑥

Taj Mahal is about as authentic as Indian gets in BA. The tandoor, a clay oven typical of Northern India, is the showpiece; the vegetables, meats and even the bread (chapati) pass through there. Beginning with the appetisers (lamb kebabs, and chicken marinated

A bar with a view

Sula

Want to get high? Bars with rooftop terraces are increasingly popular, so now you can pick a perch from which to sip your spirits while having a smoke and experiencing BA from above. Here are some of the best views.

The bird's nest view

Head to **Sula Bar** (p128) and strut up the side staircase to the impeccable crimson-lined alabaster jungle garden rooftop and take in the quintessential BA residential streetscape of low 1960s-era apartment buildings.

The bright lights, big city view

Bask in the glory of modernisation from the apex of Palermo's streamlined Asian-chic **Belushi Martini Bar** (p125) – the skyscrapers and construction cranes twinkling on the near

horizon are BA's humble version of Shanghai's superstructure-splattered Bund district. The jet-set crowd on the slick hardwood terrace consists of befittingly upward-striving B-list celebrities, blatantly augmented models, and their playboy arm candy.

The downtown view

Raise your glasses to the silhouettes of city centre office towers and the grid of power lines overhead at **Le Bar** (p61) in the Microcentro. And once you've tired of gawking at the downtown sights, the walls of the floor cushion-lined third-floor terrace sport the funky handiwork of a few adept street artists.

The product-placement view

Scoff at the queuing crowd at Club Niceto from atop **Carnal** (p125) before heading down to join 'em. Unless you enjoy watching westbound commuter trains rattle by on the tracks below, across the way, jockey for position at one of the coveted canopied terrace tables for a starlit cocktail.

The inward view

San Telmo's brand-new baby **70 Living** (p75) has a peaceful upstairs garden patio – a rarity in the crowded barrio. The rear view over the zone's labyrinth of *conventillo* housing is carefully disguised by a tall bamboo fence; best turn your gaze indoors to the interesting bunch populating the second-floor bar, or, on a slow night, straight out the street side balcony doors overlooking the ever-bustling calle Defensa.

CLUNY
RESTO DE CHARME

El Salvador 4618/22 | Palermo Soho | Tel. 4831-7176 / 4833-4275 | www.cluny.com.ar | info@cluny.com.ar
Valet Parking | Smoking Section | Credit Cards: Visa, Amex, Master | Mo/Sa: Midday till close

in Indian herbs), you'll be impressed by the varieties of flavours.

Tegui

NEW *Costa Rica 5852, y Angel Carranza, Palermo Viejo (5291 3333).* **Open** from 8.30pm Mon-Sat. **$$$**. **Argentinian**. Map p87 D1 ⑬ See box p109.

El Trapiche

Paraguay 5099, y Humboldt, Palermo Viejo (4772 7343). Subte D, Palermo. **Open** noon-4pm Mon-Sat; 8pm-1am Mon-Thur; 8pm-2am Fri, Sat; noon-5pm Sun. **$$$**. **Argentinian**. Map p87 D2 ⑲

Surrounded on all sides by ultra-fashionable foreign food haunts, brightly lit El Trapiche is unstintingly Argentinian. The grilled meat is magnificent, from the fillet steaks to what is probably the best *matambrito de cerdo* (pork flank) in town, and the mountainous desserts include the classic Don Pedro (whisky, ice-cream and hot sambayón) and a stunning ice-cream with fresh berries.

Wherever Bar

Santa Maria de Oro 2476, y Santa Fe, Palermo Viejo (4777 8029/www.wherever.com.ar). Subte D, Palermo. **Open** 10am-8pm Mon, Tue; from 10am Wed-Fri; from 9am Sat. **$$**. **Pub**. Map p86 C3 ⑨⓪

What's on the menu at this neighbourhood pub? If it's Thursday, it's Noche Inglesa – a night of British rock music, frequented by far more locals than tourists, with a guaranteed degree of alcohol-induced chaos. There's a wide selection of whiskies, from aged (and pricey) Macallan to more affordable classics, plus classic pub fare of tapas, sandwiches and pizza, as well as more filling meals of *ojo de bife* (ribeye steak) and *bife de chorizo* (sirloin).

Shopping

28 Sport

*Gurruchaga 1481, entre Cabrera y Gorriti, Palermo Viejo (4833 4287/www.28sport.com). Open 11am-8pm Mon-Sat. Map p86 C1 ⑨①

Reinforced stitching, leather lining and bronze eyelets are hallmarks of a wellmade shoe and hark back to an era when footwear was made with durability in mind. And that's exactly the ethos of this company, which bases its designs on original 1950s sports footwear. With rubber soles and a multitude of colours, these leather shoes and lace-up boots will appeal to fans of Camper's classic 'Pelotas'.

Alto Palermo

Avenida Santa Fe 3253, entre Coronel Diaz y Bulnes, Palermo (5777 8000/www.altopalermo.com.ar). Subte D, Bulnes. **Open** 10am-10pm daily. Map p86 A3 ⑨②

Popular with families and gaggles of giggling mall rats, this consumer mecca contains most of Argentina's top chains, such as Las Pepas, Ricky Sarkany, María Vazquez and Rapsodia. Missing your skinny lattes? Head for the Starbucks here.

Amor Latino

El Salvador 4813, y Gurruchaga, Palermo Viejo (4831 6787/www.amorlatino.com.ar). **Open** 10.30am-8pm Mon-Sat; 2-9pm Sun. Map p86 C2 ⑨③

Any aspiring *Belle de Jour*-era Catherine Deneuves should hot-foot it to this lingerie store, one of three BA branches, where the collection inspired by Buñuel's classic film is waiting to tantalise you. Sensual pieces in classic black and white combinations, chic polka-dot prints or hot pink will bring out your inner seductress, and masks, garters and sequinned or tasseled pasties are perfect for any femme fatale.

Balthazar

Gorriti 5131, entre Thames y Uriarte, Palermo Viejo (4834 6235/www.balthazarshop.com). **Open** 11am-8pm Mon-Sat. Map p86 C1 ⑨④

Balthazar offers a range of striking shirts in high-quality Italian fabrics. This is an urban dandy's candy store, with multicoloured striped shirts a popular choice, as are the sleek ties and blazers – and even the heat of a scorching *porteño* summer shouldn't put you off purchasing an alpaca scarf.

Bensimon

Honduras 4876, entre Armenia y Gurruchaga, Palermo Viejo (4833 6857/www.bensimon.com.ar). **Open** 11am-8.30pm Mon-Sat; 2-8.30pm Sun. **Map** p86 C1 ⑨⑤

A sort of BA Banana Republic with more vivid colors and a touch of street cred, Bensimon, one of several in the BA chain, is among the best places to find cool casualwear. Jeans and faux-velvet blazers share shelf space with sweatshirts and T-shirts with a distinct rock 'n' roll edge. Socks, underwear and assorted accessories are also on sale.

Bolivia

Gurruchaga 1581, entre Gorriti y Honduras, Palermo Viejo (4832 6284/www.boliviaonline.com.ar). **Open** 11am-8pm Mon-Sat; 3-8pm Sun. **Map** p86 C1 ⑨⑥

For the fashion-conscious man, Bolivia offers an abundance of tempting items.

From the striped or checked trousers to the Liberty print shirts, there are plenty of individual garments. A new line of tailored dark jackets has been added, but Bolivia hasn't turned over a sombre new leaf: there are plenty of skinny jeans in red, yellow or fuchsia for trendy rocker types.

Other locations Nicaragua 4908 (4832 6409).

Boutique del Libro

Thames 1762, entre El Salvador y Costa Rica, Palermo Viejo (4833 6637/www.boutiquedellibro.com.ar). Subte D, Plaza Italia. **Open** 10am-10pm Mon-Thur; 10am-11pm Fri; 11am-11pm Sat; 2-10pm Sun. **Map** p86 C1 ⑨⑦

The walls of this shop are crammed with books ranging from English literature to Argentinian art and design. Mingle with other intellectuals in the café at the back of the store.

Balthazar p115

Buenos Aires trash design

Tota Reciclados

Now you can enjoy your BA shopping spree while helping to save the planet. Compared with much of the world, Argentina has been somewhat slow off the starting block when it comes to eco-awareness, but a growing number of green initiatives are helping to cultivate consciousness as well as promoting the work of industrious local designers.

In November and December 2008, Festival Sustentable, BA's first event devoted exclusively to environmentally conscious Argentinian design, was a major step in that direction. Pablo Ferraro was one of the young designers showcasing eco-friendly garments and accessories. Opting for responsible production in an industry infamous for polluting practices, Ferraro uses neither chemical bleaching processes nor toxin-heavy inks. His cotton bags, babywear and soft furnishings with retro-inspired prints are available at **TiendaMALBA** (p124) and are also featured in **Fabro** (p118), a recently established Palermo store committed to promoting innovative national design. While stock here is not solely eco-themed, the focus is on high-quality objects and low-impact materials, from furniture made of recovered wood scraps to bags fashioned from recycled advertising banners.

Some designers have taken to recycling as much out of necessity as environmental awareness. Economic instability and limited access to resources have encouraged ingenuity, particularly during the challenging times that followed 2001's debilitating financial crisis. Design collectives Mínima Huella and Contenido Neto have formed mutually beneficial alliances with the city's *cartoneros*, or street-combing refuse collectors, using readily available waste materials to produce functional household articles and even furniture. Mariana Cortés, the designer behind fashion label **Juana de Arco** (p121), uses textile offcuts to create accessories – and jobs – with her Proyecto Nido enterprise. **Tota Reciclados** (p124), works with found items, proving there's cash in trash with their coveted jewellery, and at the quirky workshop-cum-store **Objetos Encontrados** (p121), a group of artists demonstrates that there's more to recycling than just righteousness by transforming discarded elements into souvenirs and pieces of decorative whimsy.

Cora Groppo

El Salvador 4696, y Armenia, Palermo Viejo (4833 7474/www.coragroppo. com). **Open** 11am-8pm Mon-Sat. **Map** p86 C1 ❾❽

Cora Groppo ❾❽ likes to have fun with form, as evidenced in her trademark voluminous clothing and love of layering. Gathers produce billowing shapes, while piping and stitching add decorative detail. Grey, beige and brown tones feature alongside black, white, cream and patent elements, with a baroque twist and a medley of superimposed layers.

Creative Circus

Costa Rica 4645, entre Gurruchaga y Armenia, Palermo Viejo (4833 7990). **Open** 2-8pm Mon-Fri; 2-9pm Sat; 3-8pm Sun. **Map** p86 C2 ❾❾

This spacious Palermo Viejo store features hip clothing for guys and girls, plus bags and other accessories from various designers, including Guadalupe Martiarena's 'pe' label. There are also music CDs.

Fabro

NEW *Nicaragua 4677, entre Armenia y Gurruchaga, Palermo Viejo (4831 8723/www.fabrolab.com).* **Open** 11am-8pm Mon-Fri; noon-9pm Sat, Sun. **Map** p86 C2 ❿⓿⓿

Uniting the best of local design – much of it with an eco-conscious slant – this spacious Palermo store features a host of tempting items, from funky furnishings and quirky books to jewellery by Metalistería and Nadine Zlotogora's highly desirable womenswear. Browse at leisure or ask the friendly, enthusiastic staff for advice if you can't decide between cute stationery from Monoblock or an iconic Argentinian mate gourd given a modern twist by Nobrand. With plans afoot for workshops and rotating exhibitions, this is definitely one space to watch.

Boutique del Libro p116

Félix

Félix

Gurruchaga 1670, entre El Salvador y Pasaje Santa Rosa, Palermo Viejo (4832 2994/www.felixba.com.ar). **Open** 11am-8pm Mon-Sat; 3-8pm Sun. **Map** p86 C1 **101**

Bensimon (p116), but with more cash and more class. Hip and upscale, or at least skillful enough to create that impression, the collection of skinny trousers, vests and loose-fitting long-sleeved jersey are spot-on garb for BA's best beach parties. There's a children's branch at El Salvador 4742 (4833 3313).

Humawaca

El Salvador 4692, y Armenia, Palermo Viejo (4832 2662/www.humawaca. com). **Open** 11am-8pm Mon-Sat; 2-7pm Sun. **Map** p86 B2 **102**

This brand's BKF leather backpack has become a classic, completely representative of the Humawaca style. Architect-turned-designer Ingrid Gutman uses local leather to create original bags, purses and wallets that are both creative and useful. There are briefcase-style bags ideal for transporting a laptop in the chicest possible way, and smaller items like key rings and notebooks are also available.

Josefina Ferroni

Armenia 1471, entre Gorriti y Cabrera, Palermo Viejo (4831 4033/www. josefinaferroni.com.ar). **Open** 2-8pm Mon; 11am-8pm Tue-Sat. **Map** p86 C1 **103**

Peep-toe platforms and brightly coloured heels, especially in lipstick-red, are Ferroni hallmarks. For sophisticated footwear with a subtle twist, try the gold craquelure-effect sandals with toe post and a delicate ankle strap, or the peep toes with a retro heel. Beautiful leather bags are another example of Ferroni's high-quality products.

Juana de Arco

El Salvador 4762, entre Gurruchaga y Armenia, Palermo Viejo (4833 1621/ www.juanadearco.net). **Open** 10am-8pm Mon-Sat. **Map** p86 C1 ❿④

Ten years ago, Mariana Cortés, the designer behind the label Juana de Arco, began creating designs from scraps of fabric. Born of the need for frugality, her creative experiments have developed into multicoloured patchwork confections. Underwear is something of a speciality here, as is the fun, feminine and comfortable collection of sleepwear, which includes pedal-pusher sleepshorts and loose harem pants. Comfortable cotton bras, camisole tops and organic cotton knickers complete the picture.

Kosiuko

Córdoba 4299, entre Pringles y Lavalleja, Palermo Viejo (4866 3805/ www.kosiuko.com.ar). **Open** 10am-7.30pm Mon-Sat. **Map** p86 B1 ❿⑤

Dress like an extra from *Almost Famous* with Kosiuko's 1970s-influenced collection. This successful chain brand constantly refreshes itself and doesn't leave boys out of the picture, with jeans, jackets and plenty of printed t-shirts.

Lo de Joaquín Alberdi

Jorge Luis Borges 1772, entre El Salvador y Costa Rica, Palermo Viejo (4832 5329/www.lodejoaquin alberdi.com.ar). **Open** 11am-9.30pm Mon-Sat; noon-9.30pm Sun. **Map** p86 C1 ❿⑥

In the heart of Palermo, this turn-of-the-century house is a great place to discover and enjoy Argentina's wines. The passionate team can recommend a suitable bottle from the extensive catalogue of *bodegas*, and you can choose to sample it on the premises if you can't wait until you get home. Wine tastings are also held here.

Miles Discos

Honduras 4912, y Gurruchaga, Palermo Viejo (4832 0466/ www.milesdiscos.com.ar). **Open** 10am-10pm Mon-Sat; 11am-9pm Sun. **Map** p86 C1 ❿⑦

Browse in this relaxed record store, and check out some non-mainstream music at the listening posts, from rare jazz to tango, passing through gospel, rock, world music and solo artists. The shop is housed in the same building as Prometeo Libros, which has a reasonable range of Latin American authors translated into English. At the Miles Cine store at Gurruchaga 1580, pick up some flicks or movie memorabilia, and stay for a coffee in the patio bar.

Mishka

El Salvador 4673, entre Armenia y Malabia, Palermo Viejo (4833 6566/www.mishkashoes.com). **Open** 10.30am-8.30pm Mon-Sat. **Map** p86 B1 ❿⑧

At Mishka they know how to interpret current trends with a tongue-in-cheek retro slant, with original footwear that appeals to everyone from teens to trendy twentysomethings, to a more mature customer with an appreciation for subtle creativity. A sensible heeled lace-up is given a twist with a two-tone woven raffia upper; pretty pumps are sprinkled with just the right amount of sparkle; and the brand's bags are irresistible.

Objetos Encontrados

Thames 1721, entre El Salvador y Costa Rica, Palermo Viejo (4831 6058/ www.objetosencontrados.com) **Open** noon-8pm Mon-Sat. **Map** p86 C2 ❿⑨

This all-in-one workshop, gallery and store will appeal to anyone nostalgic for their days of childhood creativity. Check out the quirky items a group of artists has lovingly crafted from found objects and/or purchase a voucher to attend one of the workshops.

Papelera Palermo

Honduras 4945, entre Gurruchaga y Borges, Palermo Viejo (4833 3081/ www.papelerapalermo.com.ar). **Open** 10am-8pm Mon-Sat; 2-8pm Sun. **Map** p86 C1 ⓶⓪

This super stationer has everything the page-obsessed could possibly desire: handmade paper in all shapes, sizes and textures; an impressive array of design and art books; and

Papelera Palermo p121

workshops on skills including book-binding, printing, origami, calligraphy, paper making, drawing and painting.

Paseo Alcorta

Salguero 3172, y Figueroa Alcorta, Palermo (5777 6500/www.paseoalcorta. com.ar). **Open** 10am-10pm daily. **Map** p86 B5 **111**

Paseo Alcorta, considered by many shopping buffs to be the best mall in BA, contains the gigantic Carrefour hypermarket as well as plenty of local clothing brands, from children's shops Cheeky and Mimo & Co to womenswear stores Ayres and Awada.

Penguin

NEW *Gurruchaga 1650, entre Honduras y El Salvador, Palermo Viejo (4831 7575/ www.originalpenguin.com).* **Open** 10am-8pm Mon-Sat; noon-8pm Sun. **Map** p86 C1 **112**

This well-established American brand brings its iconic polo shirts and other fine quality garments to Palermo. Knitted sweaters, short-sleeved shirts, hoodies and retro-style accessories, including belts, watches and sunglasses, are all available.

Puro Diseño

Gorriti 5953, entre Arévalo y Ravignani, Palermo Viejo (4776 8037/ www.purodiseno.com.ar). **Open** 11am-8pm Mon-Fri; noon-8pm Sat. **Map** p87 D1 **113**

Formerly located in Recoleta, Puro Diseño continues to offer a large selection of products from Argentina's top designers. Chic homeware is combined with quality leather goods, and 2009 brings the incorporation of furniture and clothing in an extended floor space.

Qara

Gurruchaga 1548, entre Honduras y Gorriti, Palermo Viejo (4834 6361/ www.qara.com). **Open** 11am-9pm Mon-Sat; 4-8pm Sun. **Map** p86 C1 **114**

Qara's American designer Amanda sells high-quality leather bags to urbanites wishing to transport their belongings in style, with details including special pockets for a mobile phone or a Blackberry.

Chasing beauty

Visitors have long flocked to BA to indulge in hot tango nights, succulent steak and an endless supply of red wine, and in recent years, bargain-seeking travellers have added cosmetic surgery to the to-do list. From arm lifts and chin implants to liposuction and breast augmentations, cosmetic surgery has long been huge with locals – at a fraction of what it would probably cost back home. A facelift in Argentina can run to around US$5,000 compared to US$10,000 in the US. Breast augmentations here typically start at around US$3,000 (US$4,000 in the US), and rhinoplasties, US$2,500 (US$5,000 in the US). Of course, the same dangers exist here as anywhere else, so anyone interested in getting a nip and a tuck should always do their homework and proceed with extra caution.

For those less inclined to drastically alter their appearance, *depilación*, or waxing, is also big in BA. As a rule, it gets lathered on and ripped off in one ruthless motion. Many salons claim to use 'organic' wax recipes, with secret ingredients that vary from foodstuffs to plant extracts. You'll find a waxer at most hair salons, and Lulu of London (Rodríguez Peña 1057, 4815 8471, www.luluoflondon.com.ar) offers good, professional service. For around AR$30, you can be hairless in the time it takes to say 'full Brazilian'.

BUENOS AIRES BY AREA

Sabater Hermanos

Gurruchaga 1821, entre Costa Rica y Nicaragua, Palermo Viejo (4833 3004/www.shnos.com.ar). **Open** 10am-8pm Mon-Sat; 2-8pm Sun. No credit cards. **Map** p86 C2 **115**

Run by the third generation of Sabater family soap makers, this funky shop/workshop is another soap version of a pick 'n' mix counter. With coloured soap flakes, cookie-cutter shapes, golf balls and soapy 'hundreds and thousands', you never need to buy a boring bar of soap again. For rebels (or teenagers), there are Black Sabbath or marijuana leaf squares, and don't miss the options with cheeky phrases in Spanish like 'Doesn't wash your conscience'.

Sugar & Spice

Guatemala 5419, entre Humboldt y Juan B Justo, Palermo Viejo (4777 5423/www.sugarandspice.com.ar). **Open** 9am-1.30pm, 2.30-7pm Mon-Fri; 9am-1pm Sat. No credit cards. **Map** p87 D2 **116**

When Frank Almeida couldn't find cookies like the ones he liked back home in Chicago, he enlisted the help of his wife Fabiana and they started baking them themselves. The couple has since branched out into pound cake – called *budin* here – as well as brownies, biscotti and stollen. (They supply Starbucks too.) Indulge yourself with a chunky chocolate chip cookie, the buttery banana walnut pound cake or with some fruity *pan dulce* – a local favourite.

TiendaMALBA

MALBA, Figueroa Alcorta 3415, entre Salguero y San Martin de Tours, Palermo (4808 6550/www.malba.org.ar). **Open** noon-8pm Mon, Wed-Sun. **Map** p86 B5 **117**

If you visit MALBA (p102), be sure to drop into this store. Along with average museum items like mugs and postcards, the shop stocks a range of accessories and decorative objects from local designers like Humawaca, Vaca Valiente and Nobrand. Original jewellery includes mesh bracelets

from Francisca Kweitel, and there are also must-wear T-shirts from Doma.

Tota Reciclados

First floor, Jorge Luis Borges 1978, entre Nicaragua y Soler, Palermo Viejo (4899 1813/www.totareciclados. com.ar). **Open** 2-7pm Tue-Sat. **Map** p86 C2 **118**

Valeria Hasse and Marcela Muñiz began their enterprise by selling their original necklaces made from cast-off materials in shops like Condimentos and Benedit Bis. Following their success at Buenos Aires Fashion Week, the designers opened their own studio. Their highly original accessories with a touch of kitsch combine all sorts of discarded elements, from antique fabrics to metal.

Vicki Otero

El Salvador 4719, entre Armenia y Gurruchaga, Palermo Viejo (4833

Trosman at Patio Bullrich p97

5425/www.vickiotero.com.ar). **Open**
11am-8pm Mon-Sat. **Map** p86 C1 **119**

Vicki Otero is considered a pioneer in
the Buenos Aires fashion world. She
opened her Palermo boutique in 2002
and ever since has continued to produce
flattering cuts in contrasting textures
with a prim but unconstrained look. Her
collections have featured 1950s-style silhouettes and strong use of black and
white. Selected pieces are also sold in
San Telmo's Ffiocca.

Nightlife

Belushi Martini Bar

NEW *Honduras 5333, y Godoy Cruz,
Palermo Viejo (4831 8665/
www.belushi.com.ar).* **Open** from 8pm
Thur-Sat. **Map** p86 C1 **120**

Blending chic terrace cocktails with
a busy dancefloor, this typically
packed bar-disco attracts well-dressed

Palermo-ites in droves. Belushi's
terrace is filled with drinkers no matter what the time, while the dancefloor
doesn't get busy until around midnight. The drinks are pricey, but you
get what you pay for: excellent cocktails made by proper bartenders.
General admission runs at around
AR$30 and includes a drink. See also
box p113.

Carnal

*Niceto Vega 5511, y Humboldt,
Palermo Viejo (4772 7582/
www.carnalbar.com.ar).* **Open** from
7pm Mon-Sat. **Map** p87 D1 **121**

Alfresco drinking is what it's all about
at Carnal, particularly during the warm
nights of summer, when swarms of
frisky locals invade the roof terrace
and downstairs bar. There's a healthy
dash of posing going on, but it's a
friendly vibe and the place is bustling
with good-looking, flirtatious young

Niceto Club

porteños. You should either book ahead or get there for an unusually early 10.30pm. See also box p113.

Club Aráoz

Aráoz 2424, entre Güemes y Santa Fe, Palermo Viejo (4832 9751/www.club araoz.com.ar). Subte D, Scalabrini Ortíz. **Open** *dinner* 10pm, *dinner show* midnight, *club* 1.30-7am Thur-Sat. **Map** p86 B3 ⓬

Weekends here are commercial dance; but Thursday is Aráoz's night to shine, with Lost Culture Club – the best spot in the city for upscale hip hop and

R&B. Over-21s only; ladies free before 2.30am; or call to be put on the Lost list.

Congo

Honduras 5329, entre Godoy Cruz y Juan B Justo, Palermo Viejo (4833 5857). **Open** from 8pm Mon-Wed; from 9pm Thur-Sat. No credit cards. **Map** p86 C1 ⓭

Possibly the bar king of the Palermo Viejo jungle. For all the laid-back charm of the cosy, brown and beige leather-clad interior, the true magic of Congo resides in its spot-lit summer garden, which ranks among the city's best outdoor drinking spaces. Expect to queue after midnight.

Crobar

Paseo de la Infanta, Avenida del Libertador 3883, y Infanta Isabel, Palermo (4778 1500/ www.crobar.com). **Open** from 10pm Fri, Sat. **Map** p87 D4 ❷

Crobar – southern sister to the North American super clubs of the same name – draws a regular crowd of devoted party people. A network of overhead balconies, walkways and VIP areas are cantilevered over the main dancefloor, with four well-attended bars serving up decent drinks at a premium. Saturdays can be hit-or-miss: better to shell out the hefty entry fee on Friday nights for the international DJ sets.

Mundo Bizarro

Serrano 1222, y Córdoba, Palermo Viejo (mundobizarrobar.com). **Open** 8pm-3am Sun-Wed; 8pm-4am Thur; 8pm-5am Fri, Sat. No credit cards. **Map** p86 C1 ❷

An institution since 1997, Mundo Bizarro might have changed its location, but it can't change its spots as one of the city's great hedonistic, rocking hotspots. Artwork on the blood-red walls gives the place a bohemian vibe that extends to the menu. After 1am, it's a heady mix of music, great cocktails (there are over 50 on the menu) and sociable people.

Niceto Club

Niceto Vega 5510, entre Humboldt y Fitz Roy, Palermo Viejo (4779 9396/ www.nicetoclub.com). **Open** from 12.30am Thur, Fri; from 1am Sat. **Map** p87 D1 ❷

At the enduringly popular Niceto, which celebrates its tenth birthday in 2009, the two rooms, Side A and Side B, pump out an eclectic programme of local and international performers, together with shimmering party nights. The Thursday night fusion of glittering over-achiever Club 69 (Side A) and urban beats masters Zizek (Side B) is one of the city's best nights, full stop. Friday's multifaceted INVSN

kicks off the weekend, and monthly reggaeton, dancehall, and indie rock parties are crowd pullers, with fun-loving throngs generally peaking around 3am.

Rumi

Avenida Figueroa Alcorta 6442, y La Pampa, Palermo (4782 1307/www. rumiba.com.ar). **Open** *dinner* from 9.30pm, *club* from 1am Tue-Sat. **Map** p87 F4 ❷

Rumi's strict door policy and queues from around 2am make it a good idea to turn up early for dinner first. Once inside, you'll be privy to one of the most glamorous club scenes in BA. Big names grace the DJ booth, but bigger names mingle on the dancefloor – a favourite haunt for many a model, celeb and young socialite.

Sitges

Avenida Córdoba 4119, entre Palestina y Pringles, Palermo Viejo (4861 3763/ www.sitgesonline.com.ar). **Open** from 10.30pm Wed-Sun. **Map** p86 B1 ❷

One of BA's few options for gays and lesbians looking for a bar stool where they can kill an hour or two before hitting the dancefloor. Some nights, drag comedy, musical numbers and strippers who grin and bare all liven up the mood. Friday nights $AR25 buys you all the booze you can handle.

Sugar

Costa Rica 4619, y Armenia, Palermo Viejo (mobile 15 6894 2002/www. sugarbuenosaires.com). **Open** from 12.30pm Tue-Sat; 12.30pm-10pm Sun. No credit cards. **Map** p86 C2 ❷

A lively, expat-run bar, Sugar makes a cosy change from the area's penchant for the white and minimalist. It's a welcoming venue for a lazy evening's drink during the week, with happy hour from 9pm to midnight and selected drinks at a dangerously bargain basement AR$5.

Sula Bar

Guatemala 4802, y Borges, Palermo Viejo (4776 8704). **Open** from 9pm Tue-Sun. **Map** p86 C2 ❸

Hipódromo Argentino de Palermo

This corner bar is one of the more stylish joints in the neighbourhood. Dark wood and blood red mark out an understated theme, allowing the backlit bar to hog the limelight. A DJ spinning lounge electronica sits at one end of the L-shaped bar, while the easygoing staff shakes up cocktails in the remainder. The glamorous upstairs space is for private parties or admiring some of BA's most gorgeous works of art – all human, of course.

Tiki Bar

Niceto Vega 5507, y Humboldt, Palermo Viejo (4776 4778). **Open** 9pm-4am Tue-Thur; 9pm-5am Fri, Sat. No credit cards. **Map** p87 D1 ⬤
It's hard to make a Polynesian-themed bar decorated with palm trees and coconuts not resemble a set from a Disney Channel series, but Tiki Bar does the job nicely, leaving the clichéd Hawaiian theme in Hawaii. The menu offers finger food and a few main courses, but if you want a spot on the terrace, be sure to make a reservation – the tables go quickly.

Único Barra

Honduras 5604, y Fitz Roy, Palermo Viejo (4775 6693). **Open** 8.30am-6am Mon-Fri; 8.30pm-6am Sat, Sun. **Map** p87 D1 ⬤
One of the most enduringly popular bars in Palermo Hollywood, mainly thanks to its relentless enthusiasm for round-the-clock intoxication, Único is a surefire bet for any night of the week. Come to this location of the three-branch chain for an early evening nibble or for a full-blown night of immorality.

Arts & leisure

Campo Argentino de Polo de Palermo

Avenida del Libertador 4300, y Dorrego, Palermo (4777 6444/www. aapolo.com). **Map** p87 E3 ⬤

This wonderful polo field in Palermo has a capacity of 45,000. Tickets for tournaments, played in November and December, are available from Ticketek (5237 7200).

Hipódromo Argentino de Palermo

Avenida del Libertador 4101, y Dorrego, Palermo (4778 2800/ www.palermo.com.ar). **Open** from 2-10pm Mon, Fri-Sun. No credit cards. **Map** p87 E4

This palatial horseracing venue can hold up to 100,000 spectators, though it only really gets packed out for the 'Gran Premio Nacional' held in November. Other meetings take place on Mondays, Saturdays and Sundays. Betting is on the tote system, and no alcohol can be purchased at the track.

Salón Canning

Scalabrini Ortiz 1331, entre Gorriti y Cabrera, Palermo Viejo (4832 6753). **Open** *Milonga* 11pm-4am Mon-Fri.

Classes 7-11pm Mon, Tue, Fri; 9-11pm Thur. No credit cards. **Map** p86 B1

This large hall gets taken over by a variety of different *milongas*. Particularly popular are the Monday- and Tuesday-night events, known as Parakultural and organised by Omar Viola, an MC with an edge.

Tango Cool

Avenida Córdoba 5064, entre Thames y Serrano, Palermo Viejo (4383 7469/www.tangocool.com). **Open** *Classes* 8pm Wed, Fri. *Milonga* 10pm Wed; 11pm Fri. No credit cards. **Map** p86 C1

This is a friendly and informal *milonga* with good beginners' classes in English. Start the night with a class, and then dance away with an international crowd into the early hours. Occasionally there are live music and shows on Fridays and a tango-themed art space to browse, as well as a restaurant and bar.

La Viruta

Armenia 1366, entre Cabrera y Niceto Vega, Palermo Viejo (4774 6357/ www.lavirutatango.com). **Open** from 8pm Wed-Sun. *Milonga* midnight Fri-Sun. *Classes* Tue-Sun, times vary (check website). No credit cards.
Map p86 C1 🥢

These *milonga* nights take place in a homely community centre. Dancers of all ages happily come together for tango, with a sprinkling of salsa and even rock 'n' roll jiving should the tango get a bit dull. There's also a restaurant and bar.

Las Cañitas

This emerging Palermo sub-barrio is best known for its blocks of stylish cafés, restaurants and bars. As a gastronomic and bacchanalian destination, it's still no match for Palermo Viejo, and the entire affair has a slightly collegiate frat-boy/sorority-girl feel.

Eating & drinking

Moshi Moshi

First floor, Ortega y Gasset 1707, y Soldado de la Independencia (4772 2005/www.moshi-moshi.com.ar). **Open** from 8.30pm Tue-Sun. **$$$.** **Japanese**. **Map** p87 E3 🥢

Practise your chopstick skills here with beautifully presented sushi rolls and oriental dumplings, or focus on the fancy finger foods like the *ebi no somen*, an artistic combination of shrimp wrapped in fried noodles. The mixed tempura is light and fluffy, and the *sukhothai*, a fishy thai curry with lime, prune and rice, is highly recommended. Perhaps the restaurant's best feature is the sake bar with smooth, strong cocktails.

Novecento

Báez 199, y Argüibel (4778 1900/ www.bistronovecento.com). **Open** from 8.30am-2am Mon-Sat; 10am Sat-Sun. **$$.** **Argentinian**. **Map** p87 D3 🥢

Soul Café

The flagship restaurant of a chain that has branches home (Punta del Este and Córdoba) and away (Miami and New York), Novecento is a thriving bistro with a menu that includes dishes like penne with wild mushroom and grilled chicken with guacamole.

Soul Café

Báez 246, entre Arévalo y Arguibel (4778 3115). **Open** from 7pm Tue-Sun. **$$.** **International**. **Map** p87 D3 🥢

Playing groovy tunes and serving up fusion dishes, this Las Cañitas hotspot attracts a young and sociable crowd. Grazing on sushi to a funk-soul soundtrack keeps these socialites happy before they head to the clubs. The

atmosphere is friendly and chilled, and
the food is excellent.

Sushi Club

*Báez 268, entre Arévalo y Arguibel
(0810 222 7874/www.sushiclubweb.
com.ar). Subte D, Carranza.* **Open**
from noon daily. **$$$**. **Japanese**.
Map p87 E3 **141**

The selection at this cutting-edge sushi
chain is fresh and beautifully present-
ed. The sushi *libre* what to go for if you
want to eat unlimited amounts of maki,
nigiri and sashimi. **Other location**
Ortega y Gasset 1812 (4771 1010).

Van Koning

*Báez 325, entre Arévalo y Chenaut
(4772 9909).* **Open** from 7pm daily. No
credit cards. **Pub**. Map p87 E3 **142**

If the flashier Las Cañitas bars don't
appeal, duck through the door of this
hugely popular (especially with Dutch
expats) atmospheric pub for a pint . It
has its very own microbrewery with
three ales to choose from.

Nightlife

Kandi

*Báez 340, entre Arévalo y Chenaut
(4772 2453).* **Open** 8pm-2am Mon-
Thur, Sun; 8pm-5am Fri, Sat.
Admission minimum spend AR$10
after midnight. **Map** p87 E3 **143**

This two-floor bar with fluorescent
panelling and cool crowd is a top spot
to round off a classy binge, find last-
minute love or play a game of pool.

Abasto

West of the Centre

The western barrios of Once and Abasto represent real-world BA, where camera-wielding, Bermuda shorts-wearing tourists are in short supply and European influences are minimal. The area lacks the chi-chi appeal of the northern barrios and the south's bohemian old-world charm, so it's not necessarily a priority on any visitor's itinerary. Once (it's pronounced with two syllables and is literally the Spanish word for the number 11) is a hub of commercial commotion, while things calm down slightly in Abasto, one of several barrios rich in tango history – and second, perhaps, only to San Telmo in that regard. Boedo is an up-and-coming destination for more adventurous visitors, while further from the centre, Almagro, Caballito, Villa Crespo and Chacarita offer

more of a true neighbourhood vibe and a peaceful, easy feeling that's in striking contrast to the frenzy of their sister barrios.

Once & Abasto

Once's hustle and bustle is more Grand Central Station at rush hour than Champs-Elysées. That said, the area has sporadic points of beauty: the ornate orange-and-brown-hued building that houses the **Palacio de Aguas Corrientes** (which looks more like a castle than the headquarters of BA's water works), and **El Abasto**, one of BA's five great shopping malls. That the late tango great Carlos Gardel called Abasto home gives the barrio a certain cultural cachet as well.

Sights & museums

Museo Casa Carlos Gardel

Jean Jaures 735, entre San Luis y Viamonte, Once (4964 2015/ www.museos.buenosaires. gov.ar/gardel). Subte B, Carlos Gardel. **Open** 11am-6pm Mon, Wed-Fri; 10am-7pm Sat, Sun. **Admission** AR$3. Free Wed. **Map** p134 B5 ❶

A long overdue tribute to one of the 20th century's greatest exponents of popular song, the Gardel museum preserves and exhibits various items and pieces of memorabilia that either belonged to or were connected with the master.

Museo de la Deuda Externa

Centro Cultural Ernesto Sábato, Facultad de Ciencias Económicas, Uriburu 763, entre Viamonte y Córdoba, Once (4370 6105). Subte D, Facultad de Medicina. **Open** 3-8pm Tue-Fri. **Admission** free. **Map** p134 A5 ❷

The Museum of Foreign Debt harks back not only to the city's golden age but to a recent and less glittering era: the economic crisis of 2001-02. The museum charts the course of the country's overdraft from the first default of 1827 to the chaos of December 2001. It all sounds pretty grim, but despite, or perhaps because of, the downbeat subject matter, the exhibits are suffused with the dark humour *porteños* are famous for. Perhaps best avoided if you work for the International Monetary Fund.

Eating & drinking

Cantina Pierino

Lavalle 3499, y Billinghurst, Abasto (4864 5715). Subte B, Carlos Gardel. **Open** 8pm-2am daily. **$. Italian.** **Map** p134 C4 ❸

This classic BA cantina has been serving authentic Italian food since 1907. Check out the tasty starters – *fritata* (mozzarella tortillas) and *chiambotta* (baked aubergine with onion, courgettes and mushrooms) – and the assortment of home-made pasta dishes.

Mochica

Agüero 520, y Corrientes, Abasto (4866 2200/www.restaurantmochica. com.ar). Subte B, Carlos Gardel. **$$.** **Peruvian.** **Map** p134 B4 ❹

Although Peruvian fare with a gourmet twist is par for the course here, ceviche is what really draws in the crowd. Raw white fish is classically marinated in lemon juice, chili, onion, and black-and-white condiments, but the house speciality fuses cream into the mix. Otherwise, there's a smorgasbord of options, from assorted rice, chicken and seafood dishes to *seco de cordero al estilo Mochica* or, simply put, dry lamb, Mochica style.

Reina Kunti

Humahuaca 3461, entre Sanchez de Bustamante y Gallo, Abasto (4863 3071). Subte B, Carlos Gardel. **Open** noon-4pm, 8pm-12.30am Tue-Sat. **$.** No credit cards. **Indian. Map** p134 B4 ❺

How you feel about Reina Kunti will depend in part on how you feel about cats roaming freely in restaurants. If you don't mind the moggies, you'll love this cult Indian veggie restaurant which does a pretty authentic – for Buenos Aires – rendition of subcontinental street food: *kachoris*, *pakoras*, *koftas* and so on. The design aesthetic is beach-after-a-shipwreck, with pirate chests, wine barrels and antique sewing machines doubling as tables. Puddings are more old deli than New Delhi: round off your feast with a Simply Marvellous truffle and a sharp, strong coffee.

Shopping

Abasto de Buenos Aires

Corrientes 3247, entre Agüero y Anchorena (4959 3400/ www.abasto-shopping.com.ar). Subte B, Carlos Gardel. **Open** 10am-10pm daily. **Map** p134 B4 ❻

This former fruit market is one of the finest examples of art deco architecture in BA and also the city's most

West of the Centre

Abasto de Buenos Aires p133

mainstream mall, with stores for all ages and tastes. It has indoor parking, a kids' play area, a cinema and more than 240 shops to choose from.

Nightlife

Vaca Profana
Lavalle 3683, y Bulnes, Abasto (4867 0934/www.vacaprofana.com.ar). **Open** from 9pm Mon-Sun. No credit cards. **Map** p134 C4 ➐
Vaca Profana is a major stop-off point for a wide range of quality local bands. Small and intimate with good drinks and tapas, it's a prime spot to

relax and get a close view of the featured musicians.

Arts & leisure

El Camarín de las Musas
Mario Bravo 960, y Córdoba, Abasto (4862 0655/www.elcamarindelasmusas. com.ar). Subte B, Medrano. **Shows** Thur-Sun. No credit cards. **Map** p134 C4 ➑
This is a sophisticated, multipurpose venue that gets rave reviews for its highbrow productions. Enjoy a reasonably priced meal or a drink in the arty restaurant before moving to the stripped-down space for the show.

Centro Cultural Ricardo Rojas

Avenida Corrientes 2038, entre Junín y Ayacucho, Once (4954 5521/ www.rojas.uba.ar). Subte B, Callao. No credit cards. Map p134 A5 ❾

This lively cultural centre, part of UBA, the immense University of Buenos Aires, shows interesting arthouse and experimental fare in its single auditorium. It's cheaper to see a film here than it is to rent one from Blockbuster.

Ciudad Cultural Konex

Avenida Sarmiento 3131, entre Jean Jaurés y Anchorena, Abasto (4864 3200/www.ciudadculturalkonex.org). Subte B, Carlos Gardel. Shows Jan-Nov daily. Map p134 B4 ❿

This trendy complex, based in a former factory, provides a gritty backdrop to a wide array of original events, pulling in a young and bohemian crowd. It's perhaps best known currently for Monday's regular *Bomba de Tiempo*, an improvisational musical show based on a group of percussionists who keep the crowd moving as they riff drummingly to the music of the week's special guest, following a system of signals developed by director Santiago Vazquez.

Club Atlético Fernández Fierro

Sánchez de Bustamante 764, entre Lavalle y Guardia Vieja, Abasto (www.fernandezfierro.com). Open from 9pm Wed; 10.30pm Sat. *Milonga* 11pm Wed; midnight Sat. Admission AR$12. No credit cards. Map p134 B4 ⓫

The Orquesta Típica Fernández Fierro holds a weekly residency here – and regular Saturday night fiestas – filling the warehouse-like space with an enthusiastic crowd and thundering, rock-inspired tango.

Cosmos

Avenida Corrientes 2046, entre Ayacucho y Junín, Once (4953 5405/www.cinecosmos.com). Subte B, Callao. No credit cards. Map p134 A5 ⓬

Both a film buff's paradise and an Avenida Corrientes landmark, Cosmos's 'cultural space' features new Argentinian releases as well as retrospectives and auteur films.

Espacio Callejón

Humahuaca 3759, entre Bulnes y Mario Bravo, Abasto (4862 1167). Subte B, Medrano. Shows Wed-Sun. No credit cards. Map p134 C4 ⓭

One of the best places in BA for gutsy and unusual new productions, this quirky theatre also offers evening classes in clowning and acting.

La Esquina de Carlos Gardel

Pasaje Carlos Gardel 3200, y Anchorena, Abasto (4867 6363/ www.esquinacarlosgardel.com.ar). Subte B, Carlos Gardel. Open 8.30pm-midnight daily. *Dinner* 9pm. *Show* 10.30pm. Map p134 B4 ⓮

It's a very touristy show, but the venue is grand, the dancers sexy and showbizzy, and the dinner involves big steaks and blood-red wine.

Hoyts Abasto Buenos Aires

Abasto de Buenos Aires shopping centre, Avenida Corrientes 3247, entre Aguero y Anchorena, Abasto (0810 1224 6987/www.hoyts.com.ar). Subte B, Carlos Gardel. Open from 11am daily. Map p134 B4 ⓯

One of the best of the multiplexes, Hoyts Abasto turns into an arthouse venue during BA's excellent BAFICI Film Festival.

El Portón de Sánchez

Sánchez de Bustamante 1034, entre Córdoba y San Luis, Abasto (4863 2848). Shows 10pm Wed-Sun. Closed Jan. No credit cards. Map p134 C4 ⓰

The dance-heavy programme features troupes such as Grupo Krapp as well as plays that fall at the pricier, more polished end of the indie spectrum.

Sabor a Tango

General Juan Perón 2535, y Larrea, Once (4953 8700/

www.saboratango.com.ar). Subte A, Pasco or Subte B, Pasteur. **Open** *Dinner* from 8.30pm daily. *Show* 10pm daily. **Map** p134 A5 ⑰ This is a glamorous setting for a first-rate tango show that features expert dancers, gaucho music and Argentinian folklore as well as a live orchestra. Check it out on a Saturday night to catch the Italia Unita *milonga* in full swing.

Tanquería El Beso

1st floor, Riobamba 416, entre Corrientes y Lavalle, Once (4953 2794). Subte B, Callao. **Open** *Classes* 1pm Mon-Fri; 5pm Mon-Wed, Fri; 8.30pm Mon, Wed, Fri, Sat; 8pm Sun. *Milonga* 9pm Tue; 10.30pm Wed; 6pm Thur; 10.30pm Fri, Sat; 10pm Sun. No credit cards. **Map** p134 A5 ⑱

This is a bijou setting for nightly dances and classes of a high standard held by La Academia Tango Milonguero, part of Susana Miller's highly-regarded academy.

Almagro, Caballito, Villa Crespo & Chaarita

Commercial chaos gives way to a tranquil neighbourhood vibe in the barrios west of Abasto. Though they are no match for Palermo's various residential enclaves, Villa Crespo in particular benefits from the overflow of Palermo's trendy restaurants and bars. Once Palermo moves out of its current

Palacio de Aguas Corrientes p132

Thymus

reconstruction phase, the gods of urban development will no doubt set their sights on Villa Crespo and beyond. So here's a word of advice to potential investors in Buenos Aires real estate: go west while you still can.

Sights & museums

Arte x Arte

Lavalleja 1062, entre Córdoba y Lerma, Villa Crespo (4772 6754/ www.artea.com.ar/artexarte). **Open** *Apr-Dec* 1-7pm Mon-Sat. Closed Jan-Mar. **Map** p135 D4 ⑲

With its five salons, a library, laboratories and an auditorium, Arte x Arte's claim to be the largest South American gallery space – with 1,800 square metres (19,355 square feet) – sounds plausible. It's dedicated exclusively to photography, video and digital art.

Cementerio de la Chacarita

Guzmán 630, y Federico Lacroze (4553 9034/9038/4553 0041 tours). Subte B, Federico Lacroze. **Open** 7am-6pm daily. **Admission** Free. **Map** p135 F2 ⑳

Now far more expansive than Recoleta's exclusive necropolis, with numbered streets and car access to its thousands of vaults, this cemetery is largely for ordinary folk. Still, a number of popular heroes have wound up here, including Carlos Gardel, Alfonsina Storni and aviation pioneer Jorge Newbery.

Museo Participativo de Ciencias Naturales Bernardino Rivadavia

Avenida Angel Gallardo 470, entre Warnes y Marechal, Caballito (4982 1154/4494/www.macn.gov.ar). Subte B, Angel Gallardo. **Open** 2-7pm daily. **Admission** AR$3; free under-6s. No credit cards. **Map** p135 D2 ㉑
This natural history museum is thrilling for kids who are dotty about dinosaurs. For a more hands-on activity, the museum offers two-hour workshops in paleontology (9am, 10.30am, 2pm and 3.30pm).

Eating & drinking

Almacén Secreto

Aguirre 1242, entre Darwin y Humbolt, Villa Crespo (4775 1271/ http://almacensecretoclub.blogspot. com). **Open** noon-4pm Mon-Fri; from 8pm Thur-Sat. No credit cards. **$$**. **Argentinian**. **Map** p135 E3 ㉒
Northern Argentinian dishes such as empanadas tucumanas, tamales and the gorgeously greasy *provoleta de cabra* (grilled goat's cheese) are on the 'El norte' portion of the menu. From 'El centro', try the *carne al horno de barro* (meat slow-cooked in an adobe oven), and from 'El sur', the *cordero patagónico* (Patagonian lamb). Also on the menu: live music nights and art workshops.

Cantina Los Amigos

Loyola 701, entre Malabia y Acevedo, Villa Crespo (4774 0402). **Open** from 7.30pm Mon; 12.30-3.30pm, from 7.30pm Tue-Sat; 12.30-4pm Sun. **$$**. **Argentinian**. **Map** p135 D3 ㉓
Buzzing with a late-night good-time vibe, Cantina Los Amigos is packed

with local families, TV stars and footballers. Order a selection of starters and then go for a pasta special or whatever's sizzling on the grill.

Casa Felix

Address given with reservation, Chacarita (4555 1882/www.diego felix.com). **Open** from 9.30pm Thur-Sat. **$$$**. **Eclectic**.
See box p143.

La Cava Jufré

Jufré 201, y Julián Alvarez, Villa Crespo (4775 7501). **Open** 11am-1.30pm, 7pm-midnight Mon-Sat. **$**. **Wine bar**. **Map** p135 D3 ㉔
A genuine find for wine enthusiasts, this corner of Villa Crespo has been taken over by Lito, an amateur wine enthusiast and photographer; and if you enjoy sitting around tasting and discussing wines, you're in.

Kensho

Zárraga 3799, y Estomba, Chacarita (4555 0421/15 3085 7827 mobile/ www.kensho.com.ar). **Open** 8.30pm-midnight Thur-Sat. **$$**. No credit cards. **Vegetarian**. See box p143. **Map** p135 F3 ㉕

Sarkis

Thames 1101, entre Jufre y Lerma, Villa Crespo (4772 4911). **Open** noon-3pm, from 8pm daily. No credit cards. **$**. **Middle Eastern**. **Map** p135 E3 ㉖
Sarkis's authentic Levantine cuisine and brilliant prices mean it's packed pretty much every night. The huge menu offers tasty dips, snacks, soufflés, raw mince and kebabs. Most of the listings have no translation, not even into Spanish, so grab some friends, ask for a miscellany of starters and a cheap bottle of wine and have a thoroughly enjoyable dinner.

Thymus

Lerma 525, entre Malabia y Acevedo, Villa Crespo (4772 1936/ www.thymusrestaurant.com.ar). **Open** from 8.30pm Mon-Sat. **$$**. **Argentinian**. **Map** p135 D3 ㉗
A few observations: the simplest, best ingredients come together to taste fresh

BUENOS AIRES BY AREA

and bold in the salads here; the new kobe beef with *chimichurri*, confit of orange and a baked potato is worth travelling far and wide to try; the rabbit and *foie gras* terrine with fig and Dijon mustard purée and the beef tartare are both expertly assembled. Don't forget to leave room for the 'coulant' chocolate cake with orange blossom ice-cream.

Verdellama

Jorge Newbery 3623, entre Charlone y Roseti, Chacarita (4554 7467/www.comidaconvida.com.ar). Subte B, Federico Lacroze. **Open** noon-6pm daily; 6pm-midnight Thur-Sat. **$.** No credit cards. **Vegan.** **Map** p135 F3 ㉘
Verdellama's following of diners and fans goes well beyond the vegetarian and the health-conscious. From miso soup to butternut squash ravioli and apple tart, every dish is created according to the philosophy of 'life food'. The mushroom stir-fry with jasmine rice and courgette spaghetti are guilt-free dishes, or try the pizza made without cheese or flour – the house's brilliantly inventive pie is piled with avocado and jalapeño peppers.

Las Violetas

Rivadavia 3899, y Medrano, Almagro (4958 7387/www.lasvioletas.com). **Open** 6am-1am Mon-Thur, Sun; open 24hrs Fri, Sat. **$$.** **Cafe.** **Map** p134 B3 ㉙
This French-style café has been in business since 1884, and its bustling atmosphere, great-value refreshments and attentive service keep the trade flooding in. Soaring ceilings, stained-glass windows and pristine waiters combine to create a very special spot.

Shopping

Murillo 666

Murillo 666, entre Acevedo y Malabia, Villa Crespo (4855 2024/www.murillo666.com.ar). Subte B, Malabia. **Open** 9.30am-8pm Mon-Sat; 10am-7pm Sun. **Map** p135 D2 ㉚
On the stretch of calle Murillo between Scalabrini Ortiz and Gurruchaga, there

are plenty of outlets that offer leather jackets at below-bargain-basement prices. Murillo 666 stands out for its huge selection in an imposingly large store. Myriad options include a variety of jackets for men and women, as well as handbags, belts, wallets, luggage and even sofas.

Nightlife

878

Thames 878, entre Loyola y Aguirre, Villa Crespo (4773 1098). **Open** from 7pm Mon-Fri; from 8pm Sat-Sun. No credit cards. **Map** p135 E3 ㉛
Ring the bell at the unmarked door, and you'll be invited into a slick, low-lit space with comfortable couches, a well-stocked bar and more than a few reminders of its early days as a carpentry workshop. This is one of the coolest, least publicised bars in the city.

Amerika

Gascón 1040, entre Rocamora y Estado de Israel, Villa Crespo (4865 4416/www.ameri-k.com.ar). Subte B, Medrano. **Open** from 1am Thur-Sun. **Map** p134 C4 ㉜
This is easily BA's biggest gay club, regularly drawing thousands of boozed-up, party-hungry punters of increasingly mixed and flexible sexual orientations. Featuring electronica and cheesey pop, it has two dancefloors, four bars, regular live shows, strippers, all-you-can-drink nights (Fridays and Saturdays), flirtatious bartenders and a very packed (men only) dark room.

Casa Brandon

Luis María Drago 236, entre Lavalleja y Julián Álvarez, Villa Crespo (4858 0610/www.brandongayday.com.ar). Subte B, Malabia. **Open** from 7pm Wed-Sun. **Map** p135 D2 ㉝
Where's a girl to go when she just wants to have fun? Try this four-level house – named after Brandon Teena, the transgender teen played by Hilary Swank in the 1999 film *Boys Don't Cry*. It's like a community centre, art

Home cooking

Casa Coupage

A new wave of local and expat chefs have hatched the city's latest culinary scene with *puertas cerradas* (closed door) restaurants. Several times a week, these free-spirited cooks whip up a new menu and open their homes to serve multi-course meals to a limited number of diners. One of the latest arrivals on this by-reservation-only scene is **Kensho** (p141), an underground restaurant in Colegiales where former Bio head chef Máximo Cabrera treats guests to four courses of *cocina para despertar* (wake-up food). A passionate vegetarian with Buddhist leanings, Cabrera uses his organic, meat-free menu to showcase the best that local producers have to offer. Local, organic products also take center stage at **Casa Felix** in Chacarita (p141), where chef Diego Felix prepares five courses of Latin American-inspired cuisine. From black bean and plantain empanadas to grilled *surubí* (South American catfish) and passionfruit cream, Felix's dishes

capture flavours unique to the South American continent.

At **Casa Saltshaker** (p89), guests gather around a communal table on Friday and Saturday nights at New York native Dan Perlman's Barrio Norte garden apartment. Perlman concocts elegant theme dinners inspired by semi-obscure events, such as French writer Simone de Beauvoir's 100th birthday. Oenophiles will appreciate the offerings at **Casa Coupage** (p105), where owners Santiago Mymicopulo and Inés Mendieta welcome guests into their stylish Palermo apartment for comparative wine tastings and modern Argentine fare by chef Martin Lukesch. The menu – a series of creative riffs on traditional ingredients like quinoa and Patagonian crab – revolves around wines from Mymicopulo and Mendieta's personal cellar. Like the folks behind the other *puertas cerradas*, the Casa Coupage team aspires to 'surprise your senses' in a convivial and intimate atmosphere.

gallery, bar-restaurant, lounge, disco and performance space all rolled into one. Come to collect information, gape at the shock art on display in the ground-floor gallery, indulge in some sapphic socialising (of course, boys are invited too!) over cocktails at the bar above, catch a gay tango show, listen to the DJ's selection of pop and dance tunes, or just enjoy the people-watching.

La Catedral

Sarmiento 4006, y Medrano, Almagro (mobile 15 5325 1630). Subte A, Castro Barros or Subte B, Medrano. **Open** *Classes* 8pm, 10pm Mon-Sat; 7.30pm, 9.30pm Sun. *Milonga after classes.* No credit cards. **Map** p134 C3 ❸

The atmosphere at this underground venue is pitched somewhere between post-punk/neo-goth and circus/music hall. The BA tangopolis doesn't get any cooler than this.

Arts & leisure

Actors Studio

Avenida Díaz Vélez 3842, entre Medrano y Salguero, Almagro (4958 8268/www.actors-studio.org). Subte A, Castro Barros. **Shows** Fri-Sun; call ahead. No credit cards. **Map** p134 B3 ❸

Alongside a varied programme featuring new versions of classics and a diverse selection of outrageous original works, the studio – aptly, considering its name – also runs acting classes.

Cine Club Eco

2nd floor, Avenida Corrientes 4940, entre Lavalleja y Julián Alvarez, Almagro (4854 4126). Subte B, Malabia. **Open** usually 8pm or 9pm at weekends; call ahead. No credit cards. **Map** p135 D3 ❸

If Bergman and Polanski retrospectives get your pulse racing, get down to Cine Club Eco. The entrance price includes an invitation to a post-screening discussion and coffee.

Boedo

Puerto Madero

Along the River

Money may well talk, but in the area adjacent to the Rió de la Plata, it rules. Resident foreigners who want to make their fortunes and run, and not necessarily rub shoulders with *porteños* (who tend to stay away in droves), generally end up on riverside turf. Popular with business travellers and teeming with glossy hotels, nightclubs and eateries, all somewhat lacking in local flavour, Puerto Madero, in particular, screams tourist trap. The restaurant tango shows are more Vegas than turn-of-the-19th-century BA, and you might forget you're in the capital, some of the buildings rise skyscraper high. But despite the lack of home-grown culture – blink and you might forget you're in South America – the quality of the area's swanky eating, drinking and lodging offerings are first-class, and you won't get a better view of the Rió de la Plata without leaving the ground.

Puerto Madero & Costanera Sur

Size matters in Puerto Madero, and the proof is in the **Hilton Buenos Aires** and **Faena Hotel + Universe**, two of the capital's most opulent buildings. Those who prefer to travel cruise- and resort-style, without getting bogged down in cultural details, will find everything they need right here.

Sights & museums

Buque Museo Fragata Presidente Sarmiento

Alicia Moreau de Justo 900, y Belgrano, Dique 3, Puerto Madero (4334 9336/9386). Subte B, LN Alem. **Open** 9am-8pm daily. **Admission** AR$2; free under-5s. **Map** p146 B3 ❶
This frigate, built in Birkenhead, was used as a training ship from 1897 to 1961 and is now a museum full of photos, maps and domestic objects, with the cabins and dining rooms restored and intact.

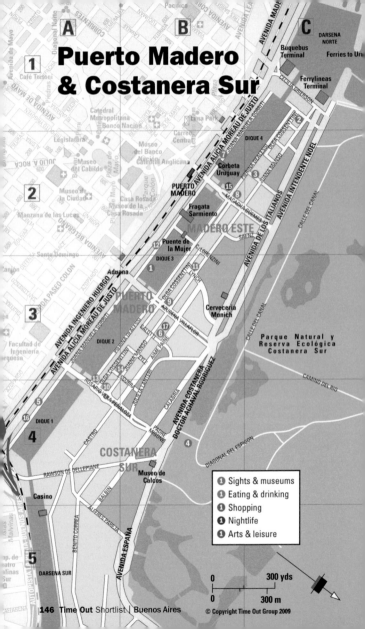

Puerto Madero
& Costanera Sur

A **B** **C**

DARSENA NORTE

Buquebus Terminal

Ferries to Uru

Ferrylineas Terminal

Café Tortoni

Catedral Metropolitana
Banco Nación

Luna Park

Legislatura

Correo Central

DIQUE 4

Museo del Banco

Catedral Anglicana

Corbeta Uruguay

Museo del Cabildo

PUERTO MADERO

Museo de la Ciudad

Casa Rosada
Museo de la Casa Rosada

Fragata Sarmiento

MADERO ESTE

Manzana de las Luces

Puente de la Mujer

DIQUE 3

Aduana

PUERTO MADERO

Cervecería Munich

DIQUE 2

Facultad de Ingeniería

Parque Natural y Reserva Ecológica Costanera Sur

DIQUE 1

COSTANERA SUR

Museo de Calcos

❶ Sights & museums
❶ Eating & drinking
❶ Shopping
❶ Nightlife
❶ Arts & leisure

Casino

DARSENA SUR

0   300 yds
0   300 m

© Copyright Time Out Group 2009

Colección de Arte Amalia Lacroze de Fortabat

NEW *Olga Cossettini 141, Puerto Madero Este (4310 6600/www.* coleccionfortabat.org.ar). *Subte B, LN Alem.* **Open** noon-9pm Tue-Fri; 10am-9pm Sat, Sun. **Admission** AR$15; AR$7 reductions. **Map** p146 C1 ❷

The Argentinian and international works at this gallery are all part of the privately owned treasure trove of the country's richest woman. Look for the psychologically complex paintings of Carlos Alonso and the highly versatile work by Antonio Berni.

Puro Remo

Juana Manso, y Victoria Ocampo, Dique 4, Puerto Madero Este (6397 3545/www.puroremo.com.ar). **Open** 7am-7pm daily. **Admission** varies. **Map** p146 C2 ❸

This highly professional kayak and rowing outfit offers tourist services in addition to classes, including trips north to the lush Delta or the scenic stretch of water just north of town.

Reserva Ecológica Costanera Sur

Avenida Tristán Achaval Rodríguez 1550, entre Brasil y Rosario Vera Peñaloza, Costanera Sur (4893 1588/0800 444 5343). **Open** *Apr-Sep* 8am-5.45pm Tue-Sun. *Oct-Mar* 8am-6.45pm Tue-Sun. **Admission** free. **Map** p146 B4 ❹

Within this nature reserve's boundaries, four lakes, giant *cortaderias* (foxtail pampas grass), willows and shrubs provide natural habitats for more than 200 bird species. Iguanas can be spotted scuttling across the hard earth, but on weekends you're more likely to see joggers, cyclists and picnickers, when up to 15,000 visitors descend on the reserve. Moonlight tours are arranged one night per month, when the moon is fullest.

Eating & drinking

Antares

NEW *Alicia Moreau de Justo 1808, Dique 1, Puerto Madero (4315 6371/ www.cervezaantares.com).* **Open** from noon daily. $$. **Bar. Map** p146 A4 ❺

Click and save

Instant delivery means that even visitors can take adavantage of Argentina's famously cost-saving version of eBay. Like its US and UK counterparts (with fewer kitschy curios and mostly fixed prices), **MercadoLibre** (www.mercadolibre.com) is an online marketplace where more than 32 million registered users buy and sell new and used goods, including electronics, DVDs, clothing, books and even cars, at rates well below retail. Since launching in 1999, it's become a major international player: revenues for the first nine months of 2008 topped $100 million, and it now dominates Latin America's online shopping market. So pervasive is the Mercado Libre trend that its desktop icon is built in to many computers sold in BA. If you go to BA's Barrio Norte Apple store, you'll end up spending AR$2,000 (US$575) on a new iPod, and those electronic shops in Microcentro only *promise* the best camera prices in town. On Mercado Libre, you can find iPods for half the Apple store cost and major-brand digital cameras for half *that*. Once you agree on a method of payment for your purchase with the vendor (usually cash, but more are accepting credit cards), pick the item up in person, or have it hand delivered to you at your hotel, never dealing with a sales assistant who won't take 'No, I'm just looking' for an answer.

El Bistro

This modern, industrial-looking space is dominated by eight copper vats that contain some of the best beer in BA. The varieties include Scotch ale, honey beer and cream stout. The food is mostly hearty Bavarian fare, but also includes tapas, *tablas de picadas* (appetiser plate of cheese, meats and olives) and main courses cooked using the house beers.

El Bistro

Faena Hotel + Universe, Martha Salotti 445, Dique 2, Puerto Madero Este (4010 9200/www. faenahotelanduniverse.com). Subte B, LN Alem. **Open** 8pm-1am daily. **$$$$. French.** Map p146 B3 ❻
From an aesthetic perspective alone, there is simply no other restaurant in Argentina quite like El Bistro; it is exuberant French designer Philippe Starck at his finest. The concoctions on the tasting menu are equally singular – a regular menu is also available – from the 'spherifications' of olives to the foams of Spanish omelette. These are innovative touches in what is an otherwise resolutely Argentinian menu.

Cabaña las Lilas

Alicia Moreau de Justo 516, Dique 4, Puerto Madero (4313 1336/www. laslilas.com.ar). Subte B, LN Alem. **Open** noon-3.30pm, 7.30pm-1am daily. **$$$$. Argentinian.** Map 146 B2 ❼
It's a tourist trap for sure, but it's got an atmospheric dockside location and a jumbo wine list. But what really matters is the meat. Whatever part of the cow ends up on your plate, it will be unforgettably tender.

I Central Market

Pierina Dealessi, y Macacha Güemes, Dique 4, Puerto Madero Este (5775 0330/www.icentralmarket.com.ar). **Open** from 8am-midnight daily. **$$. Argentinian.** Map p146 B2 ❽
The twin to i Fresh Market (*see right*), this sleek Manhattan-style venue boasts a minimalist dining room facing out over the docks of Puerto Madero. The cuisine is traditionally Argentinian – empanadas and steak figure heavily – but the empanadas are filled with apples and brie and paired with crisp chardonnay; and the steak is served with baby scallops for a twist on surf-and-turf.

I Fresh Market

*Azucena Villaflor, y Olga Cossettini,
Dique 3, Puerto Madero Este (5775
0335/www.ifreshmarket.com.ar).* **Open**
8am-midnight daily. **$$. Argentinian.**
Map p146 B3 **9**

At this modern New York-style deli,
healthy breakfasts (smoothies, cured
ham and scrambled eggs), lunch (pas-
trami and pickles on rye, smoked
salmon bagels) and dinner (modern
Argentinian dishes and own-made pas-
tas) are all good. The evening menu
includes a grilled peppers, aubergine
and courgette risotto with green tea
crème brulée the perfect topper.

Minna

*Olga Cossettini 1691, y Rosario Vera
Peñaloza, Dique 2, Puerto Madero Este
(5787 3090/www.minnacocinapasion.
com).* **$$$. Argentinian.** Map p146 A4 **10**

The restaurant takes its title from the
lunfardo (BA slang) for woman, it has
named each dish after a lady, and calls
the whole dining experience here
cocina pasión (passionate – cooking).
Forget the theme, though – the square-
shaped stone-baked pizzas here are
excellent, as is the pasta. And with the
help of the exuberant sommelier,
Fernando, you can pick your wine from
a rack of over 900 Argentinian bottles.

Nanatsu

*Olga Cossettini 1185, y Marta Lynch,
Dique 3, Puerto Madero Este
(5530 0202/www.nanatsu.com.ar).*
Open noon-4pm, 8pm-midnight daily.
$$. Japanese. Map p146 B3 **11**

This Asian fusion restaurant serves
creative Japanese-inspired dishes such
as breaded flash-fried salmon rolls,
tempura sushi and many varieties of
cooked fish, delicately presented with
tangy sauces. Roasted shitake mush-
rooms, shrimp paste wrapped in
cucumber and white salmon dishes are
good options for a light lunch.

La Parolaccia

*Alicia Moreau de Justo 1052, Dique 3,
Puerto Madero (4343 1679/4345 4742/
www.laparolaccia.com).* **Open** noon-

midnight daily. **$$$. Italian.**
Map p146 B2 **12**

Serving delicious home-made pastas
and risottos with seasonal ingredients,
this chain satisfies the strongest of
Italian cravings. If you fancy a reliable
fish dish, these guys know what
they're doing. La Parolaccia del Mare
(Alicia Moreau de Justo 1170), a few
doors down, specialises in seafood.

Rëd Resto & Lounge

*Hotel Madero, Rosario Vera Peñaloza
360, Dique 2, Puerto Madero Este
(5776 7676/www.hotelmadero.com).
Subte B, LN Alem.* **Open** noon-3.30pm,
from 7.30pm daily. **$$$. Argentinian.**
Map p146 A3 **13**

Rëd, at the Hotel Madero, is cool and
classy without being over the top or
stuffy. Chef Steven Jung adds personal
touches to French cuisine, ranging
from red tuna with a roasted vegetable
tian to braised Patagonian lamb with
caramelised onions.

Tea Connection

*Loft 3, Olga Cossenttini 1545, Dique 2,
Puerto Madero Este (4312 7315/www.
teaconnection.com.ar).* **Open** noon-9pm
Mon-Fri; 10am-9pm Sat-Sun. **$$. Tea
house.** Map p146 B3 **14**

This airy, modern tea house offers a
range of delicious teas and infusions.
Teas to take home are sold in pretty
tins with labels like 'Bliss' (green tea
with mint) and 'Rooibos', a South
African blend believed to soothe an ail-
ing or party-weary body. The menu
includes a range of snacks and light
meals, from sweet potato and coriander soup to coconut muffins and devil-
ishly dense chocolate cake, served with
a shot of lemon-scented rice pudding.

Nightlife

Asia de Cuba

*Pierina Dialessi 750 y Macacha Güemes,
Puerto Madero Este (4894 1328/
www.asiadecuba.com.ar).*
Open 1-4.30pm, from 9pm Mon-Sun.
Map p146 B2 **15**

Wednesday nights are the main event
at Asia de Cuba, when the 'after office'

Costanera Norte

crowd descends early and stays late. Though this dockside spot has experienced a little fall from grace with the BA clubbing 'in' crowd, its sushi, decent drinks and dancefloor remain popular with executives and tourists from Puerto Madero's swanky hotels.

Arts & leisure

Cinemark 8

Alicia Moreau de Justo 1920, Dique 1, Puerto Madero (0800 222 2463/ www.cinemark.com.ar). **Open** from noon daily. **Map** p146 A4 ⑯

This modern docklands complex has eight screens and a restaurant. It shows a mixture of Hollywood and Latin American new releases, as does its ten-screen sister branch near Alto Palermo shopping centre (Beruti 3399, 0800 222 2463).

Rojo Tango

Faena Hotel + Universe, Martha Salotti 445, Dique 2, Puerto Madero Este (4010 9200/www.rojotango.com). Subte B, LN Alem. **Open** 8pm-midnight daily. *Dinner* 8.30pm. *Show* 10pm. **Map** p146 B3 ⑰

From the moment you enter Faena Hotel + Universe, you realise that Rojo Tango is not your average dinner and show. You'll be greeted with a glass of champagne before an excellent three-course meal is served, setting the scene for a sexy and intimate show, albeit one that doesn't really break any rules.

Costanera Norte

It's not exactly must-see BA, but when one tires of the capital's central pleasures, there are at least two good reasons to beeline north of town: Aeroparque Jorge Newbery, BA's city airport, with flights to and from Argentina's other provinces; and the 'beach' clubs, where *porteño* families go to beat the oppressive summer heat.

Sights & museums

Tierra Santa

Avenida Costanera Rafael Obligado 5790 (4784 9551/www.tierrasanta-bsas.com.ar). **Open** *May-Nov* 4pm-12.30am Fri-Sun. *Dec-Apr* 9am-9pm Fri; noon-11pm Sat, Sun. **Admission** AR$20; AR$8 under-11s. **Map** p151 B1 ⑱

This Holy Land extravaganza begins with a son-et-lumière show celebrating

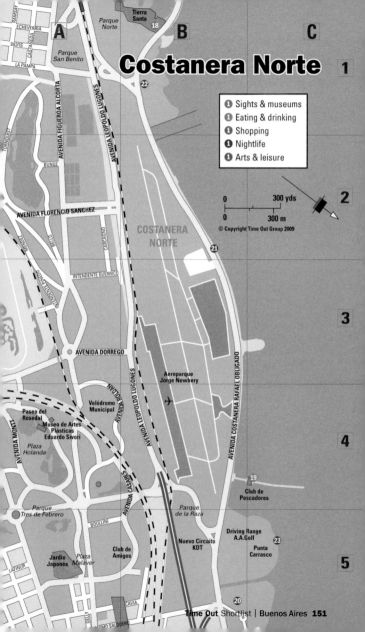

Costanera Norte

Tierra Santa **18**

Parque Norte

Parque San Benito

A **B** **C**

1

AVENIDA FIGUEROA ALCORTA

AVENIDA LEOPOLDO LUGONES

ECHEVERRIA

RAMSAY

SUCRE

CASTAÑEDA

LA PAMPA

22

- **1** Sights & museums
- **1** Eating & drinking
- **1** Shopping
- **1** Nightlife
- **1** Arts & leisure

0   300 yds

0   300 m

© Copyright Time Out Group 2009

2

AVENIDA FLORENCIO SANCHEZ

TORQUIST

BUNGE

BELLO

JORGE NEWBERY

CANCARO

COSTANERA NORTE

21

INTENDENTE GUERRICO

3

AVENIDA DORREGO

AVENIDA LEOPOLDO LUGONES

NEWTON

Aeroparque Jorge Newbery

AVENIDA COSTANERA RAFAEL OBLIGADO

Velódromo Municipal

AVENIDA

Paseo del Rosedal

Museo de Artes Plásticas Eduardo Sívori

AVENIDA MONTT

Plaza Holanda

AVENIDA CASARES

4

19

Club de Pescadores

Parque Tres de Febrero

BOULINI

Parque de la Raza

Jardín Japonés

Plaza Malaver

Club de Amigos

Nuevo Circuito KDT

Driving Range A.A.Golf

23

Punta Carrasco

LAFINUR

CAVIA

GUIDO SALDUERO

20

GELLY

5

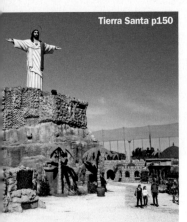
Tierra Santa p150

the Nativity. As the Angel of the Anunciation descends from a neon-lit sky, locals in Middle Eastern garb herd visitors into the 'world's largest manger'. The *pièce de résistance*, however, is the Resurrection, which takes place every 45 minutes, weather permitting, when an 18-metre Jesus rises from the park's central mountain.

Eating & drinking

Muelle de Pescadores
Avenida Costanera Rafael Obligado, y Avenida Sarmiento (4773 1354/www.club-pescadores.com.ar). **Open** 8am-1am Tues-Sat; 8am-8pm Sun. **$$$**. **Argentinian**. **Map** p151 C4 ⑲
The 1930s faux-Tudor blast from the past perched on a long wooden jetty offers a waterfront view on three sides. Skip lunch and go for a bottle of cold Trumpeter Chardonnay and a *picada* – a selection of cheeses and cold meats.

Nightlife

Caix
Complejo Costa Salguero, Avenida Costanera Rafael Obligado, y Salguero (4805 6069/www.caix-ba.com.ar). **Open** 12.30-6am Wed, Fri, Sat; 9am-3pm Sun. **Map** p151 B5 ⑳

The surreal scene here packs in hundreds of can't-stop-won't-stop clubbers on Sunday mornings, winding down only when the DJ pulls off his headphones at around 3pm. The action takes place upstairs – there is a second airier room which looks out over the water and offers some respite for the sweat-sodden crowd.

Jet Lounge
Avenida Costanera Rafael Obligado 4801 (4872 5599/www.jetlounge. com.ar). **Open** from 12.30am Fri, Sat. **Map** p151 B2 ㉑
An exclusive private lounge and club located on the Costanera, Jet Lounge has played host to some of BA's most exclusive events, including fashion parties, premieres and high-profile music events. In the early evenings it's a relaxed lounge-bar, complete with cocktails, sushi and a beautiful marina view. As the night continues, the vibe peps up with house tunes.

Pacha
Avenida Costanera Rafael Obligado, y La Pampa (4788 4280/ www.pachabuenosaires.com). **Open** *mid Feb-Dec* from midnight Fri; from 1.30am Sat. **Map** p151 B1 ㉒
BA's outpost of Ibiza's clubbing giant – pronounced Pachá by locals – overlooks the river and remains a sure-fire destination for partying, especially on Saturday nights. Expect international names – Sander Kleinenberg, Dave Clarke et al – in the large, sweaty main room, which has several bars. The patio DJ upstairs tends to play softer, funkier tunes, for sunglass-clad clubbers to get their groove on under the stars.

Rouge
Punta Carrasco, Avenida Costanera Rafael Obligado, y Sarmiento (4806 8002/www.rougebuenosaires.com.ar). **Open** from 1am Sat. **Map** p151 C5 ㉓
Friday nights are back down at Punta Carrasco in the disco formerly known as Mint. The main room hosts house while the river-view terrace lightens up the wee hours of the morning with hip hop and dance tunes.

Belgrano

Further Afield

Most visitors stick to BA's tried-and-tested tourist circuit, but there is plenty of life off the beaten path. Colegiales is like a residential extension of Palermo. Formerly a separate municipality from the capital, Belgrano is home to many *porteños* as well as BA's very own Chinatown, a strip of Chinese restaurants on and around calle Arribeños. Zona Norte, from Olivos to San Isidro, is the part of town that much of the city's high society calls home.

Colegiales, Belgrano & Nuñez

Eating & drinking

Don Chicho
Plaza 1411, y Zarraga, Colegiales (4556 1463). Subte B, Tronador. **Open** 8pm-midnight Mon; noon-3pm, 8pm-midnight Tue-Sat; noon-3pm Sun. **$**. No credit cards. **Italian**.

Two pasta cooks quickly shuttle back and forth from the kitchen to the tables, rolling out, cutting and hand forming every order of pasta *al momento*. There's no menu, so just take the suggestions off the board out front or whatever the waitress recommends.

Lotus Neo Thai
Arribeños 2265, entre Olazabal y Mendoza (4783 7993/ www.restaurantelotus.com.ar). **Open** from 8.30pm Mon-Sat. **$$**. **Thai**.
Pull up a floor cushion to relish traditionally Thai flavours – lemongrass, coriander, ginger, coconut milk, mint, peanuts – or head for the terrace to eat in the open air. Start off with skewers of chicken served with sweet and sour cucumber sauce, then try the stir-fried prawns with shiitake mushrooms and baby corn in oyster sauce.

Manero
Monroe 895, entre Dragones y Husares, Nuñez (4787 4848/ www.manerorestaurant.com). **Open** 8.30pm-1am daily. **$$**. **Argentinian**.
The breads and fish dishes on the Mediterranean-inspired menu, all

prepared here, mean an almost 24-hour day for the oven; and the place has its own market garden in which vegetable and herbs destined for the pot are raised. For starters, try *mollejas* (sweetbreads) and for a main course, the incredibly tender *bondiola* (pork) with pear chutney.

Palitos

Arribeños 2243, entre Mendoza y Olazabal, Belgrano (4786 8566). **Open** noon-3pm Tue-Fri; noon-5pm Sat, Sun; 8pm-midnight daily. **$$**. No credit cards. **Chinese**.

Eager punters at this Taiwanese restaurant in BA's Barrio Chino are prepared to queue for the sizzling fried whole shrimps and the sweet and sour chicken. And as long as you can wrench your mind away from Bambi, you'll find house speciality *ciervo salteado con verdeo* (sautéed venison with spring onions and ginger) a successful dish.

Pura Tierra

3 de Febrero 1167, entre Federico Lacroze y Teodoro García, Belgrano (4899 2007/www.puratierra.com.ar). Subte D, Olleros. **Open** from 8pm Mon-Sat. **$$$**. **Argentinian**.

The starters and puddings are the highlights here. Kick things off with some *mollejas* and caramelised red onions, drizzled with a light syrup of sugarcane honey, lime and thyme. Then try the wonderfully tender rabbit, seasoned with fennel, lemon and almonds, accompanied with sweet potatoes and a tomato and garlic confit.

Ruffino

Sucre 646, entre Figueroa Alcorta y Catañeda, Belgrano (4782 9490). **Open** noon-1.30am Mon-Fri; noon-2am Sat, Sun. **$$$**. **Italian**.

This Belgrano joint is the last word in posh pizza in BA. Ruffino's oven-baked, thin-crust pizzas are delicately topped with extras such as rocket, sun-dried tomatoes and just the right amount of cheese. Other dishes include saffron risotto, grilled fish and home-made pastas.

Sucre

Sucre 676, entre Figueroa Alcorta y Castañeda, Belgrano (4782 9082/www.sucrerestaurant.com.ar). Train to Scalabrini Ortiz. **Open** noon-4pm, from 8pm daily. **$$$**. **Argentinian**.

Order anything off the nuevo-pan-Latino menu and you'll be happy; but if you'd like a little direction, then the grilled swordfish with artichoke pesto linguini is a fish-and-pasta combination that may have been made in heaven. This kitchen turns out modern interpretations of *ceviche* (marinated raw fish), risotto, grilled salmon and slow braised pork, plus carpaccio of octopus with niçoise vinaigrette.

Shopping

Burdel

2nd floor, Gorostiaga 1559, entre Migueletes y Libertador, Núñez (4776 3757/www.burdelsite.com). **Open** 3-8pm Mon-Sat.

Burdel's current collection is both sexy and chic: French lace and Italian satin are combined in flirty, feminine pieces, and the sensual loungewear is offered in a variety of shades. There's also erotic literature and a smooth soundtrack, *L'amour Dans la Première Étage*, featuring Billie, Edith and Ella.

DC Petite Boutique

2nd floor, Zapiola 2196, entre Mendoza y Juramento, Belgrano (4542 3528/www.disenioclub.com.ar/petite_boutique.htm). **Open** 2.30-7.30pm Mon-Fri. No credit cards.

Located on the second floor of an old mansion, Petite Boutique displays clothes and objects by more than 30 Argentinian designers. Among knick-knacks such as magnets and accessories, there are undies, chunky jewellery, women's clothing, woolly hats and woven bags. Colour, texture and shape are jumbled up in this space.

Mercado de las Pulgas

Conde y Dorrego, Colegiales (5382 6234). **Open** 10am-7pm Tue-Sun.

This flea market is full of antique furniture and household items with

Mad about polo

It's still no match for a football showdown between Boca Juniors and River Plate, but polo is fast becoming one of Argentinian sports lovers' next favourite things. The Argentinian Open at Campo Argentino de Polo de Palermo (p129), has become the most prestigious polo tournament in the world. And the sport's media profile is growing too: what happens in the stands of a Triple Crown Championship match often receives as much attention as the action on the field.

The three-part Triple Crown play-off, contested by the Tortugas Open, the Hurlingham Open and the Argentine Polo Open Championship, makes and breaks top players while thrusting free publicity onto their cortége of socialite VIPs. Polo matches, many of which also are played in San Isidro and neigbourhoods like Tortugas and Hurlingham on the outskirts of the capital, have become a major site for star spotting, with top BA models,

actors, designers and TV personalities all embracing the current polo craze.

Fashion has been synonymous with polo since Ralph Lauren trademarked his clothing line with the legendary emblem of a polo player. In 2005, famed Argentinian polo player Ignacio 'Nacho' Figueras brought the logo to life when he was named the luminary face to model some of RL's most profitable collections. Aside from bringing international attention to the sport, Nacho has helped carry polo fashion off the field and onto the runway, and as such major Argentinian fashion labels as La Dolfina (p95), La Martina and Etiqueta Negra, all available at most of BA's major malls, jump on board the polo craze. Matches are played throughout the year, but the Triple Crown season runs from September to December. Tickets can be purchased through Ticketek (5237 7200, www.ticketek.com.ar).

pieces from the 1800s to the 1970s. Packed with atmosphere, it's a good alternative for vintage fans tired of San Telmo.

Ricky Sarkany

Crámer 3664, entre Crisólogo Larralde y Jaramillo, Núñez (4701 4133/ www.rickysarkany.com). **Open** 9am-7.30pm Mon-Fri; 9am-1pm Sat.

Sarkany adapts European trends for *porteño* tastes. Fringed suede sandals come in hot pink adorned with rock 'n' roll studs, and there are be jewelled, snakeskin-effect and animal-print options, plus more subtle variations. Bags, sunglasses, perfumes and clothing also form part of Ricky's world.

Nightlife

Estadio Obras Sanitarias

Avenida del Libertador 7395, entre Núñez y Manuela Pedraza, Núñez (4702 3223/www.estadioobras. com.ar). **Tickets** AR$20-$65. No credit cards.

Argentinians do love their guitar music. Hence the enduring popularity of this so-called 'temple of rock', which opened in 1917 and can hold 5,000 souls. Eric Clapton, James Brown, The Ramones, Megadeth, Manu Chao and most of BA's hottest bands have all played here. Renovated toilets and a new air-conditioning system have relieved the place of some of its traditional drawbacks.

El Teatro

Federico Lacroze 3455, y Alvarez Thomas, Colegiales (4555 1145/ www.elteatroonline.com.ar). **Open** from 9pm Wed-Sun. **Tickets** AR$10-$20. No credit cards.

Set in a spectacular old theatre equipped with two bars, El Teatro is decidedly a rocker joint: the bars don't have imported whiskey, just beer and basic drinks. But the great acoustics combined with good sound make a gig here a decent outing. On Saturday nights, a crowd of boys and girls – some a little on the young side – converge here for the gay and lesbian pop-and-rock Ambar La Fox party.

Arts & leisure

Estadio Monumental

Avenida Figueroa Alcorta 7597, y Udaondo, Núñez (4789 1327/ www.cariverplate.com.ar). **Tickets** AR$10 for guided tour, 2pm and 4pm, Tue and Fri only.

The Monumental – home to Club Atlético River Plate, the eternal rivals of Boca Juniors – was the setting for the opening and the final of the 1978 World Cup. It's also the largest stadium in the country. Big names such as Madonna, Keane and Red Hot Chili Peppers have also played to crowds of 60,000 and upwards here, and more concerts and festivals are planned for 2009.

Mataderos & Liniers

Shopping

Feria de Mataderos

Lisandro de la Torre y Avenida de los Corrales, Mataderos (www.feriade mataderos.com.ar). **Open** *Jan-Mar* 6pm-1am Sat; *Apr-Dec* 10am-9pm Sun.

At this rural-style fair located in the far west of the city, gauchos show off their skills with guitars and horses, and day trippers indulge in country food and browse through the predominantly gaucho-themed flea market. Folk bands perform on a small central stage and locals join in on the *chacareras* (country dances).

Zona Norte

Shopping

Galpón Chic

Primera Junta 1118, Bajo San Isidro (4747 3930/www.galponchic.com.ar). **Open** 11am-7pm Tue-Sat.

In this large ex-shipyard in lower San Isidro, you'll find all sorts of chic and trendy items ranging from iron furniture and recycled antique pieces to chandeliers, jewellery, arty sculptures and paper imported from Europe.

Feria de Mataderos

There are designer shoes and leather jackets, and Galpón Chic also has an art gallery and a wedding-list service.

Arts & leisure

Catedral de San Isidro

Avenida del Libertador 16199, y 9 de Julio, San Isidro (4743 0291). Train Mitre or de la Costa to San Isidro/bus 60, 168. **Open** 8am-8pm daily. **Admission** free.

Classical performances are usually at 4pm on Sundays, from April to December; arrive well in advance if you hope to secure a good seat.

Hipódromo de San Isidro

Avenida Márquez 504, y Santa Fe, San Isidro (4743 4019/4011/www. hipodromosanisidro.com.ar). Train from Retiro to San Isidro. **Open** 9am-11.30pm daily. **Admission** AR$1-$5. No credit cards.

Hosting races on Wednesdays and during weekends, this *hipódromo* is the only grass horseracing track in Argentina. Its biggest calendar event – the Gran Premio Carlos Pellegrini – takes place in December each year.

San Isidro Club

Blanco Encalada 404, entre Sucre y Darregueira, San Isidro (4766 2030/4763 6374/www.sanisidroclub. com.ar). Bus 60 (Panamericana line). **Tickets** AR$5, AR$2.50 7-15s; free under-7s. No credit cards.

The Argentinian rugby season runs from March to November. On the domestic scene, two teams from the affluent northern suburb of San Isidro dominate: Club Atlético de San Isidro (CASI) and the San Isidro Club (SIC).

Tren de la Costa

Avenida Maipú 2305, Olivos (4002 6000/www.trendelacosta.com.ar). From Retiro, Ramal 2 train on Mitre line to Olivos. **Open** 7am-10.30pm Mon-Thur; 8.30am-11.30pm Fri-Sun. **Return ticket** AR$20 non-residents; AR$12 residents; free under-3s.

On this lovely 25-minute train ride from Olivos to Tigre, you can get on and off at stations along the route, where there are cinemas, restaurants and shops. San Isidro station has the most sightseeing and entertainment options close by, and it's also the best way to reach BA's riverbank beaches.

home

14 ROOMS
4 SUITES
SPA
POOL
RESTOBAR
GARDEN

WWW.HOMEBUENOSAIRES.COM

HOTEL
home
BUENOSAIRES

Honduras 5860 (1414) Palermo Viejo Bs. As. Argentina
tel (5411) 4778 1008 • fax (5411) 4779 1006
info@homebuenosaires.com
www.homebuenosaires.com

Essentials

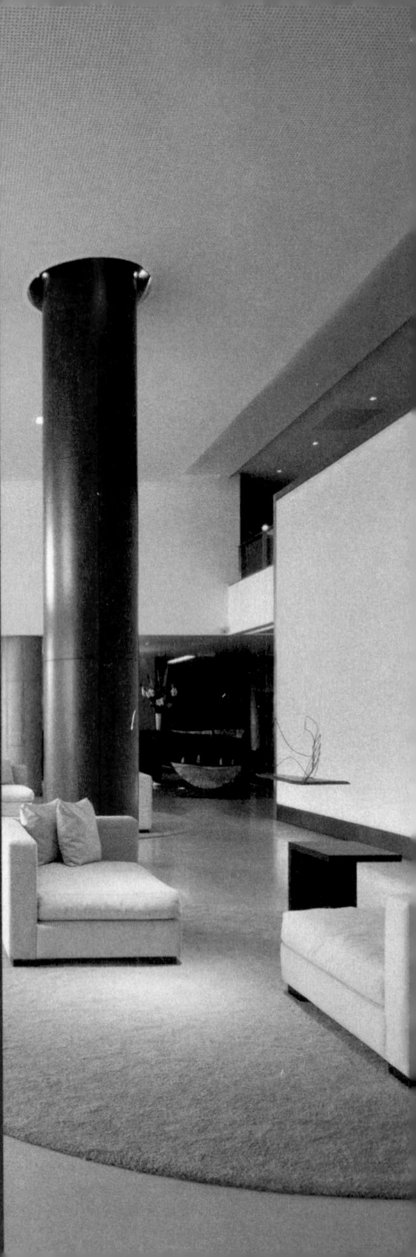

Blue Soho Hotel p173

Hotels

Several years into Argentina's recovery from the 2002 economic crash, Buenos Aires continues to offer a sophisticated urban experience at a relatively low cost – with the notable exception of hotel expenses. Translation: If mid- to high-end lodgings are your thing, get ready to pay for them. The good news is that as the current global economic situation plays out, hotel prices are remaining more or less static.

The Microcentro is one of the best locations for business travellers and anyone whose priority is being near important historical attractions. **Casa Calma**, a recent arrival to this neck of the woods, offers a sumptuous hotel experience and a welcome measure of tranquillity, despite its location in the noisy downtown area. But there is something for every taste throughout BA, from grand old ladies like the Microcentro's 100-year-old **Marriott Plaza** to such hip young things as **Mine** and **Glu**, boutique hotels across town in trendy Palermo. If you're prepared to splurge, settle down in the chic barrio of Recoleta. You can sleep like royalty at **Four Seasons** or over at the **Alvear Palace**, virtually a national institution. On the other end of the scale is San Telmo, the old colonial-style part of the city, which is now blooming with boutique hotels.

Do your homework

New hotels often offer special introductory rates, and spending quality time online might help you

find some bargains. Hoteles con Encanto de Buenos Aires (www.buenosairescharming hotels.com) is a loose collection of Palermo's most popular boutique hotels, including 1555 Malabia House, Bo Bo Hotel and Home Hotel Buenos Aires.

The peso hovers at a rate of around 3.5 to one US dollar, the currency in which almost all hotels quote their official 'rack rates'. You can often get good deals by booking online and through third-party sites, so shop around. It's a good idea to ask if the prices include VAT (known as IVA in BA and charged at 21 per cent) and breakfast. The following listings fall into four categories: deluxe (over US$250 – around AR$880 at press time – for a double room) $$$$; mid-range (US$150-$250/AR$530-$880) $$$; moderate (US$80-$150/AR$280-$530) $$; and budget (under US$80/AR$280) $.

Centre

Casa Calma

NEW Suipacha 1015, entre Santa Fe y Marcelo T de Alvear, Retiro (5199 2800/www.casacalma.com.ar) Subte C, San Martin. **$$$$**.
Looking to escape the big-city traffic and pollution, the headlines, the heat or whatever? A few days decompressing in this oasis of tranquillity should do the trick. The establishment's 'wellness' and premium suites come with their own sauna and jacuzzi, and all rooms are spacious, with a Scandinavian air. It's a new-age haven, where ambient forest sounds play softly in all the hallways and you can order a massage as well as purchase items from the 'wellness boutique' gift basket.

Castelar Hotel & Spa

Avenida de Mayo 1152, entre Salta y Lima, Congreso (4383 5000/www.castelarhotel.com.ar). Subte A, Lima. **$$**.

ESSENTIALS

Five-star hostels

Trip Recoleta

With the recent thinning in the ranks of super-rich globetrotters, the frugal traveller is suddenly looking smarter. And in Buenos Aires, an increasing number of hostels are combining budget appeal with the cool, urban style and decor one would expect from a boutique hotel. You might still have to sleep in a room with snoring strangers, but the rest of the time you can hang out on a roof garden or watch movies on a plasma-screen TV, lounging on retro space-age chairs. And if you like, you can probably skip the snoring strangers: in addition to dormitories, most of these 'boutique hostels' have a single room, a double and sometimes even a suite of some kind. So if you don't feel like skimping on modern amenities and hip ambience while following the backpacker party trail, one of these hostel-boutique hybrid hotels might be just the ticket.

Even the dormitory of the new **Elefante Rosa Hostel** – the Pink Elephant (p179) – is designed in the 'approved' boutique manner.

Located in Boedo, a well-placed but less touristy barrio than Palermo or San Telmo, it includes single and double rooms as well as a loft apartment which might feel like your own little place in BA.

With six interweaving staircases, the interior of the **Ostinatto Hostel** (p169) looks a little like an Escher sketch; but one with an in-house art gallery, a screening room and a cool piano bar. There's also a spacious apartment on the penthouse floor.

Some of the grandest views in Buenos Aires can be enjoyed from the rooftop bar (and grill) of **Trip Recoleta** (p179), a popular new hostel. There's 24-hour check-in available and the helpful staff can organise everything from kayaking to Spanish lessons.

A *porteño* breakfast (coffee and croissants) and Wi-Fi access are included in the price at **Antico** (p168). The bar and breakfast room in the first-floor courtyard is an inviting meeting place.

In business since 1929, this hotel is a successful blend of period atmosphere and modern amenities and facilities. Some of the interior rooms have limited light; fortunately, the 44 with a view overlook the tree-lined Avenida de Mayo. Meanwhile, there's an elegant cocktail bar adjacent to the old-school lobby, conference facilities and, in the basement, a Turkish spa with steam rooms, a sauna and massage facilities.

Claridge

Tucumán 535, entre Florida y San Martin, Microcentro (4314 7700/ www.claridge.com.ar). Subte B, Florida. **$$$$.**

This 1946-vintage hotel is popular with travellers who value a style that was already considered traditional long before anyone put the words 'boutique' and 'hotel' together. The grand Greco-columned entrance leads into the lobby; beyond is a mock-Tudor bar and restaurant. Most of the hotel's 152 rooms are smaller than you'd expect but well decorated.

Elevage

Maipú 960, entre Marcelo T de Alvear y Paraguay, Retiro (4891 8000/ www.elevage.com.ar). Subte C, San Martin. **$$$.**

Mostly business travellers seem to rub pinstriped shoulders at the Elevage, and it's little wonder considering its array of conference facilities, plus a private screening room and a cosy subterranean bar, suitable for clinching that big deal. Recently renovated, Elevage eschews boutique style flourishes in favour of a more traditional look. The outside heated pool is vast by BA standards, as is the breakfast buffet. The suites on the newly created Executive floor are particularly pleasing, with old-school (but sparkling new) bathtubs.

Marriott Plaza Hotel

Florida 1005, y Marcelo T de Alvear, Retiro (4318 3069/www.marriottplaza. com.ar). Subte C, San Martin. **$$$$.**

Designed by Alfred Zucker, the who had a hand in the New York Metropolitan Opera House, the Marriott is celebrating its bicentenary in 2009 and has the distinction of being the first true luxury hotel in South America. The location, overlooking Plaza San Martin, is arguably the best in the city, and the entire place oozes old-world charm. The Plaza Bar, for instance, is a Bauhaus-esque design treat, while the Plaza Grill is like the banquet hall of an Austro-Hungarian count.

Rooney's Boutique Hotel

Sarmiento 1775, y Callao, Tribunales (5252 5060/www.rooneysboutique hotel.com). Subte B, Callao. **$$.**

This lovely boutique hotel, a stone's throw from the Obelisco, has a literary past: the building was once the residence of the writer and poet Leopoldo Lugones. Today, 14 rooms and suites still contain original wood floors, gilded mirrors, high ceilings and chandeliers. Guests have access to a lounge bar, café and tango patio, where free lessons are held nightly.

Sofitel Buenos Aires

Arroyo 841, entre Suipacha y Esmeralda, Retiro (4131 0000/ www.sofitelbuenosaires.com.ar). Subte C, San Martin. **$$$$.**

Perfectly encapsulated in a 1920s-era art deco tower, this hotel with its glass-roofed lobby and chess board-patterned floor will whisk you back to the jazz age. While the rooms are quite small, they are also perfectly formed. In the on-site library, which holds 20 people, guest speakers talk about Argentinian wine (Mon), art (Wed) and history and architecture (Sat), and the hotel's eatery, Le Sud, is one of the best French restaurants in the city.

South of the Centre

1890 Hotel Boutique

Salta 1074, entre Carlos Calvo y Humberto 1°, San Telmo (4304 8798/ www.1890hotel.com.ar). Subte C, Constitución. **$$.**

The owners like to think of this restored 19th-century house as a 'hotel with the spirit of a home'. With its long wooden dining table, tall windows and relaxing patio garden, it certainly feels like home. All six rooms contain original features as well as contemporary touches, such as modern air-conditioning and heating.

Antico

Bolívar 893, entre Independencia y Estados Unidos, San Telmo (4363 0123/www.anticohostel.com.ar). **$.**
No credit cards.
See box p165.

Axel Hotel Buenos Aires

Venezuela 649, entre Chacabuco y Perú, San Telmo (4136 9393/www.axel hotels.com). Subte E, Belgrano. **$$$.**
There's nothing particularly Argentinian about the Axel, South America's first all-gay luxury hotel. So don't look for any local flavour in the Axel Kitchen, a restaurant with few design flourishes; the Axel Bar & Chillout, a lounge with a VIP vibe; or the Axel Sky Bar, site of a grand swimming pool whose transparent bottom is visible from the lobby below. The minimalism extends to the rooms, bright and modern with a glass shower planted in the middle.

Boquitas Pintadas

Estados Unidos 1393, y San José, Constitución (4381 6064/www. boquitas-pintadas.com.ar). Subte E, San José. **$$.** No credit cards.
Owned by a hip young couple, this self-proclaimed 'pop hotel' is more like a cultural space than a typical B&B. The decor of the five spacious suites is constantly changing, with anything from shanty-town art to abstract sculpture. Outdoor patios, an unfussy atmosphere and huge all-day breakfasts help lure a largely bohemian clientele. Expect a unique experience rather than stinging power showers.

Casa Bolívar

Bolívar 1701, y Finochietto, San Telmo (4300 3619/www.casabolivar.com). **$$.**
No credit cards.
A charming apartment hotel, gay-friendly Casa Bolívar is set in a converted mansion with 14 rooms, open patios, a new gym and some eye-catching interior design touches. Rooms vary in size (some are big enough for three) but are all cosy and well equipped, with full kitchen facilities and Wi-Fi just a few of the extras.

La Cayetana Historic House

México 1330, entre San José y Santiago del Estero, Monserrat (4383 2230/www.lacayetanahotel.com.ar). Subte E, Independencia. **$$.**
Opened in 2005, this thoughtfully restored 1820s home is nestled on a back street behind a plain wooden door, and a buzz-to-enter policy adds to the sense of sanctuary. Beyond the ivy-clad courtyard and its 200-year-old fig tree are 11 suites, each with individual quirks – a spiral iron staircase in one, a clawfoot bathtub in another – and each boasting lovely design touches such as high bare-brick ceilings, original mosaic flooring and restored period furniture and furnishings.

The Cocker

Avenida Juan de Garay 458, entre Defensa y Bolívar, San Telmo (4362 8451/www.thecocker.com). **$$.**
No credit cards.
In a grand and beautiful old house, this excellent-value San Telmo hotel has, since its opening in 2006, been blazing a trail as one of the most original and finest boutiques in the neighbourhood. Named for a much-loved spaniel that once lived here, the Cocker boasts a restored interior complete with grand piano, a series of leafy roof gardens and terraces and a new yoga space.

Hotel Babel

NEW *Balcarce 946, entre Estados Unidos y Carlos Calvo, San Telmo (4300 8300/www.hotelbabel.com.ar).* **$$.**
This recently renovated *conventillo*-style house welcomes visitors from all parts of the globe, maintaining the tradition of a hodgepodge of languages that inspired its name. The nine air-conditioned, Wi-Fi-equipped rooms surrounding a small, private patio are compact and pared-down; the discreet decor has a retro air and the prevalence

Home Hotel Buenos Aires p176

of dark wood – a design feature common to the entire hotel – adds warmth to the overall environment.

Milhouse

Hipólito Yrigoyen 959, entre Tacuarí y Bernardo de Irigoyen, Monserrat (4345 9604/4343 5038/www.milhousehostel. com). Subte C, Avenida de Mayo. **$.** No credit cards.

Conveniently located between San Telmo and Microcentro, this is the city's liveliest and most popular hostel, so be sure to book well in advance. Always buzzing with a good vibe, Milhouse also offers tango classes and tours.

Moreno 376

Moreno 376, entre Balcarce y Defensa, Monserrat (6091 2000/www.moreno buenosaires.com. Subte E, Bolívar. **$$$.**

An art deco exterior forms the shell of this seven-floor boutique hotel, with an interior design that's starkly modern and minimalist. There are, however, a few touches left over from the roaring 1920s, such as original stained-glass windows and wrought-iron lifts. The rooms are all sizeable, and the best have original artworks, whirlpool baths and a balcony or views of the dome of the San Francisco church next door.

Ostinatto Hostel

Chile 680, entre Perú y Chacabuco, San Telmo (4362 9639/4300 4525/ www.ostinatto.com). **$.** No credit cards. See box p165.

Posada Gotan

Sánchez de Loria 1618, entre Pavón y Juan de Garay, Boedo (4912 3807/ www.posadagotan.com). Subte E, Boedo. **$.** No credit cards.

If you don't need to be in the midst of everything, then take the road less travelled to this boutique hotel in Boedo. The building is evidence of the city's Italian immigrant roots, constructed in 1890 by the grandparents of the current owner, Gabriela. Charming reminders of the hotel's roots coexist comfortably with contemporary comforts such as Wi-Fi, air-conditioning and a home theatre with a large-screen plasma TV.

Ribera Sur Hotel

Paseo Colón 1145, entre San Juan y Humberto 1°, San Telmo (4361 7398/ www.riberasurhotel.com.ar). **$$.**

This boutique hotel, built from the shell of a turn-of-the-20th century townhouse, is a showcase for voguish design. All of the 16 rooms have pleasing design touches like colourful

ESSENTIALS

Mapuche rugs draped across the king-size beds, pastel tones, fat pillows and wooden furnishings. Paseo Colón may not be anyone's idea of the Riviera, but Ribera's room rates trounce most others in this category.

North of the Centre

1555 Malabia House

Malabia 1555, entre Gorriti y Honduras, Palermo Viejo (4833 2410/ www.malabiahouse.com.ar). **$$$.**

This boutique benefits from its owner's inherent flair for design, evident in the use of colour and the play of natural light. Three mini gardens combine to create a relaxed oasis, while three of the 14 rooms are categorised as classic and the remainder as modern – all have queen-size beds, air-conditioning and private bathrooms. Though the building has undergone a transformation, it truly remains an urban sanctuary.

248 Finisterra

Báez 248, entre Arguibel y Arévalo, Las Cañitas (4773 0901/www. 248finisterra.com). Subte D, Carranza. **$$$.**

Pitched squarely at the young and restless who populate the area, this 11-room boutique hotel is in the approved style, with minimalist decor and unobtrusive fittings, well-chosen antiques, and a lot of beige and white. The hubbub of café society below can be viewed from an aloof distance, with a glass of wine in the rooftop jacuzzi.

Alvear Palace Hotel

Avenida Alvear 1891, entre Callao y Ayacucho, Recoleta (4808 2100/ www.alvearpalace.com). **$$$$.**

The clue is in the word 'palace' – which is not, in this case, pretentious hyperbole. The Alvear, which fills half a block of BA's most exclusive street, Avenida Alvear, reeks of old-school class, and it's perhaps the grandest hotel in all of the capital. The 210 rooms – 100 of which are suites – include antique French furniture and

Southern comfort

The Buenos Aires hotel scene is evolving, and it has nothing to do with talk of a recession. Even before people started using the 'R' word, five-star customers had been demanding more space for less money.

The team that set up OasisBA (4831 0340, www.oasisba.com) seemed to think this was a reaonable request and went about setting up a new style of apartment rental service. A week's stay in one of OasisBA's smart luxury apartments will come to less than a few nights in a five-star hotel. The properties range from between US$325 a week for a studio near Plazoleta Cortázar in Palermo Viejo to US$1,000 a week for a fabulous pad on the 34th floor of a high rise in Puerto Madero. You can book online, be met on your arrival with the keys, and then be left to your own devices. If so much independence is a little daunting, Oasis BA will go out of its way to ensure that you have a pleasant stay in BA. Through its weekday concierge telephone service, the staff can arrange restaurant or club reservations, and help you book personal services, such as hair salon appointments and your own private chef. In other words, it's not entirely unlike staying in one of BA's luxury hotel, except there's more privacy (which means no knocking on the door by housekeeping at inopportune moments), and it's a little easier on the finances.

Hermès bathroom goodies scattered around the jacuzzis. A buffet lunch or afternoon tea in the bird-cage-like La Orangerie bar and terrace is the best way for non-guests to soak up the hotel's ambience.

Art Hotel

Azcuénaga 1268, entre Arenales y Beruti, Recoleta (4821 4744/ www.arthotel.com.ar). Subte D, Pueyrredón. **$$.**

Modelled on the European hôtel de charme concept, this handsome establishment has no trouble at all living up to its name. A regularly changing art exhibition occupies the ground floor of this impeccably converted century-old townhouse, and paintings by Argentinian artists adorn every room. A few of the 36 guest quarters are on the cosy side of small; but making up for it, six of them can be combined with adjacent rooms to create family-sized quarters.

Bernarda House

Uriarte 1942, entre Soler y Nicaragua, Palermo Viejo (4774 8997/www. bernardahouse.com.ar). Subte D, Plaza Italia. **$.** No credit cards.

Five rooms are spread over three floors in this charming B&B, on a tree-lined street. The converted house's hardwood floors, exposed brick and vintage furniture add to its appeal, as does the artwork, painted by Bernarda herself. Soak in the antique claw-foot tub or take a relaxing dip in the pool.

Blue Soho Hotel

El Salvador 4735, entre Armenia y Gurruchaga, Palermo Viejo (4831 9147/www.bluesohohotel.com). **$$$.**

There are nice, whimsical touches in the decor and amenities of this youth hostel-turned-boutique hotel, such as cordless phones and DVD players. In three of the suites, you can pull open wooden shutter doors on to a balcony overlooking the leafy street below. There's a lively downstairs bar where breakfast is also served, and an upstairs terrace, suitable for watching the sun go down.

Blue Tree Hotel

Laprida 1910, entre Pacheco de Melo y Peña, Recoleta (5199 8391/ www.bluetreehotel.com). Subte D, Agüero. **$$$.**

The Buenos Aires branch of this Brazilian hotel chain gets one thing absolutely right: an American-style breakfast buffet with eggs, bacon and sausage. The size of the breakfast is compensation for some of the 45 rooms, which are on the small side, though suites on the eighth floor come with spacious balconies. The location is a sedate, residential area of Recoleta. Inside, it's a stylish black and white affair with a polished marble lobby.

Bo Bo Hotel

Guatemala 4882, y Thames, Palermo Viejo (4774 0505/www.bobohotel.com). Subte D, Plaza Italia. **$$$.**

Bo Bo stands for bohemian-bourgeois and, true to its name, a sense of hip, affordable luxury runs throughout the property. Each of this boutique hotel's seven rooms represents a 20th-century art or design movement, and the top-priced Argentinian deluxe suite benefits from a lagoon-sized jacuzzi. The cool, friendly and efficient staff bring international experience from five-star hotel chains, and there's a top-notch contemporary restaurant downstairs.

Cabello Square

Cabello 3181, entre Colonel Diaz y Ortiz de Ocampo, Palermo (4807 8277/www. cabellosquare.com). Subte D, Bulnes. **$$.**

Run by apartment rental company RentinBA, Cabello Square offers spacious two-bedroom units and fully-furnished studios, equipped to provide the comforts and conveniences of home with the luxuries of a top hotel. The two-year-old building counts a rooftop pool, gym, sauna, solarium and 24-hour doorman among its amenities, while its location in posh Palermo Chico, on the edge of Palermo and Recoleta, puts it in close proximity to many of the city's best art museums, restaurants, shopping boutiques and bars.

ESSENTIALS

CasaSur Art Hotel

NEW *Callao 1823, entre Alvear y Quintana, Recoleta (4515 0085/www.casasurhotel.com).* $$$$.
Despite opening during the worst financial crisis since 1929, everything about this hotel brims with smooth assurance. Thoughtful professionalism is evident in everything from the disabled facilities to the monogrammed toilet paper seals. The Suite Deluxe is great value with 60 square metres and two bathrooms. A hydro massage in the spa will soothe away any remnants of big-city tension.

CE Design

Marcelo T de Alvear 1695, entre Rodríguez Peña y Montevideo, Recoleta (5237 3100/www.designce.com). Subte D, Callao. $$$.
Every detail has been tended to in the slick guest rooms and suites of CE, particularly in the enormous Plaza Suite, where a flat-screen TV swivels so you can choose your entertainment from a perch on the crisp white daybed, the kingsize 'regular' bed or from the depths of an oversized in-room jacuzzi.

Craft Hip Hotel

Nicaragua 4583, entre Armenia y Malabia, Palermo Viejo (4833 0060/www.crafthotel.com). $$$.
Hip indeed. Craft is a cool all-white art space and hotel. The works of contemporary artists are featured, and a similarly creative sensibility has been applied to ten rooms with themes like Song (featuring a mini record player – vinyl LPs are available in the lobby) and Park (boasting great views over the plaza below). The rooms are small, but the space is used wisely.

Cypress In

Costa Rica 4828, entre Borges y Thames, Palermo Viejo (4833 5834/www.cypressin.com). $.
Named for its cypress trees, one of the few features that remains from the original old house, this is a quaint B&B in the heart of Palermo. Located on an atmospheric cobblestoned street just minutes from Plazoleta Cortázar, the newly remodeled hotel has 13 minimal-

Krista Hotel Boutique p176

ist rooms at bargain rates. There's a cosy dining area, a living room with plush leather couches and plasma TV, and a rooftop terrace.

Five Cool Rooms

Honduras 4742, entre Armenia y Malabia, Palermo Viejo (5235 5555/www.fivebuenosaires.com). $$.
This venue ticks all the boutique boxes: bare pine flooring; a Zen-like gravel and bamboo-shoots decor scheme; a 1,500-square-foot (140-square-metre) rooftop terrace, a sauna and a massage parlour. In addition to the three rooms, each of which comes with its own balcony and jacuzzi, there's also a pair of suites, one of which has a private decking and living area.

Four Seasons Hotel

Posadas 1086, y Cerrito, Recoleta (4321 1200/www.fourseasons.com). $$$$.
Frequently cited as the best hotel in Buenos Aires, this is the first choice for visiting celebrities; indeed everyone from Madonna to Fidel Castro has stayed here at one time or another. Towering over Posadas and Libertad streets, the 13-floor Four Seasons

Craft Hip Hotel p175

boasts marble walls, voluminous rooms and tasteful art lining the walls of the lobby and corridors. Behind the tower is a luxurious seven-suite mansion featuring 24-hour butler service.

Glu Hotel

NEW *Godoy Cruz 1733, entre Honduras y Gorriti, Palermo Viejo (4831 4646/www.thegluhotel.com). Subte D, Palermo.* **$$$.**

The new Glu was purposefully built as a boutique hotel from the ground up, so instead of cramming the leftovers from every end-of-line designer sale into rooms the size of a closet, here the smallest room measures around 375 square feet (35 square metres), and is decorated in irreproachably minimalist style. Immaculate rosewood furnishings, buff leather sofas, velvet chairs and spotless linen bedclothes are all pleasing to the eye and to the touch. There's a rooftop jacuzzi and a spa/sauna downstairs.

Home Hotel Buenos Aires

Honduras 5860, entre Carranza y Ravignani, Palermo Viejo (4778 1008/www.homebuenosaires.com). **$$$.**

It's not, truth be told, very homey at Home – unless, that is, your house looks out onto a garden complete with an azure pool; has a restaurant that serves popular weekend brunches; and sits on a quiet street in one of the nicest parts of your city. Each room at this boutique hotel has its own distinctive look. The breakfast, included in the room rate, is presented like a tray studded with jewels: a thimble of juice here; a shot of yoghurt there; bread, cheese and jam and a morsel of chocolate ganache, and plenty of good coffee.

Hotel Costa Rica

Costa Rica 4137/39, entre Gascón y Acuña de Figueroa, Palermo Viejo (4864 7390/www.hotelcostarica.com.ar). Subte D, Scalabrini Ortiz. **$$.**

Light and airy Hotel Costa Rica is an affordable option for those wishing to get away from the headache of downtown traffic and noise. The rooms are basic but clean, and there's a rooftop terrace that's perfect for sunbathing on or enjoying a glass of wine from the bar with other guests. The unerringly friendly staff can arrange excursions to football games as well as city tours.

Kala Petit

Thames 1263, entre Córdoba y Niceto Vega, Palermo Viejo (4773 1331/www.kalapetithotel.com). **$$.**

In Palermo Soho, just blocks from Plaza Serrano, this stylish hotel is a welcome addition to the neighbourhood. It boasts six simple rooms with garden or pool view, soft colours, plush comforters and tasteful art, which all create a cosy, home-like environment. For a daytime outing, ask about the polo facilities and the boat in Tigre; or give in to Kala's knack for making you feel at home and stay put to enjoy the pool and garden, or make like the locals and sizzle up a steak on the rooftop *parrilla* (barbecue).

Krista Hotel Boutique

Bonpland 1665, entre Gorriti y Honduras, Palermo Viejo (4771 4697/www.kristahotel.com.ar). **$$$.**

The bedrooms here are large and comfortable, and although eight of the ten rooms are on the ground floor, indoor patios ensure there is plenty of light. A serene courtyard, a new massage salon and a mini spa enhance the boutique hotel's appeal.

Livian Guest House

Palestina 1184, entre Córdoba y Cabrera, Palermo Viejo (4862 8841/ www.livianguesthouse.com.ar). **$.**
Tastefully decorated with artful touches, this century-old Palermo house has six cosy and relaxing conceptual rooms that, some with a balcony or garden. Amenities and services include Wi-Fi, mobile phone rental, yoga classes, personal trainers and even personal shoppers. The owners emphasise the arts with occasional painting and photography exhibitions and live music; there are also wine tastings and a variety of activities tailored to each guest's preferences.

LoiSuites Recoleta Hotel

Vicente López 1955, entre Junín y Ayacucho, Recoleta (5777 8950/ www.loisuites.com.ar). **$$$$.**
Ubicación: it's the Spanish word for location, and this place has that, situated as it is in the middle of Recoleta. Some of the rooms even offer a rare, 'bird's eye' view of the famous cemetery. This property blends a boutique aesthetic with the amenities of a large international hotel. The facilities include conference rooms, a spa, a parking garage and even specially arranged golf tours. With its white wicker furniture and decorative swimming pool, the LoiSuites' winter garden must surely be one of the most pleasant places in town to enjoy a hearty – or healthy – breakfast.

La Otra Orilla

Julián Alvarez 1779, entre Costa Rica y Soler, Palermo Viejo (4863 7426/ www.otraorilla.com.ar). Subte D, Plaza Italia. **$$.**
La Otra Orilla is a classic B&B in a converted rustic house on a charming, cobblestoned Palermo street. The seven rooms are spread over two floors, five of which have an en-suite bathroom. Each room is fitted out according to a slightly different theme, reflected in its name: Bamboo, Verde, Violeta. The highlight, however, is the suite with a view of the garden that will almost make you forget that you're in the heart of Buenos Aires.

Mine Hotel Boutique

Gorriti 4770, entre Malabia y Armenia, Palermo (4832 1100/www.minehotel.com). **$$$.**
Atmospherically lit to accentuate the positive in both its decor and its guests, this first-class boutique hotel is decked-out in brown and neutral tones, a stone-wall motif and funky furniture that looks like it came straight out of a swinging 1960s bachelor pad. Wi-Fi, DVD players and jetted baths in all 20 rooms add a spot of postmodern flair. There's also an attractive swimming pool, though it's admittedly more suited to lounging around in deck chairs with a drink than to taking the plunge.

Park Hyatt Buenos Aires

Avenida Alvear 1661, entre Montevideo y Rodríguez Peña, Recoleta (5171 1234/ www.buenosaires.park.hyatt.com). **$$$$.**
In true belle-époque style, the entrance to the Park Hyatt is a confection of neoclassical columns, marble floors and cast-iron gates, while the rooms themselves, simple and modern, speak of a 21st-century sensibility. Boasting a vinoteca with over 3,000 bottles of Argentinian wines, a cheese room and three restaurants, the Park Hyatt Palacio Duhau, to call it by its full name, really is fit for a king – which might explain the presence of the bulletproof Duhau Suite on the penthouse floor.

Soho All Suites

Honduras 4762, entre Malabia y Armenia, Palermo Viejo (4832 3000/ www.sohoallsuites.com). **$$$.**
Each of the 21 roomy suites here is well-lit, equipped with a flat-screen TV, CD player, microwave and breakfast bar, with a cream and beige colour scheme that's more soothing than striking. The Superior suites, which can sleep up to

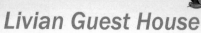

four people, have balconies facing the street, and the penthouse has its own terrace, while a sunny rooftop terrace open to all guests has a set of sun-loungers and a brand new jacuzzi.

Tailor Made Hotel

Arce 385, entre Chenaut y Arévalo, Las Cañitas (4774 9620/www.tailormade hotels.com.ar). Subte D, Ministro Carranza. **$$$**.

Tailor Made may be one of the best-equipped hotels in Buenos Aires. There's an Apple Mac in every room, a high-definition TV, an iPod dock and an IP phone for free international calls. Best of all, there are no extra charges for basic services. No US$6 peanuts here; and wait, you want a beer? No problem! Laundry? It's included in the price. Ironically, pretty much everything else in your room is for sale: the furniture, blankets, sheets, towels, pillows, photographs, books and wine.

Trip Recoleta

Vicente López 2180, entre Azcuénaga y Uriburu, Recoleta (4807 8726/ www.triprecoletahostel.com). **$**.
See box p165.

Ulises Recoleta Suites

Ayacucho 2016, entre Avenida Alvear y Posadas, Recoleta (4804 4571/www. ulisesrecoleta.com.ar). **$$$**.

If you're coming to Buenos Aires to shop until you drop, then it would be hard to think of a more conveniently located boutique hotel in which to stash your purchases. All of the rooms are equipped with kitchenettes and, for an additional surcharge, Wi-Fi. Duplexes are split between two levels with separate bathrooms for extra privacy, and the penthouse suite features a large living room topped off with a skylight.

Vain Boutique Hotel

Thames 2226/8, entre Charcas y Paraguay, Palermo Viejo (4776 8246/ www.vainuniverse.com). Subte D, Plaza Italia. **$$**.

A stylish façade gives way to a sleek, multi-textured, 15-room boutique with modern furniture, hardwood floors

and, in the rooms, high ceilings and mostly neutral tones with splashes of bold colour. The breakfast area has the vibe of a trendy Buenos Aires café; a rooftop terrace rounds off the hip ambience.

West of the Centre

CarlosVia Boutique Hotel

Lavalle 3119, entre Agüero y Anchorena, Abasto (4864 2032/ www.carlosvia.com). Linea B, Carlos Gardel. **$$**. *No credit cards.*

This 1920s mansion turned 12-room hotel features colourful tapestries, pottery and local artwork throughout. Bright pink and lime-green walls and on-site tango classes complete the boutique's unique-but-traditional spirit.

Elefante Rosa Hostel

Alberti 1191, entre San Juan y Humberto 1°, Boedo (4941 7255/ www.elefanterosahostel.com). Subte E, Jujuy or Pichincha. **$**.
See box p165.

Hotel Lyon

Riobamba 251, entre Sarmiento y Perón, Once (4372 0100/www. hotellyon.com.ar). Subte B, Callao. **$$**.

Hotel Lyon is a classy-looking joint, with brass revolving doors and psychiatrist-style Chesterfields in the lounge area. Smoking is encouraged, and the furniture is not retro – it's just still in use. The excellent, professional service makes this is a good bargain for so much space, and the apartments are genuinely attractive and comfortable.

Along the River

Faena Hotel + Universe

Martha Salotti 445, Dique 2, Madero Este, Puerto Madero (4010 9000/ www.faenahotelanduniverse.com). Subte B, LN Alem. **$$$$**.

Richly red and decadent, sleekly white and contemporary, and designed by Philippe Starck, this opulent, lavish lodging is cocooned in the shell of a red-brick former grain silo. The hotel houses the wealthy and famous in its 105 gorgeous rooms and the even wealthier in its 83 privately owned apartments. Intended to be more than just a hotel, as the 'Universe' part of the name might suggest, Faena also includes a bistro, a Library bar, an outdoor pool bar, a slick cabaret theatre and a spa, all open to the public.

Hilton Buenos Aires

Avenida Macacha Güemes 351, Dique 3, Madero Este (4891 0000/ www.hilton.com). **$$$$.**

The Hilton was built with prominent executives and affluent couples in mind. The vast glass-roofed atrium/lobby is embellished with chrome sofas, a marble reception, dazzling carpets and a pair of glass lifts. Spread over seven spacious floors, the 417 modern rooms and 17 suites all have deluxe amenities and king-size bathrooms. This acclaimed hotel has a cool location and the killer advantage of having the best hotel pool in town.

Hotel Madero

Rosario Vera Peñaloza 360, Dique 2, Madero Este (5776 7777/ www.hotelmadero.com). Subte B, LN Alem. **$$$$.**

Inconspicuously tagged on at the far end of Puerto Madero Este, this chic 193-room hotel is aimed at the discerning business traveller, although couples and families will be happy with its attractive features, which include a rooftop pool, a White bar and the open-plan Red Resto & Lounge. There's also a spa and health club, and a heated indoor pool and solarium.

Further Afield

Hotel del Casco

Avenida del Libertador 16170, San Isidro (4732 3993/www.hoteldel casco.com.ar). Train to San Isidro from Retiro. **$$$.**

San Isidro is an irresistibly quaint neighbourhood which has been a popular short excursion from BA's bustle ever since the 18th century. It's

become more attractive than ever since 2003, when this late-19th-century house was made over into a hotel with all the trimmings. With its white-washed porticoes, wrought-iron lanterns and a striking, interior glass-ceilinged patio, the hotel is charming, with amenities that include a business centre, a health club with spa and a heated outdoor pool.

My BA Hotel

Zabala 1925, entre 11 de Septiembre y Arribeños, Belgrano (4787 5765/ www.mybahotel.com). **$$$.**

There aren't many hotels dotting the residential streets of Belgrano, so My BA stands out. A smart 1940s theme means well-restored pieces of period furniture and fittings, and original artworks cheek by jowl with modern amenities. Five of the nine rooms have balconies, and there's further luxury in the fit-for-a-sultan beds. The quiet location is ideal for those who have seen the sights or couples looking to lose themselves in piles of pillows and big breakfasts. The hotel also offers free access to a nearby health club.

Pampa Hostel

Iberá 2858, entre Vidal y Crámer, Belgrano (4544 2273/www.hostel pampa.com.ar). **$.**

One of the few hostels in Belgrano, sky-blue Pampa is friendly and sophisticated. As well as its comfortable quarters and a range of modern conveniences, you can take advantage of tours, football excursions and Spanish, tango and cooking classes.

Urbanica Suites

Montañeses 2585, entre Roosevelt y Monroe, Belgrano (4787 3003/ www.urbanicasuites.com.ar). **$$.**

This Belgrano design hotel features 19 standard suites and four master suites with king-size beds, LCD TVs, private balconies, Wi-Fi, full kitchens stocked with coffee and tea, and earth-toned decor spruced up with polka dots and unusual textures. The sole drawback: the beds could be a little bit longer to accommodate loftier guests.

Getting Around

Airports

Ezeiza (Aeropuerto Ministro Pistarini)

5480 6111/www.aa2000.com.ar. 35km (22 miles) from city centre.

The official name of Buenos Aires' international airport is Aeropuerto Ministro Pistarini, although it is more commonly known as Ezeiza. All international flights arrive and depart from here, except those between Buenos Aires and Uruguay (see **Aeroparque Jorge Newbery**, p182). The airport has two interlinked terminals, A and B, in close proximity. Aerolíneas Argentinas uses Terminal B, while all other airlines operate out of Terminal A.

During rush hour, allow 1 hour 20 minutes for travel between downtown BA and Ezeiza. At all other times, plan for 30-40 minutes.

On arrival, go to the taxi desk in the arrivals hall and pre-pay a set fare of AR$80-$100 to city centre destinations. Approved and reliable operating companies include **Manuel Tienda León** (4314 3636, www.tiendaleon.com) and **Transfer Express** (4312 8883), both of which offer *remise* (minicab) services. Fares are one-way to the centre and include road tolls. Several other remise companies accept advance calls on airport pickups and drop-offs. Alternatively, call on arrival and a driver will be sent within 15 minutes. Try **Le Coq** (4964 2000) or **Recoleta VIP** (4983 0544).

Manuel Tienda León also operates a shuttle bus service to and from the airport – with a stand in the arrivals hall and outside the terminals – and its downtown office (Avenida Eduardo Madero, Retiro). Buses leave every 30 minutes from the city centre, between 4am and 10.30pm. From the airport there is a 24-hour service with buses leaving every 30 minutes. Fares: AR$38 one way, AR$69 return.

There's free pick-up and drop-off at hotels, offices or homes in a defined area of the city centre; otherwise, journeys start and finish at the firm's office on Avenida Eduardo Madero.

If you have more time than cash on your hands, take a *colectivo* (city bus) for just AR$1.50, but allow at least two hours. Bus 8 (make sure you take one that says 'Aeropuerto Ezeiza') runs to and from La Boca and Avenida de Mayo.

International airlines

In addition to these airlines, all the major Latin American airlines have services to Buenos Aires.

Aerolíneas Argentinas
0810 222 86527/4139 3000/www. aerolineas.com.ar

Air Canada
4327 3640/www.aircanada.com

Air France
0800 222 2600/4317 4700/ www.airfrance.com/ar

Alitalia
4310 9999/www.alitalia.com.ar

American Airlines
4318 1111/www.aa.com

British Airways
4320 6600/www.britishairways.com

Iberia
4131 1000/01/www.iberia.com

KLM
4326 8422/www.klm.com

Lufthansa
4319 0600/www.lufthansa.com

Swiss
4319 0000/www.swiss.com

United Airlines
4316 0777/www.united.com.ar

ESSENTIALS

Aeroparque Jorge Newbery

Avenida Costanera Rafael Obligado, entre La Pampa y Sarmiento, Costanera Norte (5480 6111/www.aa2000.com.ar).

Aeroparque Jorge Newbery, more commonly known as Aeroparque, is the arrival and departure point for all domestic flights, as well as those to and from the Uruguayan cities of Montevideo and Punta del Este. It's located on the Costanera Norte, 15 minutes from the city centre. **Manuel Tienda León** (p181) has a shuttle bus service to and from Aeroparque every 30 minutes (AR$14 one way), as well as *remise* services. **Transfer Express** (p181), operates from the airport and also offers a *remise* service to the city centre. *Remises* cost AR$25-$30. Several city buses also serve the airport; the fare is AR$1.10. The most useful is the No.33 (make sure it says 'Aeroparque' on the front), which runs to and from Plaza de Mayo. There is also a taxi rank at the airport entrance. A taxi to downtown costs AR$15-$20.

Domestic airlines

Several of these airlines also offer international routes to neighbouring countries, particularly to Uruguay. Note that non-Argentinian residents pay significantly higher prices for internal flights in Argentina.

Aerochaco
0810 345 2422/ www.aerochaco.net

Aerolíneas Argentinas
0810 222 86527/4139 3000/ www.aerolineas.com.ar

LAN
0810 9999 526 option 7/ www.lan.com

Sol Lineas Aéreas
0810 4444 765/ www.sol.com.ar

Arriving by land

Estación Terminal de Omnibus
Avenida Ramos Mejía 1680, Retiro (4310 0700/www.tebasa.com.ar). Subte C, Retiro.

Buenos Aires' bus station is in Retiro, next to the train station. There are left-luggage lockers in the station (AR$3), but they are not completely secure. Be wary of pickpockets in and around the terminal; there are frequent reports of bag snatching.

More than 80 long-distance buses operate out of Retiro. But don't panic – they are grouped together by region (for example, Northwest or Patagonia), so it's easy to compare prices and times. There are services to every major destination in Argentina as well as to neighbouring countries.

For most destinations there are two levels of service known respectively as *común* and *diferencial* or *ejecutiva*. The latter has hosts or hostesses, includes food, and has different types of seats – the most comfortable is *coche cama*, which offers larger, almost fully reclining 'bed seats'. Tickets to all destinations must be purchased at the bus station. In high season (December to February, Easter week and July), it is worth buying your ticket in advance.

Arriving by sea

Unless you are arriving from Uruguay by Buquebus or stopping off on a cruise, it is unlikely that you will arrive in BA by boat. Regular boat services run between BA and Colonia and Montevideo in Uruguay, docking at the passenger port in **Dársena Norte**, a few blocks from the city centre at Avenida Córdoba and Avenida Alicia Moreau de Justo. Cruise ships dock at the new **Terminal Benito Quinquela Martín** (4317 0671) at Avenida de los Inmigrantes and Castillo.

Public transport

Getting around Buenos Aires is relatively easy and cheap. *Colectivos* (city buses) run frequently, cover the whole capital and offer 24-hour service, while the Subte – the small but reliable underground network – is a fast alternative.

Buses

City buses are known as *colectivos*. There are 140 bus lines along a variety of routes (*ramales*) that run through nearly every city barrio (neighbourhood). Service during the day is frequent and companies are obliged to provide an all-night service with at least one bus every half hour, although not every line complies.

Bus fares within the city are either AR$1.10 or AR$1.25. Just tell the driver where you are going, and he will tell you how much to pay – make sure you have coins to hand as notes are not accepted.

Be warned that the average bus driver rarely comes to a complete stop to let passengers on and off. You need to be alert, hold on tight while on board, and be ready to yell if the bus moves off while you're hanging out of the door.

Pick up a *Guia T*, the handy guide to BA bus routes, for AR$6 from most newspaper stands. Find your destination on the maps on the right-hand pages (all of the city streets are listed in an index in the front of the guide, with street numbers, map numbers and letter-number combinations to locate your point of reference on the maps) and then, like bingo, cross reference to the bus numbers on the left-hand page. For complaints or information, call freephone 0800 333 0300.

Underground

Buenos Aires' underground train network, operating since 1912, is called the Subte. It's the quickest, cheapest and easiest way to get around the city during the day, though it can be very crowded during morning and evening peak hours. The service runs from 5am to 10.45pm (8am to 10pm on Sundays). Large parts of the city are not served by the network, including some important tourist areas such as Recoleta and Palermo Viejo. A single journey, *un viaje*, to anywhere on the network costs AR$1.10. Magnetic card tickets, for anything between one and 30 Subte journeys, can be bought at the *boleterías* (ticket offices), located inside the stations. For complaints or suggestions, contact **Metrovías** (0800 555 1616/www.metrovias.com.ar).

Trains

Trains connecting the northern suburbs with the city centre are modern (some with air-conditioning), while those serving the south are more rundown. Trains linking the capital with destinations in greater Buenos Aires province are not in great nick either, but they do have three classes: *turista* (wooden seats), *primera* (soft seats) and *pullman* (even better seats and air-conditioning).

These are the main stations:

Constitución

General Hornos 11, Constitución.
Trains from Constitución go south. **Metropolitano** (0800 122 358736, 4018 0719) runs services on the Roca line to Buenos Aires province, La Plata, Glew, Ezeiza (which is 20 minutes from the airport by a connecting bus) and Temperley. **Ferrobaires** (4306 7919) runs a long-distance service via the BA province coastal destinations of Mar del Plata, Tandil and Bahía Blanca.

Retiro

Avenida Ramos Mejía 1508, Retiro.

Trains run north and west from Retiro, actually three stations in one, known by their old names: Mitre, Belgrano and San Martín. From Mitre, **Trenes de Buenos Aires** (4317 4407, www.tbanet.com.ar) runs services to Tigre, with connections to Capilla del Señor, José León Suárez and Bartolomé Mitre (in Olivos). There is a weekly service to Rosario in Santa Fe province. From Belgrano, **Ferrovías** (4511 8833) runs trains to Villa Rosa. From San Martín, **Transportes Metropolitanos** (4011 5826) goes to Pilar.

Taxis & remises

Taxis in Buenos Aires are reasonably priced and plentiful (except in rainy rush hours). However, visitors need to be wary of being taken for a long ride, or worst of all, being robbed by an unlicensed driver. For this reason, it is recommended that you use only a radio taxi or a *remise* (licensed minicab). Both will go to nearly every destination in the city. You will need at least a few words of Spanish to book a cab by phone, though staff in hotels and restaurants will usually be happy to help. If you're in a rush and need to hail a cab in the street, try to stop a radio taxi (look for 'radio taxi' and the company name and phone number written on the doors).

Taxis run on meters: the initial fare is AR$3.80, plus AR30¢ for every 200 metres or one minute of waiting time. You are not expected to tip taxi drivers and they should give you change to the nearest AR10¢. Change is the perennial problem with taxis. Anything larger than a AR$10 bill is guaranteed to produce a sigh, and most taxi drivers would rather gargle battery acid than change a AR$100 note.

Taxis are black and yellow (radio cabs included), with a red *libre* (free) light in the front window. *Remises* look like other private cars and do not run on meters. You should agree on a price before setting off.

Radio taxis
Pídalo *4956 1200*
Radio Taxi Premium *4374 6666*

Remises
Remises Blue *4777 8888*
Remises Recoleta Vip *4983 0544*

Driving

Driving in Buenos Aires is the surest way to raise your blood pressure. Chaos rules as buses, taxis and private cars fight it out on the roads. Despite the apparent anarchy, there are a few basic rules:
• You have to be 17 to drive (16 with a parent's permission).
• Front seatbelts are compulsory.
• Under-10s must sit in the back.
• Priority is given to cars crossing other streets from the right.
• Overtake on the left – but the law bends a little to say that if the left-hand lane is moving slower than the right-hand one, you can overtake on the right instead.
• On streets (*calles*), the maximum speed is 40kmh; avenues (*avenidas*), maximum 60kmh; semi-motorways (*semiautopistas*), maximum 80kmh; and on motorways (*autopistas*), maximum 100kmh. On main national roads (*rutas nacionales*), signs on different stretches of road indicate minimum and maximum speeds, but the max never exceeds 130kmh.

Car rental

You need to be over 21, with a driver's licence, passport and credit card to rent a car in Buenos Aires. Prices vary greatly – a rough guide is AR$150-$200 per day, depending on mileage. Major car rental companies will allow you to take the car out of the country if you sign a contract in front of a public notary, which will set you back around AR\$180. You can often return the car to a different office within Argentina. You must have at least third-party insurance (*seguro de responsabilidad civil*), but it makes sense to take out fully comprehensive insurance.

Alas Rental
Aime Paine 1665, No. 805, Puerto Madero (5787 0832/ www.alasrental.com).

Avis
Cerrito 1527, y Posadas, Retiro (4326 5542/www.avis.com.ar). **Open** 8am-8pm Mon-Sat, 9am-6pm Sun.

Hertz Annie Millet
Paraguay 1138, entre Cerrito y Libertad, Tribunales (4816 8001/ www.milletrentacar.com.ar). Subte D, Tribunales. **Open** 8am-8pm daily.

Breakdown services

Only members of automobile associations or touring clubs with reciprocal agreements in other regions (FiA in Europe, FITAC in the Americas, and AA or RAC in Great Britain) can use the breakdown services of the **Automóvil Club Argentino** (4808 6200 information, 4803 3333 breakdown service, www.aca.org.ar). You will have to present the membership credentials of your local club, showing the FITAC or FiA logo, to the mechanic.

Various companies offer emergency assistance to drivers. The basic callout price is AR\$50-\$70. Try **ABA** (4572 6802), **Estrella** (4922 9095) or **Mecánica Móvil** (4925 6000).

Parking

Parking restrictions are indicated on street signs, but in general there is no parking in the Microcentro area downtown during working hours (and on some streets, there's no parking at any time). Parking is prohibited in the left lane on streets and avenues throughout the city, unless otherwise indicated.

The easiest option is a private garage (*estacionamiento privado* or *garaje*), signalled by a large blue sign with a white letter 'E' in the middle. Some barrios still have free on-street parking, though you'll probably be approached by an unofficial *guardacoche* (car-keeper, possibly a child), offering to look after your car while you're gone. You will be expected to pay a couple of pesos on your return. If you're not happy with this arrangement, find somewhere else to park.

Always take valuables out of your car (stereo included, if possible), close windows and lock all doors.

Cycling

Cycling in Buenos Aires can be a hazardous undertaking thanks to potholes, sociopathic drivers, pollution and a lack of respect for cycle lanes. However, there are pleasant cycling areas in Palermo, the Reserva Ecológica and as well as number of riverside neighbourhoods.

Walking

Despite frustrations such as broken pavements and ongoing street repairs, walking in Buenos Aires is a pleasure, and one of the best ways to get to know the city. The terrain is flat, and the block system makes it easy to navigate. Green spaces in Palermo and Recoleta make these ideal barrios for a stroll. San Telmo is also a delightful area to explore on foot. But always be careful when walking through any barrio at night, and don't carry any valuables.

Resources A-Z

Accident & emergency

All available 24 hours daily.

Ambulance
107

Fire
100
For the fire brigade you can also call:
4383 2222,
4304 2222
4381 2222.

Hospital Británico
Marcelo T de Alvear 1573,
Barrio Norte
(4812 0048/49).

Police
101
Also 4370 5911 in an emergency.

Apartment rental

ApartmentsBA.com
5254 0100/4800 1700/
646 827 8796 US/
www.apartmentsba.com

Confort Argentina
4801 5393/
www.confortargentina.com

International Nest
www.internationalnest.com

Credit card loss

American Express
0810 5552639

Diners Club
0810 4442484

MasterCard
4348 7070

Visa
4379 3333

Customs

Entering Argentina from overseas you can bring in the following items without paying import duties: 2 litres of alcoholic drinks, 400 cigarettes, 5kg of foodstuffs, 100ml of perfume. If entering from a neighbouring country, these quantities are halved. If travelling to the United Kingdom, you're allowed to bring back 200 cigarettes, 2 litres of wine, 1 litre of spirits and 60ml of perfume free of charge. The United States asks returning citizens to declare any items purchased or received as gifts during their trip.Goods totalling up to US$800 are duty-free.

Disabled

Movidisc
4328 6921/15 5247 6571
mobile/www.movidisc-web.com.ar
This company offers specially adapted vans for wheelchair users. Tours of the city are also available with advanced booking.

Electricity

Electricity in Argentina runs on 220 volts. Sockets take either two- or three-pronged European style plugs. To use US electrical appliances, you'll need a transformer (*transformador*) and an adaptor (*adaptador*); for UK appliances only an adaptor is required. Both can be purchased in hardware stores (*ferreterías*) thoughout town.

ESSENTIALS

Embassies & Consulates

Check the phone book for a full list.

Australian
4779 3500

Canada
4808 1000

Great Britain
4808 2200

Ireland
5787 0801

New Zealand
4328 0747

United States
5777 4533

Dental emergency

For emergency dental treatment, call the *Servicio de Urgencias* on 4964 1259.

Internet

Downtown and in the more affluent neighbourhoods you'll rarely be more than a block away from a café or restaurant with Wi-Fi. If you go with your laptop, be sure not to sit outside or near the door where thieves have been reported to linger. *Locutorios* (call centres) offer computers with internet and on average charge around AR$2 per hour.

Opening hours

Opening hours are extremely variable, but here are some general guidelines:
Banks Generally open from 10am-3pm weekdays, some open an hour earlier or close an hour later.
Business hours Ordinary office hours are 9am-6pm, with a lunchbreak from 1pm-2pm.

Police

Comisaría del Turista
Avenida Corrientes 436, entre San Martín y Reconquista, Microcentro (0800 999 2838). Subte B, Florida. **Open** 24 hrs daily. Phone lines 9am-8pm daily. English-speaking staff are on hand to help tourists who've been robbed, ripped off or injured.

Postal services

Correo Central
Sarmiento 151, entre Leandro N Alem y Bouchard, Microcentro (4891 9191). Subte B, LN Alem. **Open** 8am-8pm Mon-Fri; 8am-1pm Sat.

Smoking

Legislation in 2006 prohibited smoking in all public buildings, restaurants, shops, bars and clubs, as well as on public transport. Larger eating and watering holes may have a separate smokers' area, but in general, you'll have to head outside for a smoke. In most late-night bars and clubs, the ban is flagrantly ignored.

Spanish classes

Many institutions and private teachers advertise on Craigslist and in the English-language newspaper *Buenos Aires Herald*.

Ayres de Español
Gurruchaga 1851, entre Costa Rica y Nicaragua, Palermo Viejo (4834 6340/www.ayresdespanol.com.ar) Subte D, Plaza Italia. **Open** 9am-6pm Mon-Fri.

Ibero
Uruguay 150, entre Bartolomé Mitre y Perón, Congreso (5218 0240/ www.iberospanish.com). Subte A, Sáenz Peña. **Open** 9am-6pm Mon-Fri.

ESSENTIALS

UBA - Laboratorio de Idiomas, Facultad de Filosofía y Letras

25 de Mayo 221, entre Perón y Sarmiento, Centro (4343 5981/ 1196/www.idiomas.filo.uba.ar).

Telephones

Dialling & codes

To call a mobile phone, 15 must be added to the front of an eight-digit number. From overseas, dial your country's international dialling code followed by 54 11 and the eight-digit number. To call mobile phones from overseas, dial 54 9 11 and leave out the 15. To dial overseas from BA, dial 00 followed by the country code and number (Australia 61, Canada 1, Ireland 353, New Zealand 64, UK 44, USA 1).

Other useful numbers:
Directory information *110*
International operator *000*
National operator *19*

Call centres

BA is awash with *locutorios* (call centres), generally run by Telefónica or Telecom. They offer fax services and often net access and post services. Public phones are coin or card-operated, sometimes both. Phonecards can be bought from kiosks or *locutorios*.

Time

The clocks in Argentina have been known to go back and forward in a rather arbitrary manner, so time differences between BA and the rest of the world are not set in stone. Argentina is three hours behind GMT during the spring and autumn of the southern hemisphere, two hours behind the southern summer, and four hours

behind GMT during the southern winter. But this may very likely change again.

Tipping

As a rule of thumb, leave ten to 15 per cent in a bar, restaurant, or for any delivery service; in a cab, just round off the fare. In hotels, bellboys expect AR$1.50-$2 for helping with your bags. Ushers in cinemas expect the same. When checking out, it's normal to leave a small tip for the maids.

Tourist information

The tourist board website is www.bue.gov.ar, and has an English version.

Visas

Visas are not required by members of the European Community or citizens of the USA and Canada. Immigration grants you a 90-day visa on entry that can be extended by a quick exit out of the country – to Uruguay for example – or a one time only stamp authorised by the immigration service for AR$100. The fine for overstaying is AR$50; if you do overstay, arrive at the airport early so you can pay the fine.

What's on

www.nexo.org
Nexo has info on BA's gay scene, counselling and free HIV tests.

www.whatsupbuenos aires.com
Hip recommendations for eating, shopping, drinking and clubbing.

www.guiaoleo.com.ar
Reviews of restaurants across town.

Vocabulary

General expressions

hello *hola*; good morning *buenos días*; good afternoon *buenas tardes*; good evening/night *buenas noches*; OK *está bien* or *dale*; yes *sí*; no *no*; maybe *quizá(s)*; how are you? *¿cómo te va?*; how's it going? *¿cómo andás?*; Sir/Mr *Señor*; Madam/Mrs *Señora*; please *por favor*; thanks *gracias*; you're welcome *de nada*; sorry *perdón*; excuse me *permiso*; do you speak English? *¿hablás inglés?*; I don't speak Spanish *no hablo castellano*; I don't understand *no entiendo*; have you got change? *¿tenés cambio?*; good/well *bien*; bad/badly *mal*; small *pequeño/chico*; big *grande*; beautiful *hermoso/lindo*; a bit *un poco*; a lot/very *mucho*; with *con*; without *sin*; also *también*; this *este*; because *porque*; if *si*; what? *¿qué?*; who? *¿quién?*; when? *¿cuándo?*; which? *¿cuál?*; why? *¿por qué?*; how? *¿cómo?*; where? *¿dónde?*; where to? *¿hacia dónde?*; where from? *¿de dónde?*; where are you from? *¿de dónde sos?*; I am English *soy inglés* (man) or *inglesa* (woman); Irish *irlandés*; American *americano*; Canadian *canadiense*; Australian *australiano*; New Zealander *neocelandés*; at what time? *¿a qué hora?*; out of order *no funciona* or *fuera de servicio*; bank *banco*; post office *correo*

Getting around

airport *aeropuerto*; station *estación*; train *tren*; ticket *boleto*; one way *ida*; return *ida y vuelta*; platform *andén*; bus station *terminal de colectivos/omnibús*; entrance *entrada*; exit *salida*; left *izquierda*; right *derecha*; street *calle*; motorway *autopista*; no parking *prohibido estacionar*; toll *peaje*; petrol *nafta*; unleaded *sin plomo*

Accommodation

hotel *hotel*; bed & breakfast *pensión con desayuno*; do you have a room for this evening for two people? *¿tiene una habitación esta noche para dos personas?*; no vacancy *no hay habitación libre*; room *habitación*; bed *cama*; double bed *cama matrimonial*; a room with twin beds *una habitación con dos camas*; breakfast *desayuno*; included *incluido*; lift *ascensor*

At the restaurant

the menu *la carta/el menú*; appetiser *entrada*; main course *plato principal*; dessert *postre*; side dish *guarnacion*; water without gas *agua sin gas*; water with gas *agua con gas*; glass *vaso*; individual-sized beer bottle *porrón*; beer on tap *tirada*; litre *litro*; barbeque *asado*; the bill *la cuenta*; closed *cerrado*; open *abierto*

Numbers

0 *cero*; 1 *uno*; 2 *dos*; 3 *tres*; 4 *cuatro*; 5 *cinco*; 6 *seis*; 7 *siete*; 8 *ocho*; 9 *nueve*; 10 *diez*; 11 *once*; 12 *doce*; 13 *trece*; 14 *catorce*; 15 *quince*; 16 *dieciséis*; 17 *diecisiete*; 18 *dieciocho*; 19 *diecinueve*; 20 *veinte*; 21 *veintiuno*; 22 *veintidós*; 30 *treinta*; 40 *cuarenta*; 50 *cincuenta*; 60 *sesenta*; 70 *setenta*; 80 *ochenta*; 90 *noventa*; 100 *cien*; 1,000 *mil*; 1,000,000 *un millón*

ESSENTIALS

Index

ESSENTIALS